From Dits to Bits:
A personal history of the electronic computer

From Dits to Bits: A personal history of the electronic computer

Herman Lukoff

Robotics Press
Portland, Oregon

Any opinions expressed in this book are those of the author and not of the Sperry Univac Division of the Sperry Rand Corporation.

The photographs in this book are reprinted with the permission of the Sperry Rand Corporation and the University of Pennsylvania.

ISBN: 89661-002-0
Library of Congress catalog number: 79-90567

Printed in the United States of America.

First printing, 1979

Robotics Press
P. O. Box 92
Forest Grove, Oregon 97116

TO

My wife, who lived through the birth of our four children and many computers.

INTRODUCTION

by

Dr. J. Presper Eckert and Dr. John W. Mauchly
Inventors of the Electronic Computer

Herman Lukoff and I have known each other for more than thirty years. For both of us, those years have been filled with adventure and accomplishment which went far beyond anything that we could have imagined when we first met as student and teacher at The Moore School of Electrical Engineering of the University of Pennsylvania. A wartime project which might have ended with the war's end was instead the beginning of a technological revolution which has changed almost every phase of society and touched almost every "bit" of the life of any person who may read these words. The electronic computer industry, in all of its ramifications, now ranks among the largest industries in the world. A large library of publications exists on the digital computer; most writings have been technical, ranging from engineering design and application texts to training the M.B.A. for corporate gamesmanship.

With every advance in technology, there must be a story of human efforts which brought it about. Until now, that history of the computer field had not been told in human terms by any of those who helped to create that history. The fun of accomplishment kept us all busy, too busy to write about what we were doing and the fun we were having doing it. We were creating ever more capable and cheaper devices, certain that myriads of uses would be found for our "universal robots."

Now, for the first time, we can read the very human story of a really active participant in computer development. Herman Lukoff was one of the handful of engineers who worked with Pres Eckert and me at the University of Pennsylvania, designing, building and testing the first electronic digital computer.

Herm's ham radio skill and experience produced the prototype "heart-pacer" (the microsecond pattern generator) for my crucial test on the first two accumulators of the "ENIAC." Then his draft board took him away, figuring that no youth merely 21 years of age could be indispensable to any project. But after the war, he knew where his career had to be.

This is not a book about how computers work—but about how the life of one member of a pioneer development team was changed by the challenging events which brought about the "computer revolution."

John W. Mauchly

December 16, 1978

Herman's book is most interesting reading. It filled in some gaps in my knowledge and insight into the history of computing, as Herman saw the development from a somewhat different perspective from Dr. Mauchly and me.

Equally interesting were many of the phases of Herman's life, some of which I knew a little about and some of which were completely new to me. His early attempts to build small radios and later ham equipment paralleled my own development, although he probably had it tougher than I did; he had an allowance of twenty-five cents per week, while mine was fifty cents. Nevertheless, we both resorted to spending those magnificent sums on old radios which sold in this price range—just to take them apart and get the parts.

This early similarity in our backgrounds made it very easy, from the time I first met Herman, for us to communicate. We are both very practical in our view of new development, and developments we worked on together always went more smoothly than others; Herman required only some aiming and then could always continue by himself.

This is not to say that we always agreed: we did not; but when we didn't, it was as likely that I was wrong as that he was (if we were not both wrong, as is often the case in development work). In any case, his position was always well conceived, thoroughly thought out, and clearly presented, something I cannot say for too many development engineers.

Some of the things Herman referred to in this book have little to do with computers; he refers to a kissing machine or "osculometer." When I first read his manuscript, I asked him if he knew that as a college senior, I built this device for a dance. He did not. In fact, what he saw was a cut-down version of the original osculometer, lacking the "wow-wow" sound effect feature of the uncut version.

Herman has made great contributions to the computer art, not only positive contributions in the ENIAC and later in the Univac line, but also in the area, hardly ever discussed, of preventing our group from going down a wrong road and trying to use an electrostatic storage tube memory—a road which our biggest contemporaries tried to commercialize and failed, and a road which we avoided, largely because of Herman's excellent experimental ability. We knew that if Herman could not get it to work satisfactorily in the laboratory, nobody could.

In the early days of UNIVAC I, Herman was in charge of testing some of the earlier machines in a building which was also occupied (on different floors) by Pep Boys Auto Stores. The building housed their main warehouse as well as having one of their stores on the first floor, and it was called the Pep Boys Building. Pep Boys also referred to themselves as "Manny, Moe and Jack," a fact easily remembered from my childhood when I eagerly examined their large newspaper advertisements for the super bargains in electric parts. It was at this same time that General Douglas MacArthur became chairman of the board of Sperry Rand, the company where both Herman and I worked. From that point on, we referred to the Pep Boys Building as "Manny, Moe and MacArthur's."

Have fun reading this book.
J. Presper Eckert

December 19, 1978

PREFACE

Since the turn of the century, only a handful of significant developments have directly affected the everyday lives of all of us—the electric light bulb, telephone, automobile, radio, television, and most recently, the electronic digital computer, whose impact may be the most encompassing and dramatic of all. The modern computer was born as a World War II development. All of the personnel associated with the design and use of this computer, the Electronic Numerical Integrator and Computer (ENIAC), could easily fit into one room. Today the number of people involved with the computer in various ways is in the millions. A vast new industry has been launched since the delivery of ENIAC in 1946. Personnel are employed as computer operators, maintenance engineers, designers, programmers, analysts, data entry clerks, and so on. New industries have emerged to support the computer activity. Some of these are suppliers for punched cards and high speed printer paper, industry consultants, and service bureaus. Hundreds of new companies are supplying mass storage disks, tape drive units, high and low speed printers, memories and terminals of all types. The computer industry is earning gross revenues of twenty-eight billion dollars this year and still growing vigorously. It would not be surprising in a few years to find it rated with automobiles and oil as one of the top industries in the United States. In fact, the United States is the world leader in computer technology.

Changes in computer technology are occurring at an increasing rate despite the passage of more than thirty years since the invention of the first computer. ENIAC occupied an enormous room and consumed over 100 kilowatts of power. Today, a hand-held calculator can exceed the computational capability of ENIAC and requires only a few, small, internal batteries for power.

Computers have become a part of our daily lives. They print our paychecks, send us bills, keep track of how many cans of beans are on the shelf, control traffic lights, and even select our mates. They can compose music and permit man to land on the moon. Computers monitor patients in the intensive care units of hospitals, and control important industrial processes. There is hardly an important function left that isn't being carried out by computer. Automobiles now in development will come equipped with microcomputers to optimize the carburetion for least fuel consumption and pollution. Computers are now starting to appear in the home. Radar ovens use them for flexible control, and they will be used similarly in washers and dryers.

Advances in semiconductor integrated circuits in the early 1970's have permitted a whole computer to be placed on a piece of silicon the size of the head of a nail. This created a revolution in the industry. It is now possible to build a miniature computer system for a few hundred dollars. The outgrowth of this development is a whole new hobby industry involving people from every walk of life.

Thirty years ago there were no computer programming courses. Today most colleges have courses in computer science, and many liberal arts students, in addition to engineers, are required to take a term of computer programming. Even students in high schools are running simple programs in the BASIC language on remote terminals.

There have been disadvantages, however. We worry that our privacy is being invaded, that our innermost secrets will be revealed to the IRS or to our competitor. We are concerned about electrons pilfering our money through unauthorized bank transactions or by some clever clerk who can break the computer code. We get an unlisted telephone number to avoid crank calls, only to find a computer methodically dialing every number to give a recorded message. Not everything about the computer has been beneficial.

The following chapters recount the glories and frustrations of the pioneering days of computer development. I was fortunate in being there at the right time and place to witness and participate in the birth of the computer and its launching into the commercial world. The computer industry today is past the pioneering stage. It is a big business and new systems are being announced frequently. It is a pity that the engineers, systems designers, and programmers engaged in computer development now can never experience the thrill and fun (and the long hours!) that we had in the early days.

This is the story of my life, which coincidentally includes the history of the computer industry from its inception through three generations. My early years, when I was bitten by the "electronic bug," are traced to The Moore School, University of Pennsylvania, where Drs. J. Presper Eckert and John W. Mauchly initiated the development of ENIAC. After completion of the project, they left to form their own company, the forerunner of the present Sperry Univac Division of the Sperry Rand Corporation. For many of the early years, Univac stood alone in the computer industry. It was commonplace for people to use the name "Univac" synonymously with "computer." Trials, successes, tribulations, and tales about people are all part of the development of the trailblazing, early computer systems.

The title of this book, *From Dits to Bits,* may need some explanation. My hobby as a youngster was amateur radio and I communicated by the Morse code. The book tells of my evolution from the "dits" (and "dahs" of the Morse code) to the "bits" of information used in the computer.

My involvement in computer development occurred as an engineer. I have lived and worked with engineers for thirty-five years and have a deep appreciation for their situation. I think Herbert Hoover best described our profession when he wrote,

> Engineering. It is a great profession. There is the fascination of watching a figment of the imagination emerge through the aid of science to a plan on paper. Then it moves to realization in stone or metal or energy. Then it brings jobs and homes to men. Then it elevates the standards of living and adds to the comforts of life. That is the engineer's high privilege.
>
> The great liability of the engineer compared to men of other professions is that his works are out in the open where all can see them. His acts, step by step, are in hard substance. He cannot bury his mistakes in the grave like the doctors. He cannot argue them into thin air or blame the judge like the lawyers. He cannot, like the architects, cover his failures with trees and vines. He cannot, like the politicians, screen his shortcomings by blaming his opponents and hope the people will forget. The engineer simply cannot deny he did it. If his works do not work, he is damned. . .
>
> . . .unlike the doctor, his is not a life among the weak. Unlike the soldier, destruction is not his purpose. Unlike the lawyer, quarrels are not his daily bread. To the engineer falls the job of clothing the bare bones of science with life, comfort, and hope. No doubt as years go by, the people forget which engineer did it, even if they ever knew. Or some politician puts his name on it. Or they credit it to some promoter who used other people's money. . .but the engineer himself looks back at the unending stream of goodness which flows from his successes with satisfactions that few professions may know. And the verdict of his fellow professionals is all the accolade he wants.

CONTENTS

Chapter 1

THE SPARK OF INTEREST

Even as a kid, I wasn't ordinary. When I was six years old I found that I enjoyed playing with gadgets such as erector sets much more than being outside and taking a chance on being roughed up by the neighborhood kids. My parents had a grocery store on 22nd Street in North Philadelphia, just around the corner from the old Philadelphia Athletics baseball park. Twenty-second Street was the business street and the neighborhood was solidly Italian to the east and Irish to the west. There were a few Jewish friends to play with, but the environment wasn't especially conducive to playing outside. I preferred to spend my free time taking apart the motor from my erector set and devising experiments with the transformer from my electric train set. I enjoyed the electrical aspects more than the mechanical.

My parents worked hard for a living. Their store was open six days a week from 6 a.m. until 11 p.m., but by staggering their hours, and with a hired neighborhood girl behind the counter, they were able to keep going. Both my parents were immigrants, having fled the Czar's tyranny at an early age. My father had the equivalent of a sixth grade education, because he had had to go to work when he was twelve to help support his family. My mother had about two more years of schooling. Running the business was therefore quite an achievement for them, but they longed for a much better life for their children.

Dad hadn't the faintest idea of how electricity worked, and didn't understand why I was spending all my time indoors playing with it. He kept prodding me to go outside and play with the other kids. He worried about my becoming a "sissy." Dad tried his best to change my interests; he bought me boxing gloves, he sent me to summer camp, but to no avail. I became more and more introverted and interested in electricity. Of course, having the grocery store and its contents of goodies easily accessible didn't help. It was too easy for me to devour a goodie each time I walked through the store, and before long I became a fat little boy. Fat little boys become the victims of jibes and practical jokes by the neighborhood kids, and this led me to return to the solace of tinkering with electricity. Of course, I helped my parents in the store. It started with restocking the shelves. When I was a little older, I delivered grocery orders in the neighborhood with my bicycle and later I advanced to waiting on customers. Those early years made a big impression on me in the determination of my career. The tremendous number of hours that my parents worked soured me on business in general; I decided that I was going to be a technical man rather than a business man.

One of the few pleasures during the depression years was going to the movies on Saturday afternoon. Just about every kid in the neighborhood paid 10 cents every Saturday afternoon to find out how the hero got out of the villain's trap set during the preceding week's show. It was my habit, upon returning from the movies, to read the newspaper. The Philadelphia *Evening Bulletin* had a special column in the Saturday edition which was devoted to hobby radio. It frequently published circuit diagrams for newer and better crystal sets and 1- and 2-tube, battery-operated radio receivers. At first the diagrams were strange to me, but after a few weeks I recognized the symbols for a resistor, tube, crystal, and condenser (as they were called in those days). People would write in to the *Bulletin* to have their questions answered in this column. I was nine years old at the time and intrigued by what I was reading. I could hardly wait until the next Saturday, not to go to the movies, but to read the radio column in the *Bulletin.* The more I read, the more I knew I had to build a radio one day, but with my allowance of twenty-five cents a week, when would it be possible?

The opportunity finally came when I was ten years old, and had collected $10 in gifts during the holiday season. Armed with a schematic drawing of the 2-tube "Doerle" that I had gotten from the *Bulletin,* I took the trolley car to downtown Philadelphia. "Radio row" was quite popular at the time, with many radio stores, spread out between 4th and 7th Streets on Market Street selling components. Radio 437 caught my eye as it seemed to have the best display of components in their store window and the lowest prices. In the basement were all the low-priced components that I needed. Although I was a complete neophyte at the time, the salesman was most helpful and gathered all the bits and pieces I needed to build the 2-tube radio; all, that is, except the soldering iron, which was over my $10 limit.

When I got back home I studied all of the parts and the layout carefully. In fact, it was two weeks before I started building anything. I had no one to talk to; no one to question. I had to answer all of the questions myself and received some rather shaky

TWO-TUBE DOERLE S. W. RECEIVER

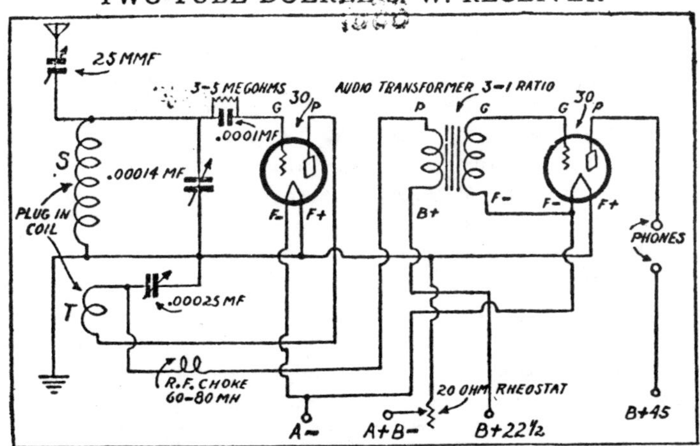

(a) Herewith is the circuit diagram of the two-tube Doerle. The values of the parts are shown on the diagram. (b) Batteries will be much better than trying to use alternating current on the filament of the 30 type tubes.—(Jack Haas)

Letters and Questions from 'Hams' and 'Fans'

(Please write on one side of paper only)

Correction

In the diagram of the crystal set of Mr. Hulfish (W3EGZ), published last Saturday, appeared a perpendicular straight black line between the .00034-mf. and .002-mf.

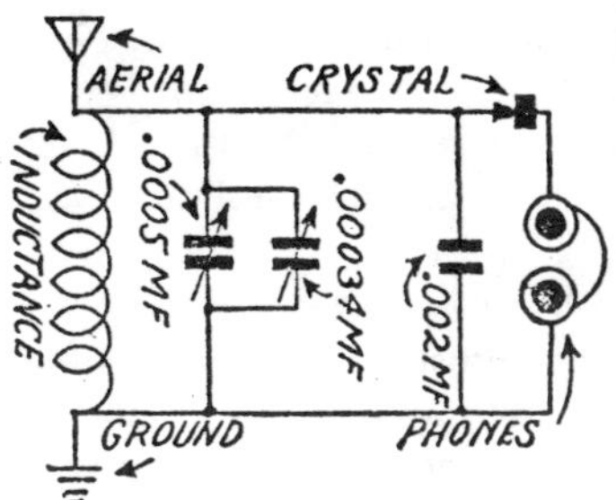

condensers. It has no place in the circuit and had been brushed out with white, but for some reason it showed through the white. The correct diagram is reproduced herewith.

Transmitter License Required

Sir: Recently I read an article which said that if a transmitter didn't send over the boundary of the State and didn't interfere with other stations, a license was not required.—CLAYTON WOLF.

An operator's license is required with all transmitters.

"1,000-Mile" Crystal Booster

Sir: I built the Maguire "1,000-mile" (?) crystal set published in The Bulletin and got very good results. I advise the rest of the fans to do the same.

Doesn't the two-tube A. C. set published February 2 have any ground?

THOMAS E. DAGER.

The two-tube A. C.-D. C. sets function without ground connection. The ground connection is optional. If set is grounded, connection should be made through the .002-mf. fixed condenser in series with the ground wire.

AMATEUR DATA: Consult stores and libraries for books—(H. N., C. B.)

BATTERY DEFECTS: Your trouble lies in poor batteries. Try a new one.—(S. P.)

UNSATISFACTORY RECEIVER: We suggest a service man check your set.—(A FAN.)

DANGEROUS FOR NOVICE: When working around the high-voltage part of a radio, it is best that one have a fair knowledge of the construction of the set. We recommend the connections be left to a service man. It is easy to ruin a good radio and expensive to replace.—(L. C.)

A hobby radio column, published every Saturday, in the local newspaper during the mid-1930's got me started.

answers. I did manage to solve the problem of what to use for a soldering iron. I stuck a screwdriver into the burner on Mom's gas range, and when it got red I figured it would melt solder. It did, but the type of soldered joint I got was something to behold. I think I invented the "cold solder joint," a term used by technicians to describe a soldered connection that looks like it is, only it isn't.

After several months of painstaking work, the day finally arrived for the test. In my anxiety to make the radio work, I inadvertently reversed the A and B batteries while connecting them. This put 45 volts on the fragile filaments of the tubes rated for 2 volts. The flash from the tubes looked as if the world had come to an end. But I had gotten that far—I couldn't quit now. Where could I get the money to replace the tubes? My stamp set! I could sell my stamp set to raise the money. One of the neighborhood kids bought it for $5, more than enough for new tubes.

Type 30 tubes were popular in those days, so there was no problem in purchasing a pair from a nearby radio store. With the new tubes in place, I cautiously hooked up the A and B batteries again. This time I could see the filaments in the tube lighting dimly. So far so good! The earphones were plugged in next, ground connected to a heating radiator, and about 30 feet of wire strewn around the room for the antenna. I was almost too afraid to listen, but I put on the earphones and then slowly turned the dial to listen for stations. Not a thing! I didn't hear a darned thing! It took another two weeks of diddling to find that another control called "regeneration" seemed to have an effect. At certain settings of the control, I was able to hear whistles. One day I discovered that if I advanced the regeneration control up to a certain point, the whistle would disappear and then voices would sound as clear as a bell. The first voices I heard, though, were foreign and speaking Italian. "Dad, Dad," I yelled, "I'm getting Italy on my radio!" My illusions were dispelled a half hour later when the announcer said, "This is WDAS in Philadelphia, your foreign language broadcast station."

It wasn't too many months later, however, that I was picking up Italy, England, Holland, and other foreign shortwave broadcast stations. I was helped by the *Bulletin's* published information on how to wind your own plug-in coils to cover the radio spectrum. The enchantment of exploring the ether to look for unknown (to me) signals was overpowering. I was then officially a SWL (short wave listener), sending reports of reception to distant stations and receiving from them in return a verification, a QSL card, for my collection.

One of my early memories was bringing the radio to a hobby show in Mrs. Coslett's fifth grade class at the T. M. Pierce

Established 1847

WILLIAM L. McLEAN - PUBLISHER 1895-1931

PUBLISHED BY BULLETIN COMPANY

FILBERT AND JUNIPER STREETS

PHILADELPHIA

ROBERT McLEAN
PRESIDENT
WILLIAM L. McLEAN, JR.
VICE-PRESIDENT AND TREASURER

November 2, 1935.

Mr. Herman Lukoff,
2853 N. 22nd street
Philadelphia, Penna.

Dear Sir:

Replying to your letter, the difference between a three-volt battery and the three volts that can be ontained from a wet storage cell is the question of amerpage (quantity). The voltage (pressure) remains the same from both sources.

Small "C" batteries are not designed for heavy duty or continued operation. The storage cell is designed for continuous operation over long periods of time. No B current flows when the A battery source of current to the set is turned off.

The primary and secondary of an audio transformer are usually indicated with the letters P and B+ for primary; G and F- for secondary. An unmarked transformer can be tested and the windings determined by the use of a pair of head phones, small dry bettery and one side of the transformer windings.

Placing the phones, battery and transformer so that they form a series circuit, the making and breaking of the circuit will cause a clicking to be heard in the 'phones. The winding that allows the greatest amount of current to flow will give the loudest click and is the primary winding. The other winding, giving much fainter click, will be the secondary.

Yours very truly,

THE EVENING BULLETIN.

PHONES
BELL LOCUST 4400
KEYSTONE RACE 5701

"IN PHILADELPHIA NEARLY EVERYBODY READS THE BULLETIN"

The only way I could get answers to my technical questions, at first, was to write to *The Evening Bulletin*.

School. It was an early start toward a career, because right then and there I knew I wanted to be a radio engineer. Later, I modified this to be an electronics engineer.

The radio waves continued to fascinate me as I explored new frequencies. One day I came across a group of men talking to each other. In fact, there seemed to be a band of stations that were engaged in conversations about their receivers, transmitters, antennas, and other technical matters. Finally, I realized that these were the amateur radio operators that I had heard about who built and operated their own radio stations. My mind was made up fast; I had to become a ham, although I didn't have the faintest idea of how to go about it.

Meanwhile, my basic 2-tube receiver expanded to four tubes, with the addition of a type 33 tube audio amplifier to drive a loud speaker, and a type 34 radio frequency amplifier to provide more sensitivity. The 30 feet of wire strewn indoors now became an outdoor elevated antenna. Most of the parts I needed for the expansion came from bicycle trips to the St. Vincent de Paul rummage house in North Philadelphia. For twenty-five cents, I would lug back an old Atwater Kent or Philco radio, and dismantle it completely to obtain the components. If I had had the foresight, I should have saved some of those old radios intact; their value as antiques today is quite high.

Hugo Gernsback's magazine *Short Wave Craft* enthralled all radio hobbyists in the 1930's.

Then I discovered *Short Wave Craft* magazine. It was a wonderful publication put out by Hugo Gernsback, and contained a wealth of information on all aspects of short wave radio. It had articles on new receiver and transmitter circuits, gave tips on how to find that elusive foreign broadcasting station, and where to write for their verification card. Frequently it contained wonderful stories of how short wave radio came to the rescue. Typically, the young hero carried his radio receiver and transmitter along on a family trip and it was only through the miracle of radio that he was able to save the family from disaster in the Okefenokee Swamp. *Short Wave Craft* magazine was so exciting that I could hardly wait for next month's issue, even if it did consume my whole allowance.

In the course of exploring the airways one evening, I came across the short wave broadcasting station W1XAL in Boston, Massachusetts, giving a lecture in electronics. I learned that a Mr. Belcher was scheduled to conduct a course in electronics for an hour each Monday evening at 7 p.m. For one dollar you could enroll and get a set of diagrams used in teaching the course. It's probably the best dollar I ever invested, because at the tender age of eleven I learned something about electronics. Mr. Belcher was a most excellent teacher, and W1XAL proved to me that learning, hundreds of miles away from the teacher, is practical. At least, it worked for me because I wanted it to.

Chapter 2

THE AMATEUR RADIO YEARS

By the age of twelve, I was determined to become an amateur radio operator, and scoured libraries for information. There wasn't too much available, but the American Radio Relay League (ARRL) did have a publication which told about the requirements for obtaining an FCC (Federal Communications Commission) license. Briefly, it called for demonstrating the capability of receiving and transmitting the International Morse Code at ten words per minute, and answering ten technical questions in essay form, explaining how a receiver works, for example.

By this time, I was attending the Fitzsimmons Junior High School and through the after hours Electric Club was able to meet some lads with similar interests. One of them, Irv Brager, has been in constant touch with me over the years and is still one of my best friends. The club sponsor was also a ham, and provided some guidance. Still, just about all of the preparation for the FCC examination was something I had to do for myself.

Learning the code wasn't easy. It took a year's effort of copying code signals from the air. At first it was a few letters here and there. Later, some of the letters formed words, and then I started copying whole sentences. The theory part came a bit easier as a result of having taken Mr. Belcher's course, but I had many new things to learn about rules and regulations and which frequencies to use.

One big help was the frequent Saturday bicycle jaunts that I took with two other club members, Carl Clauss and Irv, to visit amateur radio operators in the area. It was usually easy to spot a ham's house by its enormous antenna on the roof. Our threesome would bicycle around until we spotted a big antenna, then knock on the door. We had no invitation, but a simple explanation that we were budding hams would gain us ready admittance. Nearly all hams are helpful in furthering the careers of beginners. Irv, Carl, and I would usually stand back in amazement as we gawked at the wondrous array of electronic communications equipment. What wall space wasn't occupied by the radio equipment was usually taken over by vast arrays of QSL cards verifying contacts from all over the world.

Sometimes we would hear a very strong, obviously local signal on the air and track it down by asking hams we knew if they could identify the unknown station by its call letters. One station that used to make our receivers jump several inches off the table every time he pressed his key was Nate Shuman (W3CNP). A visit to his shack left us in a state of suspended animation. Nate was a young engineer who worked for the Philadelphia Electrical Company, and had a first-class 500-watt transmitter and a commercial receiver. It was a dream world for us and not to be obtained for many years.

Charlie Schroeder (W3ATR) near 31st Street and Allegheny Avenue had a meticulous station. He designed and built everything himself and was the model for hams in the neighborhood. Charlie was the driving force in establishing a club called the Beacon Radio Amateurs which I was invited to join after I received my license.

Sometime after I was thirteen years old, my father had a stroke. The years of hard labor had caught up with him. The doctors said he would recover; he did, slowly, but he was never one to take it easy, and before long he was back at his work in the store. He always walked with a little limp from then on.

After lunch on March 9, 1939, my father and mother drove off in their automobile for a business engagement. I had just gotten home from school when my mother came home, completely distraught. She explained that while Dad was driving, he had passed out and the car had crashed into a telephone pole. Dad was taken to the hospital by an ambulance while a taxi brought Mom home. At 4:30 that afternoon, the telephone rang; it was the hospital calling to say that Dad had just died of a cerebral hemorrhage.

The world seemed to cave in. I couldn't think of anything else but losing my father. Forty-seven seemed like an old age at the time, and I didn't realize how young he was until I passed that same milestone a few years ago. My sister, two years younger than I, grieved with Mom. Maybe having a business commitment was good for Mom, because, in short order, she was back on her feet and busy. She didn't have much time to think during the day; the nights were another story.

Slowly I returned to my studying for the FCC examination but I didn't have as much time as before. I was fifteen years old now and could help more in the store. Just after junior high school graduation early in June, 1938, Carl Clauss and I went down to the FCC office at the Customs House Building in downtown

Philadelphia. At 9 a.m. sharp, we entered the office and indicated our intention of taking the Amateur Radio Exam. The examiner first had all applicants fill out forms that looked official enough to scare any youngster out of his wits. Having the form notarized on the spot didn't help matters either. Finally he asked us to sit at a long table, put on earphones, and be prepared to copy the code on a piece of paper in front of us. He explained that the code would be sent at the rate of ten words per minute for five minutes. To pass, we had to write down solid copy for at least one minute out of the five.

He started up the punched paper tape on which the text material was recorded and in a few seconds beeps sounded in the headphones, although they were a little hard to hear over my pounding heart. I wrote down what I heard, but I was missing letters. In about thirty seconds I started to do a little better and developed more confidence. Before I knew it the exam was over. Did I pass or fail? I really couldn't tell from what I had copied—something about a ship at thirty degrees west longitude. The examiner collected all the papers and proceeded to grade them. Then he called off our names; Lukoff, pass! Clauss, pass! I couldn't believe my ears. About 50% of the applicants had failed. Then the examiner tested us on our sending ability. This part was pretty easy, and practically nobody failed. The final portion of the exam required writing answers to the technical and regulations questions. While I was reasonably prepared for this part, I really couldn't tell whether or not I had passed because the answers required were so extensive, unlike the multiple-choice questions of today's exams. I was told to go home and I would eventually hear from the FCC. Each day that passed seemed like a month.

I did use the time to good advantage. Mom had increased my allowance because I was helping out so much in the store during the summer, and so I was able to buy a gem of a commercial receiver made for amateur use. The SW3 performed outstandingly, compared to all of my homebuilt junk, and I was quite happy with it for many years.

The big job was building the transmitter. Transmitters couldn't be purchased in those days so you had to build one of your own. A wooden box that had contained dried prunes was liberated and painted black to act as the transmitter housing. Working at a grocery store had its advantages! Our dried prune customers got their prunes from bags for the next few weeks, never realizing how they had contributed to science.

The transmitter itself was just a 1-tube, crystal controlled oscillator that occupied the upper half of the prune box. Hams had discovered that one of the new beam power receiving tubes,

My wooden "prune" box transmitter is shown on the left. The one tube is in the middle section of the box, the power supply is in the bottom half, and the antenna tuner is on top. Two receivers are on the right.

the 6L6, was able to take enormous abuse. The tube was capable of twenty-five watts of output with higher than rated voltage on it. With the cost at forty-nine cents, I really didn't have much choice. The only precaution that had to be taken was not to hold the telegraph key down too long. On a long hold, the plate of the tube would get red, then white, and start to melt.

The bottom portion of the prune box contained the power supply, all 400 volts of it. After one accidental encounter with the supply, I developed a new respect for electrons, especially when they were passing through me. It really didn't feel any worse than if I'd been hit on the head by a twenty-five-pound weight. Undaunted by temporary setbacks (it was about four feet!), I hooked up the power supply to the transmitter and the transmitter output to a twenty-five-watt light bulb. It was illegal to connect the transmitter to an antenna as I hadn't yet received my license. Power was switched on, and after a little tuning the twenty-five-watt bulb glowed at full brilliance. Voila! My transmitter worked! There was nothing to do now but wait to hear from the FCC. It was a long summer.

Meanwhile my fame as a young Marconi was spreading around the neighborhood. One day Mr. Popoff, who ran the butcher shop down the street, came in and asked me if I would look at his broken radio. What did I have to lose except a reputation I hadn't even acquired? So I brought the radio back to my half workshop, half bedroom on the third floor of our house and delved into it, even though I didn't have the schematic diagram of the radio or a single test instrument to my name. I developed an approach that I fondly called the "sparking wire." It was nothing more than a foot long piece of wire, one end connected to the chassis ground; the other end was rapidly touched to a terminal. A spark told me there was voltage at that point and it usually produced a thump in the speaker. By progressing backward through the set, I was able to quickly isolate the tube stage that didn't produce a thump. On Mr. Popoff's radio, the sparking wire produced no thump or spark when touched to one of the tube's screen terminal. That gave me the indication I was looking for. There was no voltage on the screen because the screen bypass capacitor had shorted. By then my red hot screwdriver had been supplanted by a soldering iron, so the replacement of the bad component was done in short order. I returned the radio to Mr. Popoff in working order. I was a hero and $5 richer. The proceeds were used to hang up the sparking wire and purchase a general purpose test meter. I wonder if any engineer today, sitting in front of his $4,000 test oscilloscope, ever thought of using the sparking wire. One bit of advice: you have to keep the spark time short. Otherwise it tends to blow things up.

High school started in the fall. I had elected to go to the all boys Northeast High School mainly because it offered a mechanical arts option which the coed high school did not. Besides, at that time, girls really didn't mean much to me. I found electronics much more fascinating, a condition that was not to correct itself until years later.

Transportation costs to the high school at 8th Street and Lehigh Avenue were low. What could be cheaper than riding a bike for the few miles? The only thing that we had to be careful of was getting the bike wheel caught in the trolley track. When that happened, we got thrown off and it was especially treacherous in wet weather. The bicycle room in the basement of the high school was loaded with at least a thousand bikes every day. No one had money to waste on public transportation.

On September 20, 1938, I had just arrived home from school when I found a small envelope addressed to me with the words Federal Communications Commission on the outside. It was the letter I had waited ten years for, or so it seemed. Within a millisecond the envelope was opened and there in gleaming bold-face type was my operator's and station license with the call letters W3HTF. I was incredibly happy. No longer was I an ordinary mortal with just a name, I also had call letters which were to follow me for the rest of my life. I only wished my Dad were around to celebrate my moment of glory.

The Northeast High School radio club, 1939. On the first row Irv Brager (W3IDQ) is at the left, I am next to him and the club sponsor William Wilson (W3JB) is in the middle. On the second row Carl Clauss (W3HTM) is at the right and Charlie Michaels (W3IGR) is next to him.

The state of euphoria lasted for a full week (actually it's been forty years) before I got around to putting my rig (transmitter and receiver) on the air. On the fourth call, a station in Brooklyn, New York, came back to me. I probably did pretty badly in using the telegraph key because my log book shows a lapse of several days before I had the nerve to go on the air again. This time a fellow in Mayfield, New York responded.

My operating habit was to try to make contacts in the afternoons after returning from school. Soon I found I was adding three contacts a day to my log book, and getting quite used to the operating procedures. I was contacting stations located throughout the New England and Mideastern states. I frequently communicated with my friend, Carl Clauss, who had received his call letters, W3HTM, the same day I did.

The urge to do better soon hit. I could hear stations at a much greater distance than I could reach. So, I added another 6L6 tube and boosted my power to 50 watts. The log book shows many, many contacts from then until April, 1939.

Running the business all by herself proved to be too much for Mom. She found a buyer, and by the end of April we were out of the house on 22nd Street and living temporarily with our grandparents at Fifth and Snyder Avenue in South Philadelphia. I finished my junior year at Northeast High by taking the hour-long trolley ride each way. On the advice of Mr. Shubin, the realtor who lived across the street from us on 22nd Street, Mom took the money she received from selling the business, and invested it in a small apartment house. The apartment house was her sole source of income for many years. She had to live frugally because the grocery business hadn't made us rich but she and Dad did put away enough money to pay for my college education.

They were both convinced that that was what I needed even though I didn't think so. I was practically oriented and I couldn't see going to college to learn all kinds of abstract subjects that had nothing to do with electronics. I wanted to go to a two year technical school, like RCA Institute, where you launched immediately into electronics theory. My Uncle Sam, Mom's brother, was the learned member of the family because he had gone to night school and become a teacher. Mom and Uncle Sam kept trying to talk some sense into me but I fought it. Less than 10% of the high school graduates went to college then, and I didn't want to be in that group; but, being a dutiful son, I finally gave in and mentally readjusted to a distasteful future. Little did I realize what a profound effect that decision would have on my whole life. After all, I didn't think too differently from today's younger generation, who believe that parents are too obsolete to know what is best. Luckily, I listened.

Early in the summer, Mom purchased a small house, for $800, on Stanley Street in the Strawberry Mansion section of Philadelphia. It was cheap because it was a wreck, and it cost her another $1,000 to fix it up. I was most anxious to move in and set up my radio station as soon as possible, because there was no room to do so at Grandmom's. It took some begging, but Mom finally let me move in by myself a full month before the rest of the family. Living alone didn't bother me—I was sixteen years old and grown up. Most important, I was able to get my ham station set up again and get back on the air.

High school was uneventful. The school catered to the blue-collar neighborhood and didn't provide much of a challenge. I had been a meritorious student all through grammar and junior high and it was even easier for me in high school. The only activity I really enjoyed was the Monday afternoon radio club meetings. The club was supervised by a kindly old electrical shop teacher named Bill Wilson (W3JB). Every Monday afternoon we would pull the breadboard rig out of the cabinet and set it up to operate. It used voice transmission on the 5-meter amateur band which was good only for contacts around the city, but it was something new to me. There was usually a good turnout at the club meetings, and a substantial part of the fun was talking to other boys with similar interests. Charlie Michaels (W3IGR), a year behind me in school, became a good friend and worked for me many years later. I still keep in touch with Charlie, via radio, of course.

Thus, by early 1940, I was in the last half of my senior year and looking forward to graduation. I was one of the younger boys to graduate, having just turned seventeen in May.

Chapter 3

THE UNIVERSITY OF PENNSYLVANIA'S MOORE SCHOOL

There was no question in my mind as to which college I was going to attend. It had to be Drexel Institute in Philadelphia, for several reasons. First, the courses offered had a practical slant which reminded me of RCA Institute. Second, it had a co-op work/study program; that is, you worked six months in industry and then went to school for six months. This really appealed to me. Finally, I could commute to the school from my home. Drexel was the only college I applied to in the Spring of 1940, as I was fairly confident that my good grades would guarantee my admittance.

Some time in June a letter arrived from Drexel notifying me that I had been rejected. I was stunned. My world came tumbling down around me. Why wasn't I accepted? What was I to do now? Later on, my Uncle Sam discreetly found out from a Drexel official that there was great difficulty in finding jobs for Jewish boys in the engineering field and this was the primary reason for the rejection.

In desperation, I quickly filled out an application form for admittance to the University of Pennsylvania. The only thing I knew about the school was that it offered an electrical engineering course in The Moore School, and it was just around the corner from Drexel. Early in August, the University notified me that I was accepted. It was impossible for me to tell at that time that rejection by Drexel and acceptance by the University of Pennsylvania would be the most important turning point in my life. How could I know that I would be in the operating room at The Moore School for the birth of the computer several years later?

In September, 1940, I donned my dink, a small cap that all freshmen were required to wear, and reported to The Moore School. The school, located in a small building at the corner of 33rd and Walnut Streets, was devoted exclusively to electrical engineering. A gentleman by the name of Moore had endowed the school in his will with the stipulation that no females be permitted to matriculate. This didn't particularly disturb me because

The Moore School as it looked in the early 1930's. It was off in its own little world at the edge of the University of Pennsylvania campus. By the time ENIAC development was initiated in 1943, the telephone poles and vintage auto had disappeared.

I was sure I was going to have my hands full with the studies. The classes in electrical engineering were small, somewhere between fifteen and twenty students. More than half of the freshman class was there on scholarship, the kind granted for being top boy in the class. I could see I was going to have a rough time with that kind of competition. My prediction proved to be true; I found I had to spend every available hour every evening and all day Saturday and Sunday just to keep up. It was clear that my days of being meritorious were over. I wasn't dumb, by any means, and I made passing grades, but just barely. Fortunately, there were several others in my league; otherwise, I would have become completely demoralized. It took me a while to realize that the whiz kids were just academically smarter than I was, but it did not necessarily mean that they could convert the knowledge to useful application. I found that I was able to relate what I did learn to the practical phenomena I had picked up in my amateur radio days. I saw equations as real things, rather than just pure mathematical symbols.

During the first two years we had many classes outside The Moore School; but once the sophomore year was over, our class became a closely knit group. It was surprising to find this small school atmosphere nestled in a small corner of a large university.

One of the fellows in my class was Nate Pearlman (W3HUH), whom I had met on the air waves in our high school days. Nate and I were to become the best of friends through our college years, because he was my mental equal. We commiserated with each other after each tough exam. Nate was always the complainer. "I flunked, I flunked," he would yell after each exam, and yet would wind up with a C or D, like me. Once in a while we were lucky and got a B. The A's were reserved for Lee Riebman, now a Ph.D. and president of American Electronic Labs.; Ray Berkowitz, also a Ph.D. and full professor at The Moore School; and a number of other sharp lads.

All of us commuted to school except Dick Merwin. He was the only playboy who lived on the campus in a fraternity house. Dick was in Nate's and my category as far as grades were concerned. You can imagine our surprise when years later IBM sent Dick back to The Moore School and he earned a Ph.D. in Computer Science.

The Moore School was a small two-story building at the edge of the campus, isolated in a world by itself. Laboratories occupied the first floor. As a freshman, I was impressed with the large motors, generators, and panels of meters that could be seen through the doorway. I longed to be a junior or senior running experiments in one of those labs, but it would be two years of calculus, physics, chemistry, and English before I would do so. The second floor contained the classrooms, library, homeroom, and Dean Pender's office. Down in the basement, "Annie," as everyone called the differential analyzer, hummed away. There was a full-time staff who tended it. As freshmen, we didn't know too much about Annie except it was a duplicate model of the differential analyzer developed by Vannevar Bush at MIT. Naturally, on the very few occasions we were allowed to see Annie, we were amazed by the tremendous maze of shafts, gears, motors, servos, etc. Annie was an analogue computer capable of solving certain types of mathematical problems involving differential equations, but Annie had its limitations, and the crew assigned to it was constantly trying to improve the device. This was The Moore School's first introduction to computation and we had heard that Annie was somehow tied into our military defense.

Every morning students would meet at the homeroom. It was a combination study hall, recreation room, meeting room, and all else combined. Everyone got to know everyone else, although classes tended to herd together. The freshmen would, of course, look up in awe at the seasoned upperclassmen who, with immense slide rules dangling from their sides like guns, were spending nearly all their time on electrical engineering courses at The

Moore School, while we had to travel across campus for classes in College Hall, Harrison lab, or one of the other hundred-year-old ivy-covered buildings.

We struggled through the freshman year. It was tough, no question about it. I studied night and day, just living a day at a time. To stand back and look ahead would have been disastrous, and would have demoralized all but the geniuses. One of my classmates, Lee Riebman, used to go back to his home in Coatesville each weekend to work in the steel mills. How he did it, I'll never know.

With our noses in the books, most of us were oblivious to what was happening in the outside world. We didn't even have time to read the newspapers and realize the full significance of the storm clouds that had erupted into war in Europe.

Freshman year, from September, 1940, to June, 1941, was one big blur, but we managed to get through, at least most of us. The summer of 1941 proved to be interesting. It was officially designated as vacation, but I went out looking for a job. I needed whatever money I could get to help pay for some of my college expenses. I put an advertisement in the evening paper and that did the trick. The first call, I turned down. Crawling through ventilators to clean them didn't sound too appealing, but the second call got my interest. A Seeburg distributor in North Philadelphia called to see if I was interested in installing juke boxes. I figured that there ought to be some electronics in a juke box, so why not try it? The pay was $10 a week, half of which I gave to Mom. Supposedly we were on a forty-hour week but I can't ever remember working just forty hours. Most of the time it was eighty hours (without any overtime pay, of course), but the work was interesting and I didn't mind. After the first week, I became the supervisor of the installation team. A big, husky boy was assigned to me to drive the half-ton truck and do most of the heavy lifting. Those juke boxes weren't light, but Willie could manipulate them with little trouble. My job was getting the selection boxes installed in each booth, and then wiring them up to the juke box.

Sometimes remote speakers had to be installed. Wires had to be run everywhere. Nearly all of the installations were in taprooms or taverns, and running some of the wires behind the bars wasn't the most pleasant job. In fact, the stench of stale beer was so overpowering, I developed a phobia against drinking the stuff and I don't like it to this day.

To my surprise, electronics abounded in the juke box. The selection boxes, when operated, sent out a series of 70 KHz radio frequency pulses on the power line. At the juke box a radio receiver tuned to this frequency detected the pulses and counted them. Fourteen pulses would select the fourteenth phonograph record, and so forth, using a clever mechanism. The crystal pickup cartridge fed into an amplifier that modulated a small transmitter on 180 KHz. This signal, containing the audio information, was again sent into the power line. A receiver tuned to this frequency at the remote speaker and plugged into the 110-volt power line reproduced the sound. It was indeed a sophisticated and challenging system to install. The eighty hours per week passed quickly.

Before long, the Seeburg distributor found that I could repair the modules of the system more quickly than any of the longer term employees in the shop, so they gave me the tougher units to fix. The harder they were, the more I enjoyed it. After a month my salary was raised to the staggering sum of $12 per week. The summer flew by as I visited what seemed like every bar in eastern Pennsylvania. Finally it was the beginning of September and time to sign up for my sophomore year. The Seeburg distributor had to hire someone to replace me for $25 per week.

The world situation looked black, with Britain and France taking a pounding at the hands of Nazi Germany, but it was back to the books for us.

Sophomore year proved to be just as tough as freshman year. Physics and calculus kept us more than occupied. My sister would bring home her girl friends to our little house on Stanley Street in Strawberry Mansion and always find me studying in the dining room. I was so preoccupied with my studies that I soon became regarded as a piece of furniture. Even my amateur radio operating suffered, as I had time for only an occasional contact.

One Sunday afternoon early in December, I was busy at the dining room table studying as usual, when the doorbell rang. It was one of our neighbors. "Turn on the radio," he yelled, "something has happened." The radio blurted out the astounding events of Pearl Harbor. I went back to studying physics which still seemed the best path for me to follow. I knew that all of our lives were going to change drastically in the future, but I had no inkling that the crisis would spawn the computer.

Within two days the United States was at war. We knew our schooling was going to be more important than ever before.

Prior to the start of World War II, the curriculum at The Moore School was heavily oriented toward the electrical power of the utility companies. Most of the graduates went into this field. The war would change all of that. One of the first changes was expansion into communications and electronics, as industry and the military came to realize the important part these technologies would play in the war effort. The strategic role that radar, sonar, and loran were playing was becoming known. Courses were being introduced to reflect the emphasis on electronics. Government-sponsored courses to retrain engineers in industry were set up at the school under the leadership of Professor John Grist Brainerd. They were known as Engineering Science Management War/Defense Training (ESMWDT) courses.

Sometime early in 1942, during our sophomore year, the effect of the draft became noticeable. Those of us in engineering were exempt at first if we passed our courses. We were serious before, but, believe me, we were even more serious now. One flunk, and it was off to the war. We started hearing that our compatriots in the business and liberal arts schools were leaving for the service on a daily basis. One of the first occurrences of military activity on campus was the establishment of Army and Navy V12 programs. These were voluntary enlistment programs that offered officer training and completion of schooling. Many students started appearing in cadet uniforms on campus, but none of the students in my electrical engineering class volunteered. We told ourselves that engineers trained in electronics would be critically needed for the industrial war effort.

We finished up our sophomore year in June, 1942. The school administration wisely decided that with the war pressures bearing down hard, it would be prudent to continue classes right through the summer; so our schooling was accelerated, with our junior year starting immediately. By now all basic course requirements had been satisfied, and we were finally getting to the meat, the electrical engineering courses. Professors S. Reid Warren and Corny Weygandt did a great job through the heat of the summer. Although we didn't have air conditioning, we were too engrossed in our studies to know that it was hot.

Rumors started floating around school that we were going to be invaded by females. The rumor became a reality when one day a sign appeared on the men's room in this bastion of masculinity. The sign said WOMEN. Dr. Warren explained that in order to do its part in the war effort, the school had contracted to train women in computation. The women were attached to the Aberdeen Proving Grounds and were assigned to The Moore School for training in the operations of desk calculators.

Mrs. John W. Mauchly, a professor's wife, had the job of instructing the women. Two classrooms were taken over for their training, and each girl was given a desk calculator. The girls sat at their desks for hours, pounding away at the calculators until the clickety clack merged into a symphony of metallic digits. After the girls were trained, they were put to work calculating ballistic missile firing tables. Two classrooms full of the girls doing just that, day after day, was impressive. The groundwork was being established for the invention of the computer.

Later, personnel from the Women's Army Corps (WAC) at the Aberdeen Proving Grounds were assigned to The Moore School. The school was never quite the same with batteries of service-women parading through the halls. Each day they were marched out to the side courtyard for an hour of physical training. The WAC corporal barked out orders and the girls paid heed; 1-2-3-4, 1-2-3-4, around the courtyard they marched. It was quite disruptive to our lab experiments because there were windows that permitted viewing. We would roar with laughter when one of them turned right when she should have turned left; little did I realize I would have the same problem myself one day.

The junior year continued through the summer and into the fall of 1942. I was now enjoying the classwork because of its higher electrical engineering content, but it continued to be tough. Final exams were frightening. Most were four hours long and open book, so it was all a matter of who had the right book that gave a clue as to how to solve the problems. To flunk at this point would have been disastrous. However, we all got through, and finally became seniors. We were the men that we used to regard with awe when we were freshmen. But somehow, things were different now. There weren't many freshmen around, just a few who were rated 4F by their draft boards.

At the beginning of 1943 when we entered our senior year, the war was going badly for the Allies. The V12 units were pulled off the campus and sent to active duty. There weren't any civilian students left at Penn except for those classified 4F and the small number of engineering students with the draft boards breathing down their necks.

The first half of the senior year went well. We were getting Dr. Brainerd's course in Ultrahigh Frequency Techniques and Chambers' Electronics. These I gobbled up. We also had a course in AC theory by Dr. John W. Mauchly. He seemed obsessed with teaching the theory of matrices (a mathematical tool) throughout the course, and not covering too much AC theory. Lab, of course, was great and I always did well in it—better than some of our geniuses. I always remembered one startled student standing back from his lab bench trying to figure out how he had gotten shocked.

Pen Alterman was one of our more mathematically inclined classmates, and he struck up a friendship with Dr. Mauchly. At one of our bull sessions, Pen told us of Dr. Mauchly's interest in automating weather predictions. However, this would take massive amounts of computation. I distinctly remember Pen say-ing that Dr. Mauchly was interested in building an electronic calculator that would operate hundreds or thousands of times faster than the calculators the WACS were using. He spoke of placing thousands of miniature vacuum tubes in an egg crate. None of us paid too much attention at the time; it sounded like an impossible dream.

Despite the deadly serious atmosphere that the war created, The Moore School continued to have its "record hop." This was a dance held in the homeroom each year. Nearly everyone in The Moore School went, and I was coerced into doing so too. Not knowing any girls on my own, out of desperation I usually asked one of my sister's friends, but the chemistry seemed to be missing.

Being electrical engineers, the students had to display their talents at these dances, and something ingenious was always contrived. A favorite one that kept popping up at each record hop was the Osculometer. This device supposedly measured the intensity of a kiss. Needless to say, it proved very popular, in a scientific way, of course. Each couple would grab an electrode and kiss. A large meter displayed the "intensity." A few smart engineers knew that the device worked on the body resistance principle, so they would moisten their lips first and the meter would respond by going off the scale when they osculated. Their female friends were impressed. Now they had scientific confirmation!

One of the other impressive items on display was the television receiver. This may be a rather mundane thing to mention today, but there wasn't any commercial television in 1943. No one had a television set except a few vice presidents at RCA and Philco. Philco in Philadelphia, one of the pioneers in electronic television, owned and operated experimental television station W3XE. Because it was experimental, there was no fixed operating schedule. All that was required to put them on the air was a well-placed request to demonstrate television, and this was done whenever the record hops were scheduled. Usually a movie or test pattern was shown. The television receiver had been put together several years before by some upperclassmen as a project effort. The receiver worked well and it deeply impressed me. I was convinced that television was the wave of the future and I was going to build a set as soon as I possibly could.

One of the things that affected my social life and my personality was the scourge of many teenagers, acne. I started developing it in my last year of high school and by the time I reached college it was going full blast. I was too embarrassed to meet new people, felt self-conscious with my friends, and even avoided looking at myself in a mirror. Mom noticed my plight and sent me to the Skin and Cancer Hospital Clinic in downtown Philadelphia. For several years, each Saturday morning was occupied by a trip to the clinic, where I had ultraviolet light treatment on every occasion, and sometimes an injection.

Several years of treatment produced no noticeable results except embarassment from a red face and loss of study time. In my senior year at Penn, Mom decided to send me to a specialist in dermatology. After hearing about my years of frustration, he decided on a course of action that was common at that time, x-ray treatment. The danger in this form of therapy wasn't as commonly known as it is today. Each Saturday for many weeks, I went to the dermatologist's office for x-ray treatments. It seemed to help a little, but the high cost brought it to an end. I resigned myself to living with acne and letting nature take its course. In my early twenties, the affliction ebbed, leaving me with scars for the rest of my life, both external and internal.

During our senior year, The Moore School took on some "secret" government project work. Two of the large laboratories at the rear of the first floor were commandeered and declared off limits to all but authorized project workers. The projects were coded PX and PY and that is all we knew about them.

As the first half of our senior year came to a close in June, 1943, it was obvious that everyone's nerves (including the professors') were frayed from the long continuous session. We had been at it for two years since the last vacation period, and The Moore School decided a 6-week break was justified. My classmates started to make plans for the vacation period, most of them signing up to work for Seabrook Farms in southern New Jersey. It was out of doors, healthful, and a welcome break from the daily grind.

Just as I was wondering what I should do, Dr. Brainerd asked me to drop by his office. I was really worried that I had flunked his final exam or done something I shouldn't have. The answer came soon. Would I like to work on the PX project for six weeks? Would I like to work on the project! He must be kidding. Anyone would have given his eye teeth for that opportunity. But why did he ask me when there were so many smarter members of the class around? One answer was that they must need someone with practical electronic experience, someone who had held a soldering iron and had soldered wires. I was right. My amateur radio experience was going to pay off. I joyfully accepted his offer, forgetting to ask about the salary. It didn't matter; I was happy.

The first Monday in June, 1943, I reported to Project PX at the rear first floor lab. I was introduced to my boss, J. Presper Eckert, whom I recognized as one of the graduate students at The Moore School. His class was several years ahead of mine. Pres explained that The Moore School expected to get some super-super electronic development project, and that there was no test equipment in existence that was fast enough or good enough to use in developing the super-super. Our job that summer was to design the necessary test equipment.

Pres went on to explain the various modules required, for example, an oscilloscope that could be externally triggered and would display pulses up to a 1 MHz rate. Clearly, there were no commercial oscilloscopes available within an order of magnitude of that performance. My job was to design a signal generator that was continuously variable in frequency from 20 Hz to 1 MHz and had four sine wave outputs, each of which was independently and continuously variable in phase from 0 to 360 degrees. Another module assigned to someone else converted sine waves to various pulse outputs. The three modules and power supply were all to be relay rack mounted in a 4-foot high cabinet on wheels. Building six of these identical test units constituted the extent of the project.

Pres gave me several good leads on how to go about the design. He would stop around my workbench once or twice a day to see how I was progressing. I found him to be as smart as a whip and lucid in his explanations. He had a tremendous knack for being able to reduce things to a practical level, using simple engineering principles. Pres wasn't one to get lost in a myriad of equations. I developed a deep respect and great admiration for him. He knew what he was doing and I had a lot to learn from him. No wonder he was chosen as the project leader.

The project room was large, about fifty feet long and thirty feet wide. A number of Moore School graduates of previous classes worked there; Kite Sharpless, Jack Davis, and Joe Chedaker were three of the men I recognized. Bob Shaw was another lively member of the group. I had heard of him because of a long article in the evening paper the previous year. After graduating from Princeton University in 1937, he was taking graduate studies at Penn when he was hit by a rare spinal infection that left his legs partially paralyzed. He spent fifty weeks in the hospital and then many weeks at home recuperating, with his amateur radio station W3AOC as a companion. Eventually, Bob was able to get around, but at first just barely. He gave us all cause for concern as he hobbled along the hallway with his cane.

However, I really didn't have to interface with the other individuals. My project was complete in itself, and with only six weeks available to complete the work, I didn't have any time to waste. A basic decision had been made to use a Wein Bridge Oscillator, one of the designs I had studied in class. Pres derived the basic idea of obtaining 0 and 90 degree phase-shifted signals from the Wein Bridge itself, feeding these through 180-degree vacuum tube phase inverters and then applying all four signals to the 0, 90, 180 and 270 degree points on a continuously rotatable potentiometer that the International Resistor Company was willing to make for us. The design worked well. It did what it was supposed to do, which amazed me, because it was the first time I had ever designed anything that complex. The prototype was built and working within the 6-week period.

Time flew by; before I knew it, it was time to go back to school for the last half of the senior year. I had learned a tremendous amount under Pres Eckert's tutelage and I was sorry to leave. The final push started. October seemed a long way off, but the end was in sight.

During the summer I had earned enough money to engage in my fantasy of building a television receiver. A coincidental opportunity occurred. The Meissner Company had attempted to market a kit of parts for a television receiver, but the war came along and put a crimp into the introduction of commercial TV. With no end to the war in sight and no predictions of when com-

One of my first television receivers.

mercial TV might flourish, the kits were sold on a bargain basis by the M & H store near Radio Row in downtown Philadelphia. As I remember it, the whole kit including tubes sold for $40. The receiver design was complete, so I can't claim any credit for it. Putting the receiver together and making it work was a challenge, but with my knowledge of electronics, it wasn't too much of a problem. The standards in those days were quite primitive. A 5-inch cathode ray tube seemed large, and pulling the window shades down to see the picture was a ritual. The receivers used simple multivibrators for horizontal and vertical deflection, and they were easily knocked out of synchronization by the ignition noise from passing automobiles. Still, the TV receiver produced a fine picture and worked beautifully.

One of my great joys at the time was showing TV to someone who had never seen it before, and that included nearly everyone. Their amazement was something to behold when they saw small people in the box talk.

TUESDAY FEB. 17.

Time	No.	Program
3:30 - 4:25		W3XE Test Chart
4:30 - 5:30		Film
7:30 - 7:50	(7)	Bert Lynn - Inventor of the electric guitar - Foremost authority on electric music
7:50 - 8:00		Film Short
8:00 - 8:15	(8)	Shipley School of Music presents:-
8:15 - 8:30	(9)	"Double Exposure" an original play of the Elegant Eighties written and directed by Frank Vreeland
*8:30 - 8:55	(10)	WNBT Retelecast - "Our Neighbor Brazil" Part III - Julien Bryan, traveler and lecturer
*8:55 - 9:00	(11)	WNBT Retelecast - Your Income Tax
*9:00 - 9:20	(12)	WNBT Retelecast - Adrienne Ames (Private Previews)
*9:20 - 9:30	(13)	WNBT Retelecast - The Face of the War - Sam Cuff
*9:30 - 11:00	(14)	WNBT Retelecast - Adam Hats Sports Parade - Professional Wrestling direct from Ridgewood Grove

WEDNESDAY FEB. 18.

Time	No.	Program
7:30 - 7:45	(15)	Television Spelling Bee
7:45 - 8:00		Film Short
8:00 - 8:15	(16)	"Behind the Scenes of Radio" - WDAS present "The Three Keys"
8:15 - 8:25		Film Short
8:25 - 8:45	(17)	"Wally the Warden" 3rd episode of an original play written and directed by Frank Vreeland
8:45 - 8:55		Film Short
8:55 - 9:10	(18)	Frank Warner, collector and singer of American folk songs
9:10 - 9:20		Film Short
9:20 - 9:35		Women in Hale America
9:35 - 9:50		The Philco News Analyst - Ernest H. Traub
9:50 - 10:05	(19)	O. E. M. Show

Would you believe that commercial television was actually launched during World War II? These are some of the programs transmitted by Philco's station W3XE that I could watch on my home-built television receiver.

Just about that time, the Philco Corporation made arrangements with the University of Pennsylvania to televise their football games at Franklin Field on an experimental basis. Penn had an excellent football team and led the Ivy League that year and interest in football was high despite the war. After watching several games on TV that fall, I was delighted at how well they came through; you can see much better than actually being at the game. It was too good to be true. I decided to invite some of my classmates and their dates over to my house for a Saturday afternoon, and somehow we managed to scrunch into my little bedroom on the second floor. My friends broke loose with wild enthusiasm when the game started, enjoying it immensely, as I did. I am certain many of them still remember that introduction to television 35 years ago.

October rolled around, and it was time for the last set of final exams. They were always blockbusters and the 8-hour open book exams were the worst, but everyone passed. The professors probably had some compassion at that point. We graduated in October, 1943, with a ceremony at Irvine Auditorium. It was a great day! My ambition to become an electronic engineer had been achieved. I wished my father had lived to see it.

The Moore Class of 1943 was outstanding in many respects. It was the last class to graduate intact, until the war was over. Additionally, it was an odd time of the year to graduate—whoever heard of an October graduate? Finally and most important, the number of people in the class to achieve fame and distinction is probably greater than any other class.

Some of the graduates immediately joined the armed forces. Others accepted jobs in industry, not knowing how long they could hold off the heavy hand of the draft board.

Chapter 4

THE BIRTH OF ENIAC

The super-super development project that Pres Eckert had referred to during the test equipment construction phase came to pass. In response to a proposal from The Moore School, Aberdeen Proving Grounds awarded a contract for the development of an electronic computer. The device was called ENIAC, an acronym for Electronic Numerical Integrator and Computer.

The keel for ENIAC had been laid many years earlier, and had started with Dr. John W. Mauchly's interest in computation. Dr. Mauchly graduated from Johns Hopkins University in 1932 as a physicist, but his interests covered mathematics and meteorology as well. In the late thirties when he was on the teaching staff at Ursinus College in the Philadelphia suburbs, he started thinking about weather prediction. He realized that the reduction and analysis of meteorological data would take a tremendous amount of computation, which was not achievable with the best calculators of the day. So his thoughts turned to ways to speed up the calculation process. Mauchly was aware that the limitation in speed was due to the electromechanical components used in calculators. They took many milliseconds to respond. He quickly realized that an electronic circuit could respond at least a thousand times faster. In fact, physicists were using electronic circuits called "scalers" for their work in measuring radiation particles. John Mauchly knew that he had to learn more about electronics.

The opportunity came when The Moore School offered the ESMDT (Engineering Science Management/Defense Training) courses in electronics. Mauchly signed up for them, and before long, was having absorbing discussions with his laboratory instructor, Pres Eckert. Eckert had an impressive knowledge of electronics. As a graduate student at The Moore School, he had participated in several projects which furthered his electronics capability. One effort involved working on a Massachusetts Institute of Technology sponsored project on radar ranging techniques using delay lines. Another was concerned with the development of a high gain oscilloscope amplifier having a very rapid response time. Much of his time was also devoted to improving the analogue differential analyzer, Annie, which was too slow and not accurate enough for the Ordnance Department's needs. His thoughts turned more and more towards electronics as a way of improving the accuracy and speeding up the sluggish Annie, and thus the two men found a common interest. Eckert became very interested in Mauchly's concepts, and they spent many hours discussing how the electronic computer could be implemented.

Dr. Mauchly soon realized that the chances of progressing with his ideas on electronic computation were much greater at The Moore School than at Ursinus College. Soon he became a member of The Moore School staff, and used the opportunity in August, 1942, to write a memorandum advocating the construction of a large electronic computer. Although the memorandum was circulated at The Moore School, no action was taken. Fortunately, a liaison officer, Lt. Herman Goldstine, was assigned to The Moore School by the Army Ordnance Corps to coordinate all of the computational work being done there. Goldstine heard about Mauchly's idea for an electronic computer and became enthralled with it. Through his interest, Army Ordnance requested a proposal from The Moore School. Eckert and Mauchly wrote the technical section for the proposal that was submitted to Army Ordnance in May, 1943. Work actually began on the project in June, but the contract went into effect on July 1, 1943.

My work during that 6-week summer period must have been satisfactory, because, several weeks before graduation, I received an offer from Dr. Brainerd to return to the PX project. The terms of the offer were more than acceptable; I would be appointed a research associate (equivalent to a junior engineer) at a salary of $2,400 per year for a forty-four hour week. The extra hours were to be put in on Saturday which was a normal work day at most industrial plants during the war years. I was overjoyed, and didn't hesitate to accept Dr. Brainerd's offer. Actually, I considered myself the luckiest guy in the class as far as job opportunities were concerned.

The Monday after graduation, I reported to Project PX. It was good to see some of the familiar faces again, and there were also a number of new people. Some were at the engineering level; others were technicians and production supervisors. One of the supervisors whom I got to know very well was Sol Rosenthal. Sol was a fine cellist who had a physical deferment from the draft, but he soon found that making a living as a musician was a difficult matter. Sol was initially a technician, but later was put in charge of a group of women assemblers.

CONFIDENTIAL

APPENDIX A

REPRODUCTION OF A MEMORANDUM
PRIVATELY CIRCULATED IN AUGUST, 1942
MOORE SCHOOL OF ELECTRICAL ENGINEERING, UNIVERSITY OF PENNSYLVANIA

THE USE OF HIGH-SPEED VACUUM TUBE DEVICES
FOR CALCULATING

There are many sorts of mathematical problems which require calculation by formulas which can readily be put in the form of iterative equations. Purely mechanical calculating devices can be devised to expedite the work. However, a great gain in the speed of calculation can be obtained if the devices which are used employ electronic means for the performance of the calculation, because the speed of such devices can be made very much higher than that of any mechanical device. It is the purpose of this discussion to consider the speed of calculation and the advantages which may be obtained by the use of electronic circuits which are interconnected in such a way as to perform a number of multiplications, additions, subtractions or divisions in sequence, and which can therefore be used for the solution of difference equations. Since a sufficiently approximate solution of many differential equations can be had simply by solving an associated difference equation, it is to be expected that one of the chief fields of usefulness for an electronic computer would be found in the solution of differential equations.

As will be brought out in the following discussion, the electronic computer may have certain advantages other than the single one of high speed when compared with the differential analyzer of the usual mechanical construction. For instance, the mechanical analyzer has an accuracy limited by the way in which the slip and back-lash enter into its operation, whereas the electronic device, operating solely on the principle of counting, can without great difficulty, be made as accurate as is required for any practical purpose. Secondly, whatever errors are introduced by the electronic device (when it is properly operating) are mathematically determined errors which arise through the use of a difference equation in place of a differential equation; and since these errors are mathematically determined, they are reproduceable. Hence, a check calculation may be run at any time; and whatever the result may be for the first run, that result should be obtained exactly on every succeeding test run. Third, the ease with which the various components of such a computing device can be interconnected by cables and switching units makes it possible to set up a new problem without much difficulty. It is also to be appreciated that additional component parts may be built and connected in whenever more complicated problems require them, and that additional spare components may be kept in reserve and quickly interchanged with any components which fail in operation. Fourth, a convenient way of diagnosing faults and isolating defective units is available through the use of standard electric testing procedures. Fifth, not only can the regular problems which have to be solved be run through quickly on the electronic computer, but also the test problems, and hence less time is lost in discovering any failure which may develop during operation. Sixth, both the mechanical analyzer and the electronic computer require maintenance by skilled labor, but the number of persons required to turn out the same amount of finished work should be appreciably less in the case of the electronic computer.

The first page of Dr. John Mauchly's memo circulated in August 1942 which proposed the use of electronic circuits for high speed computation.

The back room in The Moore School was a beehive of activity. Each engineer had an assigned space at a work table that ran continuously around the periphery of the room. Assemblers and wiremen occupied the central floor space. A serious attitude prevailed; everyone realized the importance of his job.

Pres Eckert welcomed me back, and explained the magnitude of the project. I think at the time I was awe-struck, and not able to visualize the enormity or full significance of the project. Of course, as a junior engineer, I was just a small cog in the wheel. Pres told me that I had the responsibility for the design of the "Cycling Unit" portion of ENIAC.

Each engineer on the ENIAC project was given this laboratory note book. It contained a number of now historical documents as well as engineering design data and reports.

Some of the basic circuitry was under development by the time I arrived on the project. The basic decade counter and gate circuits had been developed, which made my job significantly easier. Also, I was given a "cookbook" which contained a storehouse of information on the reliable use of electronic components. Pres was an absolute bug on component reliability, and relentless in his pursuit of the subject. He queried manufacturers until they could no longer answer his questions.

I should explain that the philosophy of design prevalent at that time was to use the manufacturer's data, which usually consisted of a few typical curves. In most cases, industry engineers used the data directly from the RCA tube handbooks. Perhaps for most communications applications this was good enough, but Pres Eckert realized that it would not be good enough for building ENIAC. In fact, the statisticians and other prophets of gloom were already predicting that the computer would never run long enough in one stretch to produce any useful results. They were probably right if traditional design had been used. The estimate of the number of tubes to be used was somewhere around 18,000. The counter stages formed a sizeable portion of the machine. Each stage actually contained two tubes in one envelope and required seven supporting resistors, two capacitors and a neon bulb.

ENIAC was first thought of in simple form containing just 10 accumulators, with no provisions for input or output. Multiplication and division were to be accomplished by repeated additions and subtractions. That would require just 5,000 tubes. However, it was soon realized that ENIAC would be too limited in performance; therefore, the specifications were modified to include 20 accumulators, built-in multiplication, division, square rooting, and punched card input/output equipment. This raised the tube count to 18,000.

Pres recognized that a new design philosophy was required if ENIAC was to have adequate reliability. He studied each one of the components carefully and diagnosed its failure mode. He reasoned that if the characteristics changed through degradation, then allowances should be made for the degradation in the design. Any component that could fail catastrophically was ruled out or minimized. Furthermore, Pres realized that each component was a separate entity, and the circuit had to work when all components degraded in independent fashion. What came out of these considerations is known to engineers today as "worst case design." For example, the cookbook said the tube plate resistance and mutual conductance may be expected to vary ±40% from those given in the tube manual; the cutoff voltage could vary ±50%; therefore a safety factor of 2 was allowed for these variations. Tubes could be operated at one-quarter of maximum rated current and one-half of maximum rated voltage. Resistors and capacitors had similar degradation factors.

This concentration on the principles of worst case design, in my opinion, was probably the single most important factor in the success of ENIAC. The principles are still carried through on every computer designed today.

The cycling unit generated the master or control pulses that were destined for nearly all units in the ENIAC system. The pulses were repetitive, operating at a basic 100 KHz rate, but a variable frequency was also provided for test purposes. There were various combinations of pulses that I had to generate, and these changed weekly as the logic design of the system evolved. Fortunately, the design was flexible and easy to change. Ten different kinds of control pulses were required, ranging from single-pulse to 9- and 10-pulse combinations per addition time (200 microseconds). A cleargate lasting for seven pulse times was also required. All control pulses were fed by husky driver tubes into buses that encircled the machine. Two-microsecond-wide pulses could tolerate the transmission system. The cycling unit design originated with a 100 KHz crystal oscillator. This, in turn, drove a 20-stage ring counter. Pulse sequences were generated by tap-

CONFIDENTIAL

Disclosure of Magnetic Calculating machine

A simplified method of constructing a numerical calculating machine is proposed in which some of the mechanical features of an ordinary mechanical calculating machine are retained and combined with certain electronic and magnetic devices to produce a speedier, simpler machine as well as providing additional features of utility, ruggedness and ease of repair.

A continuously rotating shaft called the time shaft, driven by an electric motor, has at least some of each of the following discs or drums mounted on it:

a) Discs or drums which have at least their outer edge made of a magnetic alloy capable of being magnetized and demagnetized repeatedly and at high speed. Suitable coils and other apparatus are provided to convert electrical pulses or other wave shapes into spatially distributed magnetized sectors on the periphery of these discs, the position and/or phase of these magnetized sectors providing a method of storing, in some usable code, those characters or digits which must be used later or indicated. It should be noted that the direction of magnetization of the sectors is unimportant and may be in any direction relative to the motion or a combination of directions, this being a well known technique. This is analogous to the use of a magnetic tape to record sound except that here linearity is of little importance.
b) Discs or drums having edges or surfaces engraved in such a way as to cause voltages to be induced in a coil arranged near the disc. In any case either the disc or pole piece of the coil should be a magnet. This disc would generate such pulses or other electric signals as were required to time, control and initiate the operations required in the calculations. This is similar to the tone generating mechanism used in some electric organs and offers a more permanent way of storing the basic signals required than would be afforded by the alloy discs referred to above.
c) Discs or drums carrying characters, usually the digits 0 to 9, which can be illuminated by a light modulating device, say a neon gas discharge lamp, and so arranged that at any desired phase of the rotating shaft, corresponding to the positions of the characters, they can be flashed thus making one of the characters on the disc visible. This stroboscope principal is to be used as the high speed indication device in this calculator.

Addition, subtraction, multiplication and division would be carried out by processes of successive addition, such as is well known in mechanical calculation machines. The alloy discs or an auxillary alloy tape could be used to store function data such as a sine table. A multiplication table might be included in this manner to appreciably speed up the process of multiplication by the method of accumulation of partial products used in mechanical calculators.

The original data or numbers might be put into the machine by means of the usual keyboards, tapes or cards. These same types of tapes or cards could be used to record the calculated results.

In the above operations some means must be provided to switch the various signals from one circuit to another. This can be done rapidly by using electronic tubes as switches. A great economy in the numbers of these switching tubes can be effected by putting all the digits of a particular number on the same disc and taking them off serially through the same switching tube. This is to be contrasted to taking the n digits of a number off through n pick-up coils and through n switching tubes.

CONFIDENTIAL

Disclosure of Magnetic Calculating Machine

It has the advantage of reducing the number of tubes required but slows down the operation and may require the mechanical shaft system to be extended so that the alloy discs rotate slower and in syncronism with the indicator discs to allow any of the numbers on the discs to be indicated concurrently or serially. In addition to the above switching operations electronic tubes will be used to count and/or discriminate the pulses used in the system to allow composition of pulse groups from two or more sources and their deposition into other channels. Clearly the power circuits for such a system may be electronic tubes, selenium oxide rectifiers or similar devices.

The use of the binary number system is favored by such an apparatus since the switching circuits are no more complicated and the required pulse groups for representing the number are simpler. The counter circuit is also simpler and more reliable. Either discs of the etched or alloy type may be used to remember combinations required in the conversion from the decimal to the binary system and the reverse if such a system is used.

If multiple shaft systems are used a great increase in the available facilities and for allowing automatic programing of the facilities and processes involved may be made, since longer time scales are provided. This greatly extends the usefulness and attractiveness of such a machine. This programing may be of the temporary type set up on alloy discs or of the permanent type on etched discs.

The principal virtues of such a machine are largely due to the alloy discs which allow numbers to be stored indefinitely and to be put on and taken off by a conveniently controlled electric circuit, and that none of the mechanical parts have to accelerate or decelerate during the operation of the machine. The advantages of the electric control are not only that it allows rapid operation but that the design is simplified and capable of more readily being extended and interconnected to other apparatus.

Several economies of operation result. It should be cheaper to build, because the precision of the electric parts is much smaller than the equivalent mechanical parts. Maintenance should be reduced because of the reliability and long life of the electric parts, the residual mechanical parts having only very simple bearing surfaces capable of giving long life. The coil structure used to magnetize the alloy discs may be separate from those used to reproduce and demagnetize them, although in the interest of simplicity it should be possible to produce all these operations with the same coil assembly. An economy over card and tape machines may be effected since no materials are normally used up in the operation of the machine, only electric power is consumed.

J. Presper Eckert Jr.

J Presper Eckert Jr.

Copied on February 1, 1945
from three typewritten sheets
dated January 29, 1944

CONFIDENTIAL

A reproduction of an important document. J. Presper Eckert's disclosure of January 1944 describes means for storing data on magnetic discs and, specifically, in paragraph 3 on page 2, the storing of programs on discs. This was long before Dr. John von Neumann entered the scene. The actual text of the document is shown in the Appendix.

April 8, 1943

REPORT ON AN ELECTRONIC DIFFERENCE* ANALYZER

Submitted to the

BALLISTIC RESEARCH LABORATORY, ABERDEEN PROVING GROUND

by the

MOORE SCHOOL OF ELECTRICAL ENGINEERING, UNIVERSITY OF PENNSYLVANIA

The Ballistic Research Laboratory, APG, is currently using the mechanical differential analyzer of the Moore School of Electrical Engineering, University of Pennsylvania, in connection with the preparation of firing tables. This report has been prepared at the request of Lt. H. H. Goldstine, in charge of the Ballistic Research Laboratory's section at the University of Pennsylvania, for transmission to certain interested persons at APG.

Contents

*The word Difference has been used deliberately. Present differential analyzers operate on the basis of integrating continuously, i.e., by differential increments; the electronic analyzer, although it is believed that it would be both speedier and more accurate, would operate using extremely small but finite differences. It thus is more appropriate to refer to it as a difference analyzer rather than a differential analyzer.

The first page of the proposal to Aberdeen Proving Grounds from The Moore School to develop ENIAC. This was requested by Lt. Herman Goldstine as a result of Mauchly's memo nearly a year earlier.

ping off the ring counter at the appropriate points to set/reset flip-flops or feed gating circuits.

To aid in debugging, two other modes of cycling unit operation were required, one-addition-time and one-pulse-time. In one-addition-time mode, pushing a button provided one complete set of normal control pulses during the 200-microsecond cycle and then a stop. One-pulse-time operation did the same, but on a more detailed basis in a 10-microsecond period. The direct coupled circuits of ENIAC would permit it to reside in the "stopped" state for any length of time. Thus it would be possible to slow the machine down from its normal 100 KHz rate so the operator could push buttons and follow each step of computation by reading the neon lights in the decade counters. Actually, this slow mode of operation was an auxiliary benefit of direct coupled circuits. The prime reason for the direct coupling was to reduce the number of required components, a major feature in system reliability.

Part of the design included an oscilloscope, so that any selected cycling unit signal could be displayed. Pres made certain that I put the cycling unit through thorough tests. The unit had to work over a 100- to 500-volt range, even though the normal operating voltage was 250. The frequency range was tested well beyond its normal value. A working prototype was completed by January, 1944. While I was engaged in designing and breadboarding the cycling unit, other engineers were busy working on accumulators, constant transmitters, multipliers, and other elements of the ENIAC system.

Although I worked directly with Pres Eckert, Dr. Mauchly's ideas and presence were also felt. He was more concerned with the systems design aspect than with the nuts, bolts, tubes, and resistors. Frequently, he could be seen discussing elements of the system design with Eckert or Dr. Burks.

When most of the circuit designs were well established early in 1944, Eckert and Mauchly had time to reflect on the then current ENIAC system design and consider its shortcomings. Programming was to be accomplished by plugging many cables and transmission lines into the appropriate units of the system. This could be a serious disadvantage if there was frequent change in the type of problem being run. As a result of much serious thinking on the subject, Pres Eckert wrote a disclosure on January 29, 1944, relating to a magnetic disk calculating machine in which all numerical data and data regarding instructions for the operation of the machine were to be stored in the same type of temporary or erasable memory. Thus the stored program concept was born, but the idea was not publicized until later in the year when a consultant for Aberdeen Proving Grounds, Dr. John Von Neumann, entered the scene. He was immediately struck by the concept and became a key force in planning the systems design of a post-ENIAC computer.

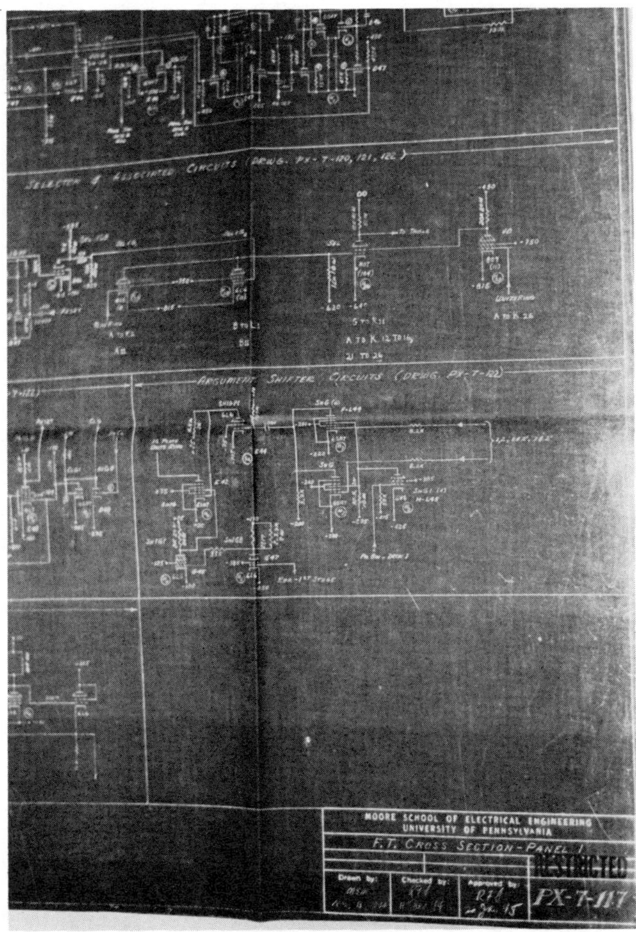

A section of one of the blueprints for the ENIAC. Note Bob Shaw's approval in the lower right corner.

In March, 1944, Pres Eckert arrived at another fundamental concept, that of using an acoustic mercury delay line as a recirculating memory for pulses representing data or instructions to be stored. This concept, too, was embraced by Dr. Von Neumann.

The work pace was relentless. Pres Eckert was a hard driver who always generated enough new ideas to keep everyone 150% occupied. The only respite we had from the serious atmosphere was provided by the sparkling antics of co-worker Bob Shaw. Bob

Photo taken of Dr. J. Presper Eckert in front of ENIAC Cycling Unit.

ENIAC was a large machine. This shows less than one-half of it.

Lt. Herman Goldstine looking at the tube (back) side of the ENIAC.

delighted in taking the small neon bulbs used in the counter units and plugging them directly into the 110-volt power strip that encircled the lab. A brilliant purple flash would occur, followed by a loud report like a firecracker going off. Our concern was for Bob. Like most albinos, Bob had impaired vision, and his was particularly bad. His face had to be two inches away from the circuit he was working on for things to be in focus. We kept worrying about the possibility of Bob's blowing off his nose or damaging his eyes. Bob's breadboards were a sight to behold, the worst kind of mess you can image. Wires went in every direction and with hundreds of volts floating around, everyone held his breath when Bob went to work. Despite several physical handicaps, Bob Shaw was one of the more brilliant members of the project.

Early in 1944, Pres Eckert announced that we were going to build a 2-accumulator model as a test vehicle. This would be an opportunity to test our designs, both electrically and mechanically, before going ahead with the final design.

Perhaps I should take a moment to explain that an accumulator was a memory device that could store a 10-digit number plus the sign of the number. It also had the capability of adding to or subtracting from the stored number. Ten decade counter units were used to form an accumulator. Each decade counter unit was formed into a three foot long narrow chassis that plugged into an eight foot high mainframe. One out of the ten small neon lights lit on each decade counter unit to disclose the number stored. There were twenty such accumulators used in ENIAC and they were the heart (or brain, if you prefer) of the system. Thus a 2-accumulator model could test the basic processes employed in ENIAC, such as addition, subtraction, storage, and control.

I was given the job of designing and building the required power supplies. Normally this isn't too difficult a task, but this was not a normal situation. The ENIAC circuits were all directly coupled and this led to the proliferation of voltages required. I remember having to design something like twenty different voltage regulated supplies interconnected into one power supply network. Pres, of course, tracked my designs and suggested some innovations of his own.

Early in March, 1944, I arrived home one day to find an ominous letter from my draft board. What it stated was quite simple—1A. I was on Dr. Brainerd's doorstep when he arrived the next morning and explained my predicament. Dr. Brainerd felt confident that with the importance of ENIAC to the war effort and with the assistance of high level personnel at Aberdeen Proving Grounds, my 1A rating would be rescinded. I left with a feeling of hope.

One month later Dr. Brainerd gave me the news—all bad. There apparently was a U.S. Government dictum that no one under the age of 22 could be deferred. The reasoning given was that no one so young could have the maturity and background to be declared essential to an industry. Dr. Brainerd had struck out. There wasn't anything more I could do but wonder what my departure date would be. I felt sorry, unhappy, and cheated. I had only just begun to cut my eyeteeth on ENIAC and now I was to be whisked away from one of the most complex and challenging projects of the century.

In the remaining period, I worked with Jack Davis in setting up a 2-accumulator model. Some of the entrance space of adjacent project PY area was taken over for this purpose.

The inevitable "Greeting" arrived in June with instructions to report to the Bainbridge, Maryland, Induction Station on July 5, 1944.

I finished up the remaining work of interconnecting all power supplies and testing them by my termination day at the end of May. I shook hands with Pres, Dr. Brainerd, and all of my other good friends at The Moore School, and I was off to join the U.S. Navy.

I wish I could describe more about ENIAC but the shortness of my stay on the project does not permit it. For those who are interested in a documented account of the development of ENIAC, I recommend reading at least the middle section of Dr. Herman Goldstine's book.

During my one-week leave from boot camp in September, I dropped by to see how the project was progressing. Jack Davis proudly showed me the 2-accumulator model—now working. It was an exhilarating sight. Jack demonstrated it by placing numbers in each accumulator. The neon bulbs testified to this. By pushing a button, he made the sum appear. Then, putting the switch on continuous mode, the accumulators added at the 100 KHz rate, producing just a blur on the neon bulbs. The significance of what I saw was momentous. Several basic principles of digital computation were proven. The 2-accumulator model was a success and now the project was engaged in building the final product.

Chapter 5

TIME OUT FOR THE NAVY

By mid-1944 the armed forces were fully stocked with commissioned officers, and my attempts to obtain a commission were unsuccessful. Luckily, through a special Navy program, I was destined to be more than a swabbie. Applicants had to pass either the Eddy test or have a valid amateur radio license to be accepted for the Radio Technician program. A one-year training course was part of the program. That was the best opportunity I could see, so I applied. I hoped I might learn something, although I was a little skeptical.

The morning of July 5, 1944, I kissed my mother goodbye and headed for the train station. A 3-hour ride brought me and a number of young looking kids to Bainbridge, Md. It was a staging area and we waited around for the groups to form. After three long days, my name popped up on a bulletin board in the middle of a long stream of names. Next morning, several hundred of us were loaded aboard the troop train for a long trip to the famous Great Lakes Naval Training Center, where we did our boot training.

The Great Lakes facilities sprawled for many miles. All you could see were barracks after barracks followed by several drill and training fields. First we were assigned to our "home," and then introduced to our company leader, Whitey. He was a small guy with a powerful voice and not too much upstairs, but he was eminently successful at his job. Later I learned that Whitey had collected more "Roosters" than any other platoon leader. Roosters were white penants with red roosters and were awarded to the best platoon at each Saturday morning's inspection. Initially I couldn't have cared less about the roosters, but that was Whitey's secret of success, he made you care.

The first several days were indoctrination. We were issued our seabags and clothing supplies, taught how to roll and store them, given our money's worth on haircuts, and lined up for all the required shots. Sure enough, only the husky guys keeled over, just like the movies. Soon we settled down to the serious business of boot training, the majority of which consisted of marching to cadence with a wooden gun. This went on for hours, day after day. Whitey's "hup-2-3-4, hup-2-3-4," droned on and on. Right face, left face always produced a few embarrassed faces. The July sun was a killer, but Whitey forbade anyone the pleasure of fainting. He was a tough taskmaster by any method of measurement.

The evening hours were free, if you can call the time spent in cleaning up free. Nearly every night we washed clothes, and the easiest way of doing that was to walk into the shower with your clothes on and start soaping them up. When the outer layer was soapy, you would take it off and soap the underclothes. Finally you would take off the underclothes, including the stockings, and thoroughly stomp on the whole mess a dozen times. The benefit of this procedure was that you could stay quite clean without ever having to take a shower.

After a week or two, I started to recognize some of the fellows. The overwhelming majority were 18 years old, right out of high school. One fellow, Ted Mihran, had a B.S. in electrical engineering from Stanford, and later I found several more men with degrees. We kept our college degrees under cover. We could see that making this information known to a drill instructor, who had only a sixth grade education, might lead to disadvantages at boot camp.

I spent some time talking to Ted about my project work. I knew the project was classified and confidential, so I could only talk in generalities. Somehow, the atmosphere was not especially conducive for a lively discussion on electronics. A more appropriate discussion would have been "on the occurrence of fluid-filled, swollen tissues at the outer extremities."

Getting ready for the weekly inspection ritual was the big activity and it occurred on Friday night and Saturday morning. Whitey whipped us into a frenzy of activity. Work details were established, with a job for everyone. If a visitor walked in, he would have sworn that the boys were dancing. They were to some degree (a very small one); we called it the Great Lakes Shuffle. Each man had a big pad of steel wool under each shoe. By swishing his legs back and forth properly, he could maintain his balance, not lose the steel wool pads, and get the floor cleaned. After forty years of such treatment, if I were the responsible officer, I would worry about the whole bottom falling out of the Great Lakes Naval Training Center.

Every single piece of wood or glass had to be cleaned. When the barracks was in order, then came the additional chore of getting yourself in order. All clothing had to be flawless; shoe polishing was a fetish. I could swear I was walking around in two cans of shoe polish most of the time.

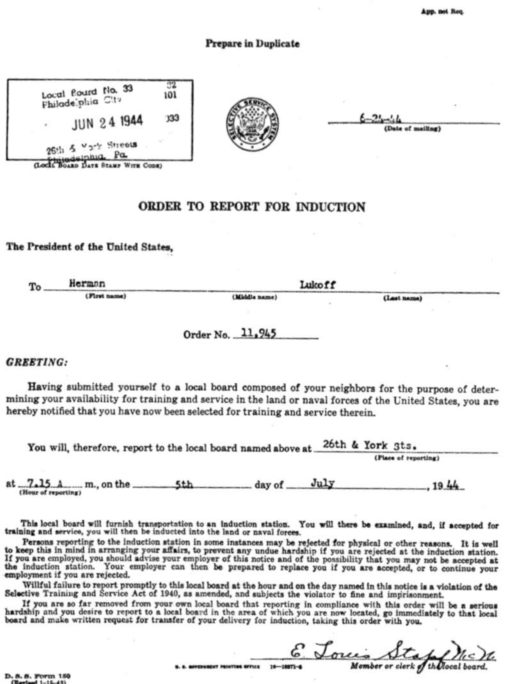

App. not Req.

Prepare in Duplicate

Local Board No. 33
Philadelphia City
JUN 24 1944
26th & York Streets
Philadelphia, Pa.
(LOCAL BOARD DATE STAMP WITH CODE)

6-24-44
(Date of mailing)

ORDER TO REPORT FOR INDUCTION

The President of the United States,

To Herman Lukoff
(First name) (Middle name) (Last name)

Order No. 11,945

GREETING:

Having submitted yourself to a local board composed of your neighbors for the purpose of determining your availability for training and service in the land or naval forces of the United States, you are hereby notified that you have now been selected for training and service therein.

You will, therefore, report to the local board named above at 26th & York Sts.
(Place of reporting)

at 7.15 A m., on the 5th day of July, 1944
(Hour of reporting)

This local board will furnish transportation to an induction station. You will there be examined, and, if accepted for training and service, you will then be inducted into the land or naval forces.

Persons reporting to the induction station in some instances may be rejected for physical or other reasons. It is well to keep this in mind in arranging your affairs, to prevent any undue hardship if you are rejected at the induction station. If you are employed, you should advise your employer of this notice and of the possibility that you may not be accepted at the induction station. Your employer can then be prepared to replace you if you are accepted, or to continue your employment if you are rejected.

Willful failure to report promptly to this local board at the hour and on the day named in this notice is a violation of the Selective Training and Service Act of 1940, as amended, and subjects the violator to fine and imprisonment.

If you are so far removed from your own local board that reporting in compliance with this order will be a serious hardship and you desire to report to a local board in the area of which you are now located, go immediately to that local board and make written request for transfer of your delivery for induction, taking this order with you.

E. Louis Staf McN
Member or clerk of the local board.

D. S. S. Form 150
(Revised 1-15-43)

For the younger generation who never heard about the famous "Greeting" from the President of the United States.

The big moment arrived at 10 a.m. Saturday morning when each swabbie stood at ease along side his bunk. At some point "Attention!" was yelled, and an officer entered the barracks with Whitey following right behind. Everyone was standing rigidly at attention as the officer initiated his thorough—nit-picking—inspection. Soon his eyes lit up—he spotted a wrinkle in a bed. A little later his eyes lit up again—he spotted a knot in a bow tie that did not meet regulations. His eyes lit up once more—a man had fuzz on the back of his neck. That did it! The rooster was shot to hell for that week. I suggested to Whitey that we might do better if we got an inspecting officer whose eyes did not light up. The poor guys that were caught were put on the s--- list, which meant you lost some privileges. Admittedly, you didn't have many to start with, and this didn't help. The next week Whitey worked everybody even harder; drilling, calisthenics, cleaning, etc. He really wanted that stringy bird. Sure enough, our platoon won the coveted rooster.

In our last week of boot camp, our wooden rifles gave way to real ones. Each day we were driven several miles to a remote part of the reservation where the firing range was located. With a minimum amount of training we shot at the bull's eye from the prone position. The first day was a disaster. We staggered back to our buses with bloody noses, bloody puffed-up lips, and battered morale. The enemy (U.S. Navy) won that battle. The trick, which we discovered soon afterwards, was to keep the gun butt tightly against the shoulder so that the recoil couldn't kick it in uncontrollable directions. After the first day, everyone did better. We even located the target that the instructor talked about.

The 6-week training period finally ended. I now knew how to put one hundred pounds of gear into a fifty pound sea bag, could tell my left from my right, and learned how to shine shoes to a high state of perfection. My Navy training so far had been a great success. I graduated as a Seaman 1/C.

After a week's leave at home in early September, 1944, I returned to the outgoing staging area at the Great Lakes facility to wait for the next assignment. While the Navy was making up its mind, it decided to keep everyone busy making best use of their talents. I was assigned to the WAVEs' chow hall. The first part sounded interesting, but it was the latter part that got me. My job was really quite simple, wiping the lipstick from the cups after they came out of the washer. Now, wiping the lipstick from 10,000 cups a day can lead one into developing a complex. It started with hating lipstick and from there it went to hating lips. I really began to worry about how far my feelings would progress when the end of the week came and I was relieved of my duties, just in time too, because I was starting to hate the hands that held the cups. The incongruity of the whole thing was that WAVEs were supposed to relieve ablebodied men for active duty. The administrators at Great Lakes seemed to have gotten the algorithm backward.

At the end of the week the sailors, including me, who were destined for the Radio Technician program were listed on the bulletin board for a Monday morning departure to the Manley School in Chicago. Manley proved to be another world, the opposite of the Great Lakes facilities in many respects. It was one of three Chicago junior high schools taken over by the Navy. Used as a one month, pre-training school, it was followed by three month primary and six month secondary schools. The total head count at Manley was small, probably several hundred. All were housed, fed, and schooled in the one building.

On our first trip through the breakfast chow line, we were stunned. Civilian servers asked us very kindly if we wanted some of this or some of that, with no limitations. It was carefully put on our trays. The other meals all proved great and a welcome change from the big base where shovelsfull of mashed potatoes were thrown at you whether you wanted them or not.

During the day we attended classes. They were very elementary, covering high school level arithmetic, trigonometry, algebra, slide rule operation, and elementary electricity. All of the fellows in my class were eighteen year olds, from many states in the union. Quizzes were given very frequently. The boys had to study furiously to pass the quizzes; failing could lead to active duty sooner than planned. It seemed unfair; here were all of these kids struggling to keep up, and to me it was as simple as ABC. What was I doing here?

Liberty was granted on Wednesday evenings and Sundays to those who passed the quizzes. I soon found near the school a small neighborhood USO, a delightful, friendly place. On each occasion there was a different group of young hostesses. After several months of nothing but males, I was more than ready to talk to sweet young things. My degree was firmly in hand, I was now free to explore the social world. Great idea! But what do you say to a girl? Somehow or other, being away from home, the friendliness of the girls, the circumstances, all acted for easy conversation. I was a terrible dancer. I figured this was the opportunity to improve. By apologizing to each girl first, I received consideration and tips on how to improve. Even I noticed the improvement.

The one month stay at Manley seemed brief, mainly because of the liberty periods. We wondered where we were headed next. The Navy had many schools scattered across the country. I hoped, I would be sent to a school close enough to home so that I might get there once in a while. My predictable luck occurred, and I wound up at the former garden spot of the Gulf Coast, Gulfport, Mississippi.

Before the war, Gulfport used to be the winter resort for wealthy Midwesterners. First the Seabees and later the Navy took over most of the town as a training center. The base was made up of many Quonset huts, used for housing, classrooms, chow halls, and just about everything you could imagine.

Down the road a few miles was the town of Biloxi, where a very large Army Air Force Base was located. With about 50,000 servicemen from each base roaming the coast, the civilians were outnumbered and didn't exhibit much enthusiasm upon seeing us. The only USO in the town of Gulfport had a dearth of hostesses; the natives probably kept their daughters locked up at night, and for very good reasons.

Each Quonset hut housed around thirty-five men in stacked bunks. I didn't know anyone in my hut, but soon enough I found that I was with some types of people I had never been exposed to before. A good number seemed to be hillbillies, or were from underprivileged sections of the country. The other possibility was that they were normal and I had led a sheltered life. Regardless, I soon learned the words to every bawdy Navy song and some that the Navy hadn't heard about. Even with today's morality, I can't repeat the words to "Lu Lu."

The primary classes were more interesting; primitive for me, complex for the others. Material started with basic electronic circuit theory and advanced to simple radio and transmitter theory. There were also some lab courses in the afternoons when the students could run simple experiments. Correlating classroom work with lab experiments was an excellent idea. To graduate, each student had to construct, debug, and tune up a 5-tube, AC/DC broadcast radio. Because it would have been impossible to supply all new parts for each radio, the old ones were used over and over. The leads on resistors kept getting shorter and shorter as they were unsoldered or clipped off. The other components were also beat up, but electrically they did work.

After the first month of instruction on what a resistor, tube, capacitor, and circuit diagram are along with some basics on how to use a soldering iron, everyone was given a basket of parts and a chassis. Some of the kids (those who knew Lu Lu best) had great difficulty in getting started. For me, it was one of my simpler projects; in fact, the parts reminded me of my junkbox at home containing parts that I had used over and over again. There were a few tricks I had learned then that came in handy now. I could extend the length on any component lead by butting a longer wire against the short wire and soldering it. A piece of spaghetti insulation was then slipped over the wire and joint and no one could tell that it wasn't the original long component lead. Another idea I used to give the radio a professional appearance was to run all components and wires parallel or at right angles to each other, but never at an intermediate angle. I also used a dab of glue to keep wires down on the chassis so they would not flop around.

Even though these procedures took longer than haywiring (wires going in every direction), which everyone else was using, I had no problem in completing the receiver in one week, and in one more day aligned it with test equipment. I hooked the antenna terminal to a piece of wire and as I fully expected, voices blared out of the speaker. I was pleased; the inside of the chassis looked beautiful.

The instructor couldn't believe it. He had never before witnessed so short a period for a construction job, nor one that looked so professional. I asked him what to do with the remaining six weeks. He suggested I help some of the other students who were far behind. The instructor disappeared with my radio and I didn't see it for a few days.

Two days later, I was notified to appear at the commander's office. He proceeded to ask me many questions, and was astounded when he found I had a degree in electrical engineering.

"What are you doing here?" he asked.

"I ask myself the same question," I responded.

He then offered me the opportunity to remain at Gulfport Naval Training Center as an instructor. I thanked him for the opportunity, but declined the offer. Secretly, I felt that any place had to be better than Gulfport.

My radio was placed on the top shelf and kept there as a model for others to emulate.

Actually, the Gulf Coast wasn't all that bad. A high concentration of service personnel made it seem worse than it was. On weekends, the sailors and soldiers would disperse, many going to New Orleans. On several occasions I hopped the train for a weekend there too—it proved to be an interesting sightseeing experience. I wasn't the drinking type or on the make, and therefore did not exercise all of the options that New Orleans had to offer. Most weekends I just lounged around the base and became bored. October, November, and December of 1944 passed slowly, but finally primary school was completed and the lists were posted for our secondary school assignments.

I was destined for Chicago again and was happy about that. At least the civilians greatly outnumbered the servicemen there. So, on a January morning of 1945 the Chicago-bound contingent boarded a troop train and headed north. Maybe it wasn't north, because twenty-four hours later the troop train was still in Mississippi. Nevertheless, we did get to Chicago and to the Navy Pier, our home for the next six months.

The Navy Pier was a structure jutting out half a mile into Lake Michigan, just a little north of the central business section of Chicago known as the Loop. The pier was a Navy Base within itself, like a small city, complete with housing, classrooms, and accommodations for thousands of men. Most of the length of the pier was devoted to barracks style housing. When the loudspeakers blared "Now hear this," you heard it, especially at 6:30 a.m. when reveille sounded. I had no problems in arising, but for some of the fellows it was torture. The world is made up of early risers and late risers; luckily, I am one of the former.

The large space heaters which hung from the ceiling had a difficult job keeping up with Chicago's wintry weather. It was then that I realized why we were issued long john winter underwear the previous summer at Great Lakes.

Secondary school proved to be much more interesting than I had originally thought. Although I had a good theoretical background, and some good practical background, I was thrust into working with equipment that I had never seen before. Radar, sonar, and loran were all new to me and I had much to learn. Even the communications equipment had many new aspects, such as high power, high and low frequency, and frequency modulation.

The schooling ran most of the day, divided between classrooms and laboratories where the actual gear was set up. Instructors would purposely place a bug (failure) into the equipment and students would attempt to isolate the problem. The classes were interesting and challenging; I must say the Navy did an excellent job of education in its secondary schools.

Not only did the schooling go well, but so did my social life. After all, we were back in Chicago. I don't know of any other city that went to the extremes that Chicago did to welcome servicemen. Anyone stationed there during the war was lucky.

The city had many USO clubs, but the biggest one of all was a multistory building on Michigan Blvd. Each floor of the building was devoted to a different facet of entertaining servicemen. One floor, the one for dancing, was loaded with hostesses; on another floor food was served; older ladies sewing buttons and stripes on service clothing occupied another floor. Pool and ping-pong tables were always available. Tickets to the best shows and even the opera were available free, although the quantities were limited. You had to go to the USO early on Saturday mornings to enjoy these giveaways. I first saw *Oklahoma* from a third row seat at one of the Saturday matinees. I was introduced to *Madame Butterfly* on another Saturday afternoon. Several times I obtained tickets for the *Chicago Theater of the Air* featuring singer Marian Clare. I used to listen to these broadcasts in my student days when romantic operettas were a means of escape.

I soon discovered there was a smaller USO in the northeast corner of the Loop that was run by the Jewish Welfare Board. This one served bagels and lox for Sunday breakfast and had hostesses of my own faith. I spent most of my free time at this USO during the cold winter months. There seemed to be an unlimited supply of girls on hostess duty. Even though I had liberty two evenings a week, as well as the weekends, I never saw the same girl there twice. Chicago had risen to the cause. If I was deprived of female companionship during my younger years, I was certainly making up for it now. At last I was getting calibrated on the types of womanhood that existed. I asked several of the girls for dates outside the USO, but I didn't develop enough interest for further follow up.

Time went by quickly with these distractions. Cruel winter melted into spring and then summer and a whole new raft of diversions appeared. A favorite one was the Edgewater Beach Hotel, a USO located on Chicago's North Shore. The setting was absolutely delightful. Nearly all of the activities were out of doors where lanterns lit up the walkways and dancing under the stars created a fantasyland. It was hard to believe that a war was going on and that we would be joining it in a few short months.

Finally, on one of my USO outings I met a girl to whom I took an immediate liking. Her name was Shirley. When I told her mine, her face lit up. "That's my brother's name," she exclaimed, "only I call him Hermie, and that is what I am going to call you." Her brother was also an electronics engineer and was undergoing officer candidate training at Fort Monmouth. Shirley lived in Chicago's West Side, and Jackson Blvd. soon became well known to me. Her parents made me feel very much at home; the weekends couldn't come fast enough. There were so many things to do and places to go; Ravinia Music Festival, Grant Park Band Shell, museums, movies, and shows. We enjoyed each other's company and soon developed an emotional feeling for each other.

My training at Navy Pier would come to an end in another month. In September, I would have a ten day leave, head back home to Philadelphia, and then leave for who knows where. Shirley already had an invitation to visit her brother at Fort Monmouth. Fort Monmouth was so close to Philadelphia that it didn't take too much to convince her to take the same train back with me in September and meet my mother.

One day in August, 1945, while we were in class at the Navy Pier, a startling announcement came over the public address system: the United States had dropped a powerful new type of bomb on the Japanese city of Hiroshima. I believe the announcement called it an "atomic bomb." The fact that an announcement was made imparted a special significance, because for the most part we were shielded from the daily battlefront events. No one had a newspaper delivered to his door, and the transistor radio hadn't been invented yet. Although I was in the war, I had scant knowledge of what was happening. We surmised that the announcement over the PA system was important.

Three days later a similar announcement was made that another "atomic bomb" had been dropped on Nagasaki. Rumors abounded that Japan might quit the war.

VJ night in the Chicago Loop was an event I will never forget. Pandemonium would be a mild way of describing it. People were dancing in the streets. Girls were running around kissing every serviceman they could find. Everyone was yelling, "The war is over!" After hours of euphoria roaming the Loop, I just barely met the curfew on returning to the Navy Pier. We were awake for hours, lying in our bunks, discussing what effect the cessation of the war would have on us. No one, of course, knew, but we counted our blessings, hoping that there was now little chance of getting killed in action.

Company 106 graduated from Navy Pier in Early September, 1945. I proudly made the transition from Seaman 1/C to Radio Technician 2/C; it felt good adding that stripe on my uniform. We were now fully trained and ready for active duty one month after the war was over. The question of next assignment was only partially answered. After the forthcoming ten day leave, we were to report to Camp Shoemaker in California. Everyone guessed that Shoemaker was the staging area for Pacific duty.

Soon Shirley and I were heading back to Philadelphia. The overnight train ride was uneventful, except that neither of us could sleep in the uncomfortable coaches. The next morning we rolled into Philadelphia, and it was good to see William Penn again atop his City Hall perch. Soon we arrived at my home. After a shower of motherly kisses, I introduced Shirley.

The two days disappeared in seconds. Before I knew it, Shirley was on the train, headed for a reunion with her brother at Fort Monmouth. I didn't know it then, but that was the last time I ever saw her.

One of the first things I had to catch up on was ENIAC. How far had the project progressed since I last saw the 2-accumulator model nearly a year ago? In my freshly pressed sailor's uniform, I entered The Moore School and headed for the rear room. When I opened the door I could hardly believe my eyes. Gone were all the workbenches that had been scattered around the room. Instead, the room was filled with wall-to-wall ENIAC. It was a monster. Black racks reached from floor to ceiling. They were arranged in a U around the periphery of the large room. Activity abounded. Several people were in the room turning knobs and looking studious. The little neon lights on each accumulator were twinkling.

Finally Jack Davis recognized me. It was a joyful reunion. He told me that ENIAC had been completed and was now undergoing programming checkout. The engineering phase was complete and it was a success. I felt good that I had played some small part in the project.

All too soon I was bidding Mom goodbye and was on the train again for the long ride across the country. This time Chicago was just a place to change trains. The ride through the western states was new, interesting, and enjoyable.

Some of my Navy Pier Company 106 friends and me enjoying Chicago's North Shore before heading for the Philippine Islands.

Camp Shoemaker was, in fact, a vast staging area, and I was able to uncover some of my Company 106 mates. We had nothing to do except scan the bulletin board each day to see if our names were posted. Finally, after three weeks of lazing in the California sun, it happened; we were put aboard large busses with our seabags and off we drove. The bus wasn't on the road more than an hour when San Francico loomed into view. Our terminus was Treasure Island in the bay.

We were again housed in temporary barracks, this time by platoon. In just a few days we found ourselves boarding a large troopship, destination unknown. I would guess that there were several thousand men aboard, and housing those men on that ship was an interesting exercise in logistics. The berths were stacked six high with only two feet or so between each berth. It was impossible to sit up in a berth and it was necessary to climb up between the rows of berths, and then slide in horizontally. It took some getting used to.

Our troopship departed Treasure Island early that next September morning. The view of the bay was breathtaking, especially steaming under the Golden Gate Bridge. After several hours, the United States was no longer visible, but other things were happening to divert our attention, like getting seasick. Some of the men were already developing wobbly legs and even wobblier stomachs. Within a day the seasickness had spread to the point where a large number of men were moaning, retching, and lying lethargically in their sacks, skipping all meals. Others, more stoic, carried buckets while they waited in the chow lines. The best way to describe seasickness is to say that you feel you would rather be dead.

After several days of pounding seas, tranquility befell us. Just about everyone was over the seasick stage and life became more bearable, or else we were getting used to it. A pattern set in of going to the mess hall, heading up to the top deck for some fresh air, taking an occasional salt water shower, and sacking out. The days were slowly passing, one by one. We had no idea where we were going. Could it be Hawaii, Japan, or one of the Pacific Isles? Each day the weather became warmer. Soon, sitting on deck for most of the day became the popular pastime. I even started to like the life and could understand the enjoyment that seafaring men found in it. Three weeks had passed and we had not seen a single evidence of land, not even one little island. Now I knew how Columbus must have felt. Finally toward the end of the fourth week, land became discernible. It took forever to cover the last few miles.

The Captain's voice boomed over the loudspeaker, "We are now approaching our destination, Samar, in the Philippine Islands." The Philippines! We had never thought of that possibility. We later learned that there was a large Navy base located on the southern tip of Samar at the native city of Guiuan. When our feet met solid ground again, after four weeks of movement, having the ground stand still was indeed a peculiar feeling. We entered the receiving station to find that again our status was temporary. From here, final assignments were made and mine was to the ship repair base on the island of Manicani, a few miles offshore.

Landing craft carried us to Manicani across the harbor full of many naval vessels. After an 8,000 mile trip I was finally at my new home. The island was only several miles wide, with the ship repair base occupying at least a quarter of it, and natives inhabiting portions of the remainder. Enlisted men lived in Quonset huts. Officers had more deluxe surroundings at the top of the hill overlooking the Quonset huts.

The next day I reported to Lt. Davis, at the large Quonset hut building near the waterfront. This was the electronic repair shop which was to be my base of operations. Lt. Davis explained that I was being assigned to the outside repair service, this was a group of radio technicians who took turns going out to ships in the harbor to repair their electronic gear. Usually it was equipment that the radio technician aboard the ship was unable to fix, or else the ship did not stock a critical repair part.

The job proved fascinating. In the morning I would board a landing craft that acted as the harbor ferry. It deposited me at the assigned ship, and then I was on my own. Sometimes I repaired a transmitter, a radar receiver, or a sonar indicator. On several occasions I had to climb eighty feet to the top of the ship's mast to repair the radar antenna motor. One moment I would look down and see that I was over water on the right side of the ship; seconds later I was over the left side. That kind of courage, however, disappears with age.

I can't remember a piece of equipment I wasn't able to repair and on most occasions I received a warming "thank you" from the ship's officers. At last I was utilizing my technical ability and enjoying it.

Sometime during the second week after arrival, I received a tremendous surprise. One of the officers, a full lieutenant, walked up to me in the repair shop and said "Hello, Herm." I was taken aback. It was Ray Attarian, a Moore School man who had been one class ahead of me. I remembered him as the fellow who cut many of his classes and spent his time playing cards in the homeroom; he remembered me as the hard working studious type.

"So this is where hard work got you," he said, as he eyed my enlisted man's dungarees while he strutted about in his officer's uniform. I only had a weak "Yea" for an answer.

There was a satisfying sequel to this event. When larger ships, like cruisers, came in to the harbor for repair, it was customary for an officer to accompany the radio technician to the ship. Sure enough, I was assigned to Ray on several occasions. Ironically, he would wind up holding the test meter for me or placing the test probe where I told him. Subtle revenge!

Life on the island was quite tolerable. The weather was tropical and ideal, with palm trees and abundant bush vegetation. The Navy had cut a road through to the other side of the island to establish a recreational area. That's where the beer was dispensed, each man being issued a chit good for three cans of beer per day. As I hated beer, I was a sought-after fellow. I gave my chit to a skinny fellow from Milwaukee who managed to collect chits from several other nondrinkers. He was able to consume an unbelievable twenty-one cans of beer a day.

The chow wasn't anything to write home about. In fact, there was a meat strike in the States which reduced our standard fare to Spam. The Spam cuisine lasted for months. I must admit that the cook was ingenious; we had Spam baked, broiled, roasted, sliced lengthwise, at a 45 degree angle, and at 75 degrees. With a little imagination it did taste different. What we lacked in meat was made up in ice cream. The Navy had a mix which was made into delicious ice cream right there on the spot, and we regularly received great gobs of it on our mess trays.

Despite the tropical paradise surroundings, something was missing. Naval authorities declared the surrounding waters polluted and so swimming was forbidden. Entertainment was provided two evenings a week with a movie shown in an outdoor theater hacked out of the jungle. The movies were several years old, not that that made any difference.

The local commandant advised all personnel that even though the war was over, they should remain on the alert for stray Japanese who had never heard of the war's end. Each enlisted man was required to stand guard duty and after two months my turn arrived. At 2 a.m. one morning, I was picked up, given a rifle by the security officer, and driven in a jeep to a desolate outpost halfway around the island. The only instructions were, "Use the rifle if necessary." No one was supposed to be out on the road at night except the patrol.

The jeep drove off and left me there, in the jungle under the stars, 8,000 miles from security. After the first half hour my sense of hearing started becoming more acute as the jungle noises intensified. I developed a nervous feeling remembering the commander's words about stray Japanese in the jungle. The second hour was worse as the strain started to set in. I was trying to put my mind at ease by thinking about Chicago when I thought I saw something move in the distance. My heart started to pound as I moved the rifle to my shoulder. I waited a bit as the silhouette got closer. Should I fire now and scare it away? The figure continued approaching as I held my hand on the trigger. When it got to within fifty feet of my post I could discern that it was a Philippine native leading a cow. I breathed a sigh of relief as I relaxed on the trigger.

"You go home right away," I barked. He didn't reply, just continued on his way. At 4 a.m., the patrol replaced me with another guard. I couldn't sleep when I got back to my hut. The night was shot.

My correspondence with Shirley had slacked off, and after a while in the Philippines, I, too, fell victim to a "Dear John" letter, only this one said "Dear Hermie." She never said why she wanted to break off and I could only surmise that she had met someone else. All further communications ceased. I felt sorry for myself, as she was the one girl I had related to.

To drown my sorrows, I thought of engaging in my old hobby, amateur radio. Several of the enlisted men were hams and they thought it was a great idea too. With the war over, the FCC authorized opening the 10 meter band. The local communications officer gave me permission to set up an amateur radio station, but he advised, "Keep it under cover." I took an old Navy transmitter used for harbor communications and converted it to the 10 meter code band. Half a dozen general coverage receivers existed in the shop, and one was appropriated for the good cause. Several Navy whip antennas were mounted on top of the building. Within a short period I had a complete station thrown together and, as luck would have it, the eleven year sun spot cycle was near its crest. I heard amateur stations from Europe, the Pacific Islands, and the West Coast of the United States. Unfortunately the skip conditions did not permit the rest of the States to come through. The transmitter and antenna worked fine and the amateur station became a major recreational outlet, with the licensed hams fighting over access to it. One of the officers, a licensed operator, found out about our operation and soon joined in the fun. Sometimes he would operate through the night and appear bleary eyed the next morning.

The amateur radio station also served a humanitarian purpose. Toward the end of 1945 and beginning of 1946, lists of personnel headed for discharge appeared weekly on the bulletin board. By the time a letter reached the home of a dischargee, he was on the front doorstep. I set up a network with stations on the West Coast who in turn could relay messages anywhere in the States. Through this service, the parents or wife of a dischargee knew of the action within a few days, rather than a month later.

The daily work and the amateur radio kept me engrossed until one day early in April, 1946, when my own name appeared on the bulletin board. The shock of going home was thrust upon me. I said goodbye to the island of Manicani and to the friends I had made there. Thirty years later for the first time I met someone who had been on the island, Dr. Richard Damon of the Sperry Corporate Research Center. He was an officer whom I remember seeing at the repair shop.

The trip back to the States gave me plenty of time to think of the future, even though the ship was faster this time and only took three weeks instead of four. I planned to go back to The Moore School first. I was on leave of absence, which in theory meant that if a position was available I could have it. But, since ENIAC was completed, would there be any project to work on? Only a trip to The Moore School could provide me with an answer.

I also had the chance to assess my one-month-short-of-two-years hitch in the Navy. On the whole it was a valuable experience, and I would recommend it to most young people, providing there is no war in progress. Aside from the technical experience, learning how to live with others and the exposure to new places and new people aided my maturity. It was a sobering experience in many respects and enjoyable in others. At first I was bitter at my poor luck in landing on the enlisted man's side of the Navy caste system but upon reflection, I have no regrets.

The train trip back across the western United States was even more fascinating than the one to California, as we wandered along the Feather River route. Three and a half days later I was in Chicago. I raced to the nearest telephone booth and called a familiar number. Shirley's mother answered. She was genuinely glad to hear from me. "How is Shirley and what is she doing?" I hesitatingly asked. Her mother replied, "Oh, Shirley is married and living in Texas." That took care of that, and I was on the train to Philadelphia a few hours later.

Chapter 6

GOOD INTENTIONS – EDVAC

I arrived home in May, 1946, just after my twenty-third birthday. My mother, sister, and other members of the family gave me a joyous welcome at our new home on 31st Street near Lehigh Avenue. Mom had remarried and moved to a larger house than the one we had on Stanley Street. My sister, Frances, had also married during the war years and was living in her own apartment. I easily settled into my own room and that weekend put my workbench back together in the basement.

Monday morning arrived. The trolley car route to The Moore School brought back memories. Dr. Brainerd was first on my list of people to see; he greeted me heartily and welcomed me back. He explained that there was a follow-on contract to ENIAC. "This computer project is called EDVAC and you are welcome to join us. Dr. Irven Travis is the contract administrator; you can see him." (EDVAC was the acronym for Electronic Discrete Variable Automatic Computer.)

I remembered Dr. Travis from my student days although I never had him as a teacher. He was glad to have me join the new project and offered me a research associate post at $2,800 per year. I didn't think twice about accepting his offer, and reported to work the next day.

Kite Sharpless and Joe Chedaker were among the old hands from ENIAC days to greet me, and I met some new members, including T. C. (Steve) Chen and Dick Weise. During the next few weeks Cy Gluck and my old classmate Dick Merwin joined the project. Kite, who was the project leader, explained things to me. Eckert and Mauchly were no longer actively engaged in the project; they were having an argument with the University over ownership of future patent rights. They had previously reached an agreement with the University whereby they owned the patent rights, but the University could license the Government or any other non-profit institution to make use of the ENIAC patent. The University was insistent upon changing this to retaining ownership of all rights, including commercial. This forced the resignations of Eckert and Mauchly in March, 1946.

Kite explained that one of the operational problems encountered with ENIAC was the large amount of time it took to reprogram the machine for a new problem. It had to be shut down for several days while many cables were replugged. It amounted to the machine's being rewired for each problem. Pres Eckert had conceived the idea of storing instructions in the memory of a computer and having these instructions carry out the rewiring at electronic speeds. To accomplish this large amounts of memory would be required, hundreds of words, and it would therefore have to be much less expensive than the vacuum tube flip-flop memory used in ENIAC. The concept that we were to exploit was the use of recirculating mercury columns. This was a follow-up on the use of a mercury column as an acoustic delay line for radar applications during the latter part of the war. To use the mercury column as a memory, an electrical pulse was transformed to an acoustic pulse by a quartz crystal placed at one end of the column. Because of the high density of the mercury, the launched acoustic pulse traveled at a low speed, taking hundreds of microseconds to reach the quartz crystal at the other end, where it was converted to an electrical impulse again. If the pulse was amplified and reshaped, it could be stuffed back into the mercury column. Thus, a pulse, once entered, could continue to circulate and be "remembered." In fact, many pulses next to each other could be put into the mercury column to represent hundreds of bits in the memory.

Mercury has the characteristic of changing its acoustic propagation time with temperature. Unless something was done to control the system, the mercury column, through temperature variation, would be too long or too short for the number of pulses it was to contain. I was given the job of devising the control system. Steve Chen and Joe Chedaker were my coworkers in trying to prove the feasibility of a mercury memory system. The approach that I decided to take was to vary the spacing between pulses in the mercury tank so that they could be spread or condensed to give the exact number of pulses required to fill the column. I started working out the details of the approach and initiated numerous breadboard experiments.

Life at The Moore School had changed considerably since the ENIAC days. Now that the war was over, the pace was much more leisurely and typical of a peacetime university. We even indulged in some academic perquisites such as having lunch in the student cafeteria at Houston Hall rather than brown-bagging it. Research personnel were also permitted to take graduate courses during normal working hours.

I had worked only a month on the project when an interesting diversion occurred. The Moore School had been asked by the

Government to put on a seminar covering computer technology. The course was to extend for a two month period during the summer, with personnel from various Government agencies invited to attend. The success of ENIAC led to Government interest in computers, and the prospect that they might be applicable to more than firing tables.

The brunt of the presentations fell on Pres Eckert and John Mauchly, but many others were signed up to contribute single lectures. Chuan Chu, who had designed the square rooter for ENIAC after I had left, was a contributer, along with Arthur Burks, Kite Sharpless, and others whom I don't remember. The seminar was an historical event. This was the first time computer technology was taught to any assemblage of people. Remember, at the time (1946) no books had yet been written nor papers given on the electronic computer art. Consequently, the officials thought it important that the lectures be recorded and published.

Dick Merwin and I were given the task of operating the magnetic wire recorder. Commercial tape recorders had not yet been perfected. Dick and I alternated days in recording. Wire recordings were not very fool proof; if you think rewinding tape on a reel that has spewed on the floor is a pain, try rewinding fine wire without getting a kink in it. Nevertheless, the recording task was completed, but the transcribing job turned into a horrendous task for the secretary. It took months to create first drafts and have these reviewed by the lecturers, but it was accomplished.

In early January, 1947, Harvard University decided to host the first computer conference. Harvard had done considerable work under Dr. Howard Aiken on relay type computers before the birth of ENIAC. The Moore School, of course, had to be well represented at the conference, and I was one of the lucky ones selected to go. The Mark I, II, and III computers from Harvard were demonstrated; although impressive, they were slow compared to ENIAC speeds. Papers were presented by people from Harvard, Penn, Princeton, and Bell Labs. In the Harvard labs, a young engineer by the name of Fuller demonstrated his "Numeroscope," electronic circuits that were capable of displaying numbers on a cathode ray tube. He was years before his time. It took twenty years for the concept to flourish.

The conference at Harvard was certainly an historic event. It verified the need for this type of communication, and became the springboard for subsequent computer conferences. Attendance has since grown from several hundred to tens of thousands.

During the fall and winter, we perfected our feasibility model of the mercury memory. My temperature compensator worked properly and we were able to get pulses to circulate in the column at a 1 MHz rate. Steve and Joe had built some test equipment to demonstrate the memory. Pulse combinations could be set up on a panel of switches on a test box to represent a number. When a button was pushed, this pulse combination was loaded in the mercury column. An oscilloscope connected to the mercury column permitted observation of the pulses in the memory and verification that the correct "bits" were being remembered. As far as I know, this was the first time a mercury memory system had been perfected.

The University also thought it was a notable achievement, and decided to demonstrate the development at the Institute of Radio Engineers (IRE) show in March, 1947, in New York City. Steve Chen and I were delegated to accompany the equipment to New York, and demonstrate it to the public for three days. We arrived the evening before the show opened, and connected up the mess of chassis, cables, and test equipment. Everything behaved as expected, so we retired for the evening.

The next day we were there at 10 a.m. to greet the thousands of attendees. No sooner was the equipment turned on than unusual things started to happen. The mercury memory would suddenly fill up with all kinds of extraneous pulses. When cleared, it would refill. I noticed that the pulses in the memory were changing rythmically every two seconds. We wondered what could be caus-

The author with an early mercury memory ready for public demonstration at the IRE show, New York City, March 1947.

ing that phenomenon. Onlookers pressed for explanation, which was embarrassing, to say the least. As I pondered the problem, the corner of my eye caught a rotating Army Signal Corps radar antenna halfway across the hall. Every time it rotated in our direction, the mercury memory pattern changed. That had to be it! I approached the radar operator, and asked him if the antenna was radiating power. Sure enough, it was. It did not make any difference to him whether the radio frequency power was on or off, so I convinced him to leave it off. That cured our problem and for the remainder of the show the memory performed without a flaw.

A week later Steve and I performed the same demonstration at the famed Franklin Institute in Philadelphia. The countenance of Benjamin Franklin smiled down upon us.

My next assignment was concerned with the development of the EDVAC central computer logic. Dick and I were given the job of developing a 4-bit parallel, floating point arithmetic unit. We were very much on our own as we evolved the laws of binary arithmetic, algorithims for multiply and divide operations, and learned about gates, half and full adders, shifters, decoders, and encoders. Many months were spent on the paper design of the logic. Each time we reviewed the drawings, we would invariably find some illogical condition we had not thought of before that required a redesign.

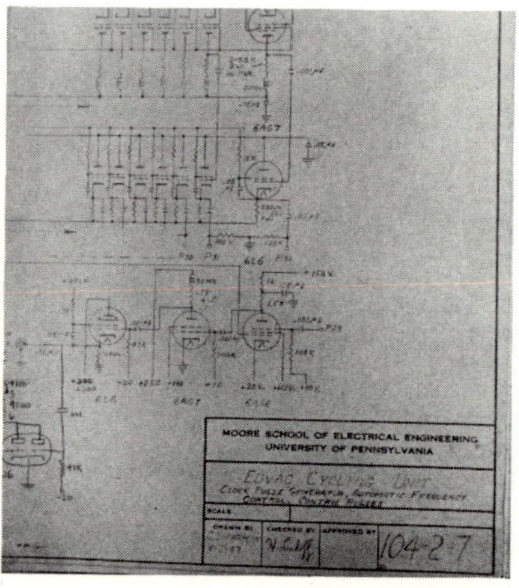

A portion of the author's design for EDVAC's Cycling Unit.

THE PHILADELPHIA INQUIRER. MONDAY MORNING. MARCH 3. 1947

EDVAC, THE NEW MAGIC BRAIN DEVELOPED AT PENN

T. Kite Sharpless, technical director of the University of Pennsylvania research group which has developed EDVAC, a new electronic magic brain, for the Army, operating a working model. The maze of coils, tubes and wires are devices for adding, subtracting, multiplying and dividing. The device memorizes a thousand 10-digit numbers.

EDVAC 'Remembers' Too

New Magic-Brain Computer Does Job 10 Times Faster

EDVAC, newspaper clipping, March 1947.

Progress, in general, was slow and seemed to lack direction, as we entered the summer. Eckert and Mauchly had long since left the University. Rumors floated around that they were organizing a business to build and sell commercial electronic computers. Kite Sharpless relinquished his position as project leader. He and three of his classmates went off to form the Technitrol Engineering Company in Philadelphia. An older ex-Navy Commander, Lewis P. Tabor, was brought in to head up the EDVAC project, but computers were new to him and he couldn't provide much direction. Dr. Travis brought aboard a relay computer expert as a consultant, but he had to make the transition from relays to vacuum tubes, and consequently was of no great benefit. Later another consultant, Sam Lubkin, proved to be very capable, knowledgeable, and argumentative.

Dr. Travis's Navy background was evident at The Moore School. He had a lieutenant, Jules Warshaw, who had everyone guessing. Every hour on the hour, Warshaw would show up at the lab door, poke his head in, look around and then disappear for another hour. We suspected that he never really did anything but report back to Doc Travis that everything was shipshape.

Early in August, 1947, Dr. Mauchly telephoned me at home one evening. He said that he and Pres had formed a company called the Electronic Control Company, and he would like me to join them as a junior engineer at a salary of $3,200 per year. That Saturday morning I went to the company office and lab. I liked what I saw. Furthermore, I was convinced that the project at The Moore School was floundering. Computer development should no longer be an academic pursuit; it was time for commercialization, time for business to exploit this modern miracle.

The following Monday morning I approached Dr. Travis, gave him my resignation, and stated my intention of leaving at the end of August. I told him I was most appreciative of the opportunity he had given me, but that the opportunity would be even greater in the new business venture. I said goodbye to all of my friends on the last working day in August, and walked slowly away from the birthplace of the electronic computer.

Subsequently, I learned that a competent engineer by the name of Richard L. Snyder was named chief engineer. He was able to deliver EDVAC to the Aberdeen Proving Grounds, much later than planned and with some residual problems. It was the last large scale computer system designed at The Moore School.

Chapter 7

ON THEIR OWN—ELECTRONIC CONTROL COMPANY

On September 1, 1947, Ted Bonn and I both reported for work at the Electronic Control Company. Ted was one of my classmates at The Moore School, and had worked on other Government projects there since graduation. The Electronic Control Company was located in downtown Philadelphia at 1215 Walnut Street on the second and third floors over a men's clothing store. The building was unusually long and adequate for the size of the company. A small machine shop was located at the rear of the second floor, with the lab area occupying most of the front of the third floor. Large glass windowpanes covered the front of the building so that it was possible to sit at a lab bench and look out over Walnut Street, one of the most elite shopping areas in town. Once a month the large windows were washed, and for days afterwards there would be disturbing thuds as pigeons tried to fly through the glass.

I was introduced to the handful of professionals who were already aboard—Al and Ike Auerbach (no relationship), Brad Sheppard, Gerry Smoliar, Frazer Welsh, John Sims, Bob Shaw, and Betty Snyder. Al Auerbach had degrees in physics and several other subjects, and was a general circuits engineer. Brad was a Moore School graduate who had worked on the early mercury memory. Ike was an ambitious young Drexel University electrical engineering graduate who was to make a name for himself in later years. Gerry had been a Signal Corps civilian employee, and had a good background in electronics, especially the power side. Frazer was an aeronautics engineer, and undoubtedly one of the cleverest fellows that I have ever run into. Even though he had no formal training in electrical engineering, his knowledge of the fundamentals and his logical thinking permitted him to hold any electronics engineer at bay. Frazer was Pres's equal in thinking ability and in most cases was the proving ground for Pres's ideas; if a flaw was there, Frazer would find it. Betty Snyder was a familiar face from the ENIAC programming group. John Sims was Pres's brother-in-law and the general

The first home of the Electronic Control Company at 1215 Walnut Street in downtown Philadelphia. A men's store occupied the first floor and we worked behind the windows on the second and third floors.

mechanical engineer for various projects. Bob Shaw, of ENIAC fame, was the logic designer, *par excellence.* A month later, Lou Wilson from MIT's Whirlwind project joined the company and shortly after that Jim Weiner, from Raytheon, became our Chief Engineer. Then there was the technician group under the capable direction of Maurice Ben Stad. Ben was a professional musician, in fact, the leading participant in the Society of Ancient Instruments, but he had to turn to other means to earn a living. Ben was a joker and a great guy. Pres, of course, was his usual effervescent and ingenious self. He was on top of everything, and never lacked ideas for the engineers to try out.

The company's ultimate goal was to develop a Universal Automatic Computer (from which the name UNIVAC originated). However, to reach that goal would require some new technological development and to support this effort, contracts with the Government were solicited. The Bureau of the Census took the lead in establishing an interest in computers. It, above all other government agencies, had an enormous problem in data reduction, and had a great deal to gain through the use of electronic computation. The officials at the Census Bureau had been turning in this direction, and through the National Bureau of Standards negotiated small contracts with the Electronic Control Company to establish the feasibility of some of the concepts. A number of the projects that we worked on were in response to these contracts. Other projects were company sponsored.

My first assignment was in collaboration with Gerry Smoliar and Brad Sheppard in designing a mercury tank memory demonstration system. The mercury tank in this case contained several parallel columns utilizing the same common pool of mercury. Gerry's approach to temperature control of the mercury tank was to electronically control an electrical heating coil wound over the tank. This was a different approach from the one I had previously used on the EDVAC project. The pulse density was also five times higher than that used at The Moore School, and consequently could contain that many more bits of information. Reducing the cost per bit of memory was the name of the game for commercial application. It still is today and probably always will be.

Eckert and Mauchly realized that the future success of electronic computers would depend on the computer's ability to communicate with man. High speed computation by itself would be of little value if information could not be gotten into and out of the

One of our first marketing brochures.

Al Auerbach (left) and John Mauchly with high speed serial adder demonstration unit.

computer rapidly. Certainly this was the case with most businesses whose records were kept on paper or punched cards. Punched cards had become the means for communicating with electro-mechanical tabulating machines and calculators, but Pres and John believed that much higher input/output device speeds were required to match the electronic speed of central processors. The solution that they favored was the development of digital magnetic tape and high speed transports for it.

A major project was initiated to develop such a tape and transport. Ted Bonn was given this assignment. Commercial magnetic tape and transports up to this time were primarily for audio recording, and were not suitable for digital (pulse) recording. The tapes and magnetic heads couldn't provide the high frequency response or reliability required, and the transports couldn't stop and start fast enough.

A chemistry lab was established for development of the tape coating materials. A major decision was made to use a metal base, because it could be easily electroplated and would not suffer from stretch to the degree that plastic based tapes did. Doug Wendell was the wizard of the test tubes and it was a matter of course to see many, many tape strips taking over Doug's lab. The chemistry lab proved its worth when the Philadelphia Transportation Com-

The Electronic Control Company's first mercury tank demonstration unit. It contained two channels for data and one for temperature control. Chief Engineer James R. Weiner is at the right and Brad Sheppard is at the left.

pany raised its trolley car rates from seven and a half cents to ten cents by changing from nickel plated tokens to copper plated ones. It was surprising how many tokens were copper plated that day in the lab!

Al Auerbach was busy designing a high speed serial binary adder demonstration unit that would work at a 5 MHz rate. Al's black panel had two rows of eight switches that could set up the two binary numbers to be added. The results of the addition, which took 1.8 microseconds, were shown visually on the oscilloscope. Al coaxed the unit to work but he soon found that 5 MHz circuitry was very touchy, and a lot of tuning was required. Nevertheless, it did demonstrate the feasibility of high speed logic circuits.

The whole attitude at Electronic Control Company was one of motivation and achievement. We knew we were doing things that had never been done before. Pres was also a hard and tireless driver. Although working hours were officially forty hours per

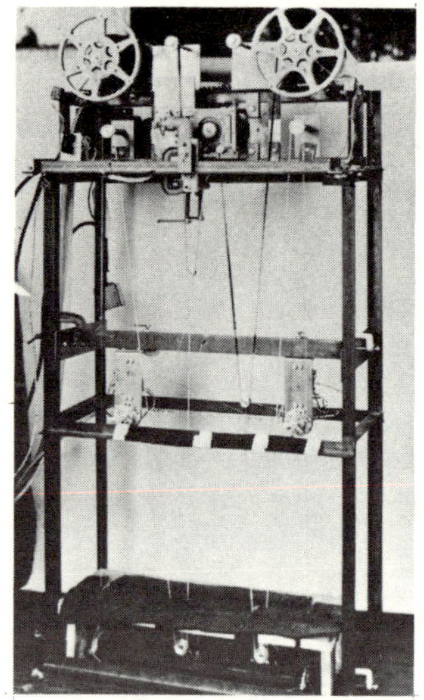

A laboratory model of the first UNISERVO tape handler. Large tape loops permitted the tape passing over the magnetic head to accelerate rapidly. A string and pulley system relayed the loop positions to two selsyn sensors in the middle of the unit.

An early project for a Government Agency that helped us develop digital tape handler techniques.

week, this was considered a minimum. Nearly all the professionals worked much more than this, without the slightest thought about overtime pay, which the company couldn't afford anyway.

We had fun too. Lunches in town were always interesting especially with Bob Shaw along. Bob was a connoisseur of exotic foods. Squid in its own ink was a favorite. Even though he survived every such culinary experiment, the rest of us suffered from impaired appetites. The small company esprit de corps brought us together for other outings such as deep sea fishing expeditions and smoker film showings at an unnamed member's home (today's X-rated films are better).

Ben Stad's group, the Society of Ancient Instruments, conducted a recital each year. (I used to needle Ben by substituting "Musicians" for "Instruments.") There was always a large company turnout for this event. One year the recital was held at the Art Center in Wilmington, Delaware. I picked up my date and headed for Wilmington. When I got to the city, I did not know which way to turn to get to the Art Center, so I stopped to ask a motorcycle policeman. "Follow me," he said. With his red lights blinking and siren screaming, he raced through the city to our destination. What a way to go! That city of Wilmington had class! My date was impressed. I was impressed.

Pres Eckert was convinced that computer memories in future systems would have to be not only less expensive, but also faster. The mercury memory was a large cost factor improvement over the vacuum tube flip-flop, but it had a speed limitation. Hundreds of microseconds might be lost while waiting for the stored information to emerge from the column. This was called access time, and on the average was equal to one half of the transit time of the mercury column. Various groups were known to be working on other approaches, mainly involving the storage of electrical charges. RCA was developing a special tube called the "Selectron." Pres wanted to investigate the possibility of storing charges on the face of an ordinary cathode ray tube (CRT), the type used in TV. It had the potential advantage of fast access time as electron beams could be deflected in microseconds. But would it work as a memory? Answering that question became my next assignment.

I designed a simple test setup for the CRT. My objective was to study the basic fundamentals of charge storage, examine the playback signals, determine the best means of storing a 1 and a 0, and learn what factors disturbed the charge. How close together could charges be stored? How long before they deteriorated? I spent weeks in running experiments designed to give me answers to these questions. Also, I wanted to try different types of CRTs to determine effects. I was most interested in small CRTs because of the advantage in space savings when many have to be utilized in a memory system.

I knew of a company that made small CRTs for its own use. Waterman Products in the Kensington section of Philadelphia made a small portable oscilloscope of their own design that used a tube two inches in diameter. But how would I get hold of one? Sometimes problems have a strange and wonderful way of getting answered.

One of our technicians, Tina Melilli, had been telling me for months about her girl friend whom she wanted me to meet, but I had paid no attention. Her friend Shirley Rosner was employed as a draftsman at Waterman Products. Coincidentally, my school buddy and amateur radio friend, Irv Brager, was employed as an engineer at Waterman Products, and I called Irv and told him of my need to try a 2-inch CRT in my experiments. Irv thought there would be no problem in getting a tube for me and promised to have one delivered by quitting time the next day.

I suspect there may have been some collusion in the event that followed, but it was for a good cause. At 5:15 p.m. the following day I was notified that someone wanted to see me in the lobby, and I found a good looking young lady in what looked like a military uniform.

"Hello," she said. "I am Shirley Rosner, I'm from Waterman Products and I have a tube for you."

"Thank you," I replied. "Oh, aren't you Tina's girl friend?"

"Yes," she murmured.

I was entranced with her friendliness and appearance. I wondered why I had not taken Tina's words more seriously before. I asked her what kind of uniform she was wearing, and she explained that she was a member of the Civil Air Patrol, and was going to a meeting of the group that evening. I thanked her again for delivering the tube and said goodbye. She looked so cute in that Tasmanian Horse Marines outfit! I knew I had to see her again.

The small CRT proved useful in some experiments. However, the electrostatic memory was giving me results I didn't expect. Signals were erratic and appeared out of nowhere. Several days later, I realized that the signals could indeed be radiated pickup. A pair of headphones substituted for the oscilloscope proved the point when music gushed forth from the phones. A radio station atop one of the nearby buildings was being picked up, rectified, and amplified by my test gear. Shielding the sense amplifier easily corrected that problem, and the responses from the CRT started making sense. Further work on the electrostatic memory was brought to a halt. I had gone as far as I could with the simple test setup and now it was time for the company to move.

The Electronic Control Company had grown by leaps and bounds after September, 1947. Many more engineers, technicians, and draftsmen had come aboard so that 1215 Walnut Street was bursting at the seams. It was evident we had outgrown our first home. In the spring of 1948, the Electronic Control Company moved into its new home on the seventh and eighth floors of the Yellow Cab Building at Broad and Spring Garden Streets, on the edge of the Center of town. The facilities were spacious and looked as if they would suffice for a while. There was little around in the way of good eating facilities, but this was compensated by other advantages. We soon found an old barber down the street who gave haircuts for twenty-five cents. He had a young blonde wife who also gave haircuts, so we always went two at a time so that at least one of us had his hair cut by the blonde.

Pres Eckert and John Mauchly, upon advice of their counsel, decided to incorporate the company. Therefore, in 1947, the Electronic Control Company became the Eckert-Mauchly Computer Corporation, and we soon developed a corporate structure. George Eltgroth came aboard as patent attorney and legal counsel. Gene Clute was controller, and Luther Harr, chief salesman.

The company was always looking for financing, a typical problem for most small companies. The Government contracts were not enough, and Eckert and Mauchly looked elsewhere for support. Two commercial companies, Prudential Life Insurance and A. C. Neilson, foresaw the need for electronic computers, and soon became involved in some development contracts. In addition, the Army Security Agency (ASA) signed for a digital encrypted communications system. All of the projects were oriented toward developing the techniques needed for the future Univac system, and all had deadlines.

Al Auerbach was working on a high speed decimal adder. It pushed the state of the art and proved to be quite a challenge. In fact, we dubbed it the "dismal" adder because of its proximity to the edge of workability. The pulse resolution was being limited by the bandwidth of the system. The project was valuable in that it showed that additional margins were needed.

Pres Eckert made a fundamental decision to use the pulse envelope (non-return to zero) system in our circuit designs. It had the advantage of requiring only one transition per pulse and therefore in theory could handle twice the data rate. On the negative side, it required a clocked system to distinguish between switching transients (glitches) and true signals. The decision was a good one and we used it with good performance advantage in our designs.

Many input/output devices and component designs were under way. Marv Jacoby was working on a method of reading one character at a time from magnetic tape in order to operate a typewriter. The problem was in starting and stopping the tape for each character and yet having the tape get up enough speed to give a decent output signal. Stopping accurately between characters was also a problem. Marv worked on a way to move the magnetic head back and forth incrementally at high speed. The "dithering" of the head produced an output signal even with the tape stationary.

Magnetic heads were also under development. To get the high data rates, we realized that the tape had to contain many parallel channels. There were many problems to be solved in developing the magnetic heads, such as physically squeezing the many transducers in, contouring the head to maintain contact with all channels on the tape, and selecting materials hard enough to give the head a decent life. With the tape moving rapidly across the head, both tended to wear.

Tape recording and playback test vehicles were constructed to handle endless loops of tape. Experiments were conducted with various recording techniques, the objective being to select one that gave highest density with high readback reliability. A sequence of pulses was recorded on the tape, and each time the loop of tape circulated, the read back signals were compared with the original information recorded. The objective was to read back many thousands of times without error.

In a remote corner of the lab another group worked on servomechanisms that could start and stop the tape rapidly. The technique being explored was isolation of a small section of tape from the large reels on which it was wound. Buffers were examined that would permit the isolated section of tape to accelerate rapidly while the reels, with more inertia, would accelerate at a slower pace.

While all of this hardware development was taking place, John Mauchly and Betty Snyder were busy studying the effectiveness of various kinds of computer instructions. The objective was to devise an instruction set that gave the greatest data manipulation and arithmetic capability in the shortest execution time.

A number of us were siphoned off to work on the ASA encryption terminal. This project consisted of developing identical terminals for each end of a communication line. Information at the transmitting end was encrypted via a continuously changing key contained on a special reel of magnetic tape. At the receiving end, an identical reel of tape decoded the received information. Because the system operated in real time, the two encryption tapes had to run in synchronism. The project was a difficult one from a technological and scheduling point of view, and we worked heroically right down to the wire. As I remember it, John Sims was spraying the cabinet grey as it was being carried out the door on shipment day. The system did work, but not as reliably as we would have liked. We learned something from each of the projects that we worked on, and this one contributed more than its fair share.

Pres Eckert's genius was very apparent to everyone as he multiplexed from project to project, asking penetrating questions and offering ingenious new approaches. Pres was the engineer's engineer; he was all-consumed with the implementation of new concepts. John Mauchly, on the other hand, was the scientist, concerned with basic phenomena, an out-growth of his education in physics. In his pre-computer years, John had researched terrestrial magnetism and then wandered into weather prediction. He had a great interest in abstract mathematics which he shared with Marv Jacoby. The two of them spent many moments trying to solve the puzzles that mathematicians have been working on for centuries. They were often seen in a corner working on challenges like Fermat's last theorem, the minimum number of colors that can be used in making a map, or searching for bounds of roots of an equation. John Mauchly's genius in science complemented Pres Eckert's in engineering.

John was always a great morale booster for everyone. His sense of humor penetrated the black clouds. He spoke in a slow, halting way as he related one interesting anecdote after another. John's interest in developing the software science led him to work with people who had similar interests, whereas the engineers worked directly with Pres in solving our circuit, mechanism, and packaging problems.

The very next day after the girl at Waterman Products had delivered the 2-inch CRT to me, I called my friend Irv Brager and asked him for her telephone number. I was too embarrassed to ask Tina. The following Saturday night I had my first date with Shirley, and we hit it off right from the start. She told me her life's history and I told her mine. Her parents were from Hungary, and had to struggle to make a living. Her father had been in the shoe repair business most of his life, but was now operating a grocery store near 40th Street and Girard Avenue. They had moved a dozen times in a dozen years, and until recently had lived two blocks away from my home in the Strawberry Mansion section of the city. Peculiar that I should meet her only now that she lived on the other side of town! After graduation from high school during the war years, Shirley decided to go to Dobbins Vocational School for training in drafting. She found that she enjoyed the work. Her first job was with the Frankford Arsenal, and at the end of the war she went to Waterman Products. There she had met Tina Mellili, and despite totally different backgrounds, they became fast friends.

Shirley had a flair for mechanical/technical work, as evidenced by her drafting capability. Mr. Rosner had two daughters and no sons, so she took over some of the chores that a son might do, such as helping repair the family car. Shirley had joined the Civil Air Patrol and was learning all of the facets of aviation required to fly a plane. My ears picked up when she said she was learning the Morse code: I was impressed.

Our first date went so well that I asked for a second, then a third, and a fourth, and pretty soon we were going steady. We had a great time together. Shirley was exactly the kind of girl I was looking for, with the same "old world" values I had. Most of the girls I had gone out with had a synthetic set of values. They wanted to be taken to night clubs, which I didn't care for, and spoke of the size of the diamond ring they would like to get. Shirley was a welcome change from that modern type.

After two months of going together, I was hooked. My mother confirmed my opinion that Shirley was the girl for me. Shirl reciprocated my feelings. She says I really never did propose to her, but in July, 1948, we reached a mutual understanding that we wanted to get married. I remember that evening well. As I floated on a wave of euphoria, I nearly went through the plate glass door in her father's store. The next day Mr. Rosner gave me permission to marry his daughter.

We were married on December 5, 1948, six months from the day we met. I can never forget our anniversary date, just two days before the anniversary of Pearl Harbor. Shirley doesn't particularly like my mnemonic aid, especially as I always tease her by mentioning the two as equal disasters. The second week of our honeymoon I spent moving in to the third floor apartment over the Rosner grocery. Her folks gave us the apartment rent free, and we lived there the first three years of our married life. Shirl was now working for the Gauge Laboratory of the Frankford Arsenal. We were able to save a large part of both salaries, and looked forward to the day when we could buy our own home.

We knew our marriage was a good one and we were very happy. I was also happy with my work. Everything was looking great!

Chapter 8

THE STORED PROGRAM COMPUTER RACE—BINAC

The Northrop Aircraft Company was one of the first commercial companies to become interested in the application of the computer. It requested a proposal for the building of a small computer, suitable for guidance of a missile by celestial navigation. The intended use was classified, but the machine they wanted built was not. Eckert and Mauchly, always on the lookout for financing, were responsive to Northrop's interest. We were looking for a test vehicle, a way of proving the hardware to be used in a Univac system. Northrop wanted a small binary computer that had high reliability. To achieve this, it was proposed that two independent central processing units (CPUs) and memory be operated synchronously, and their results compared. Any difference would signify an error. The system was called BINAC for Binary Automatic Computer.

Eckert's and Mauchly's objective was to develop a decimal machine. They believed that, although a binary computer would be simpler and consequently less costly, the disadvantages of having to convert from decimal code to binary and vice versa would be a major detriment for use in the business environment. Whether the machine used binary or decimal code had no impact on the circuit designs used. The architectural concepts would be somewhat different; however, many major aspects of a commercial Univac system could be proven with the development of BINAC. In due time a contract for BINAC was negotiated with Northrop.

Work began in the summer of 1948. Most of the engineers were assigned to BINAC projects, with Lou Wilson, Al Auerbach, Jim Weiner and Bob Shaw the major CPU designers. They, along with Pres Eckert, reached some important decisions. Logic was to be made with germanium semiconductor diodes which had now become reliable and inexpensive. A clock rate of 4 MHz was selected to give the highest circuit speed possible consistent with reliability requirements. High current required for each logic circuit was supplied by 50B5 miniature power pentode tubes that were selected because of their high volume usage in small broadcast band radios. Logic designs were evolved by one group, while another developed gating circuits, pulse formers, delay line registers, and other required circuit elements.

Development of the mercury memory was a major undertaking of another group. Building the previous demonstration unit with a few columns of memory was a start. The memory for BINAC called for many more columns (16) to occupy the common mercury pool and form the complete 512-word memory. To do this, geometries had to be accurately controlled. End plates containing the quartz crystal transducers had to be machined with greater precision so that the channels were accurately in line. Crosstalk problems caused by the many channels operating in parallel had to be resolved.

Pres Eckert and the BINAC memory.

BINAC had simple input/output means, a keyboard and a character printer. The input and output data were placed in a special register for communications to the main memory. BINAC had a tape loader input device for initially loading the program

One of the BINAC mainframes.

into the memory, and for recording data. Brad Sheppard and I were responsible for designing this portion of the system. It used more conventional techniques so we were able to complete our portion of the development early in the game, and, in fact, go on to other work while the CPU and memory groups carried on.

My next assignment was a return to electrostatic memory. The earlier experiments had been carried as far as they could go and now it was necessary to have more sophisticated test equipment, which I had to devise. In effect, I had to design a CRT memory that had a great flexibility in its modes of operation. The design allowed for deflection of the beam to 1024 positions in a 32-by-32 array. The beam alternated between a single position selected by switches and advancing through each one of the 1024 positions. Other features permitted varying duty cycles, clock rates, spacing between positions, accelerator and grid voltages, etc. The test equipment was designed to meet these requirements and constructed in rugged fashion. Without too much fuss, it was debugged and I was on my way toward exploring memory effects. The approach was to consider various means of storing 1's and 0's that could give usable signal to noise ratios. Dots and dashes were tried first, with poor results. Little dots and big dots were tried next, with good results. The big dot was obtained merely by defocusing the beam to form a blur. The dot/blur gave good memory effect but suffered by wiping out adjacent positions after a few operations. Dots and circles were tried next. These gave nearly as much signal as dots and blurs and were a big improvement in adjacent bit disturbance. The dot/circle was the system I decided to adopt for memory. Up to this time, all experiments were concerned with observing effects rather than operating the system as a memory.

The BINAC crew finished its designs, and soon hardware appeared on the floor and the job of testing began. This consisted of methodically following the signal through each one of its logic paths. In many cases the timing had to be set by adjusting taps on a delay line. There were thousands of points that had to be examined with an oscilloscope. Unfortunately, only one team could take command of the computer at a time, which slowed the testing process. The only way of getting more testing done was to go to more shifts, so two teams were kept busy. On several occasions when I arrived at work in the morning, I found Al Auerbach bleary-eyed but still chasing down a problem after the evening shift ended. The hours the engineers put in ran to seventy or more per week; their dedication to proving their designs was unswerving.

The challenges were great. The pulse former, which was supposed to restore the pulse shape after a number of logic gating transactions, proved to be tricky to adjust. Unfortunately, it had too many tuned circuits that had to be adjusted, resulting in endless "diddling." The internal registers of BINAC were composed of delay lines which had to be adjusted to an exact length. In addition, taps on the delay lines had to be set for correct timing, and attenuator networks adjusted to minimize reflections (spurious signals). Slowly parts of the system became functional—registers, arithmetic unit, and control.

Eckert-Mauchly Computer Corporation's first sales literature was issued from Spring Garden Street. It extolled the virtues of the forthcoming UNIVAC computer and spoke of circuits which could add and subtract at the rate of almost 1,000,000 decimal digits per second. A reel of magnetic tape 7 inches in diameter could contain 1,000,000 decimal digits and could be read into and out of the computer at the rate of 10,000 digits per second. Internal memory of 12,000 digits capacity was described, as well as auxiliary equipment to include UNITYPERS and UNIPRINTERS. A UNITYPER data entry device transcribed keyboard

BINAC. Two identical central processors appear in the middle, a mercury tank memory (round object) to the left, and tape loader to the right.

input to magnetic tape, and a UNIPRINTER output device performed the reverse function, transcribing magnetic tape to hard copy. The computer itself was to use less than 1,500 miniature vacuum tubes and consume only 15 kilowatts of power. Detection of errors was an important, touted feature. The first sales brochure is now a collector's treasure.

It was in the course of BINAC checkout that the company decided our quarters were too small for producing Univac systems, so in the spring of 1949 we moved to our new quarters at 3747 Ridge Avenue in North Philadelphia. The new location was interesting in many respects. It was a 2-story building that stood off by itself, and was many hundreds of feet in depth. Empty, it seemed cavernous, and it was difficult for me to believe we would ever outgrow this facility. The building had been occupied previously by a knitting mill that had inevitably moved South.

We could see that the surrounding environment would be conducive to some serious thinking. Directly across the street and on the right side, the Mt. Laurel Cemetery sprawled for blocks. A junkyard was conveniently located on the left side of the building. Between the cemetery on one side and the junkyard on the other, we joked that our "errors" could be easily taken care of, by burial

3747 Ridge Avenue, the birthplace of the BINAC and UNIVAC computers. Unfortunately, the surrounding scenery doesn't show in this photograph taken after the merger with Remington Rand.

The Mt. Laurel Cemetary was directly across the street and on one side of the building. On the other side was Charles Heavy's junk yard.

or junking. Number 3747 was located right at the bottom of a hill, which we named "Death Valley." During the heat of the summer, it felt that way.

The move was made surprisingly easily. We left Broad and Spring Garden Streets on a Friday, and Monday morning the equipment including BINAC was ready to be set up at the new location. BINAC and the electrostatic memory were assigned to the front part of the first floor. There was just one hitch which was not disclosed until Monday morning. One of our admistrative managers, in charge of the move, decided to save money by hiring open-air ice trucks for moving BINAC. The threat of exposing the delicate computer to the open skies had not occurred to him, but fortunately, it did not rain and the computer survived the indignity. However, Pres was furious when he heard about it.

After we had moved and settled in, there was a frenzied burst of effort to complete BINAC. Portions of the machine were operational. Every once in a while there would be a "Yow!" from the BINAC crew and I knew another instruction routine was functional. The second BINAC was right behind the first one. Any changes found necessary for the first unit were automatically put into the second. Short routines were now being run for minutes. Data put in the memory was holding for hours; sometimes, however, it would mysteriously disappear. Heroic efforts and many man-hours brought the first BINAC to the point where it was judged to be operational. The effort shifted over to bringing the second BINAC to the same operational state as the first, and soon it too was functional for short periods. Attempts were made to run the two BINAC computers in synchronism on the same routine; it worked, but not for as long as anyone would have liked.

Although we did not know it at the time, we were in an international race to complete the first stored program computer. A number of Englishmen had visited The Moore School in 1946 to learn of ENIAC and EDVAC computer technology. When they returned home, they had initiated EDVAC-type projects. Furthermore, there had been some earlier, highly secret, special purpose cryptoanalysis electronic machines developed during World War II which gave the British an early start in the field.

The Manchester MARK I is reported to have run its first program in June, 1948. It had a storage of 32 words, each of 31 binary bits. According to the developers, F. C. Williams and T. Kilburn, the machine was purely experimental and was on too small a scale to be of mathematical value. It was built as a pilot model for a later full-size machine. The full-size machine was developed, in cooperation with the University of Manchester, by the Ferranti Company in England, which claims this was the first commercial computer. The upgraded, commercial version was delivered to the University of Manchester in February, 1951, but it was not formally handed over for customer use until the week of July 7, 1951. (The UNIVAC I computer was formally turned over to the Bureau of the Census on March 30, 1951.) Only two MARK I computers were delivered at that time, with seven more in modified form delivered later.

The Cambridge EDSAC, which was a full-scale machine, ran its first program in May, 1949, and was formally demonstrated in June, 1949. BINAC ran programs prior to these dates, although official completion took place in August, 1949.

I recently searched the BINAC engineering log book to determine first operation and noted these significant entries.

February 7, 1949—Al Auerbach ran a small routine (five lines of coding) for filling memory from the A register.

February 10, 1949—A five-line routine was run as a memory check.

February 16, 1949—A six-line routine was used to fill memory.

March 7, 1949—Dick Baker, the Northrop Aircraft representative on site, wrote that Machine #2 performed 217 iterations of the routine on P90 (23 lines of coding for generation of squares) correctly and it was still computing correctly when stopped. This test was worked up to furnish information for John Mauchly for his paper for the IRE conference. Only one memory tank was used.

April 4, 1949—An extensive routine using 50 lines of coding to fill memory and check all instructions was run from 7:15 p.m. until 9:45 p.m. when it stopped because of a failure. On April 5th the same routine was started at 11:30 a.m. and it ran until 7:00 a.m. April 7th, with no errors.

Thus, BINAC had demonstrated for the first time a practical implementation of the stored program concept. It was truly an automatic, high speed computer which, when properly programmed, could perform a complicated set of computations by itself. BINAC had twenty instructions in its repertoire, including an unconditional transfer of control which permitted it to loop and a conditional transfer which would modify the sequence of actions dependent on meeting an equality condition. This concept is employed by every computer in existence today.

Actually, some credit for the first stored program computer should go to ENIAC. The concept of storing programs in the manually setup switches of the function tables was thought of in

ECKERT-MAUCHLY COMPUTER CORPORATION

TO Engineering Employees

DATE April 19, 1949

FROM J. Presper Eckert, Jr.

FILE

SUBJECT Saturday Work

In accordance with our discussion on Friday, April 8, 1949, the Engineering Department shall work a normal work day on Saturday. If the weather and special week-end plans should interfere in the hot part of the summer, we will get together and discuss the possibilities of a more suitable time than Saturday. However, for the present, the normal work day will be on Saturday.

sr

The amount of work to do was overwhelming and this was one of the necessary steps toward getting it done.

the basic design but not initially utilized. After ENIAC was operational at Aberdeen Proving Grounds in 1947, the concept was rediscovered. However, it was a limited stored program concept because the program could not be rapidly changed.

Jack Silver, one of our young technicians, had the job of baby-sitting the computer on the midnight shift after the exhausted engineers went home for some sleep. His job was to monitor it through the night while it ran its test routines. If the machine stopped, he had to record the condition of the various control panel indicator lights and then restart the machine. All of the information had to be recorded meticulously in the engineering log book so that the engineers on the morning shift could analyze the nature of the failures. After a while, the job got to be rather boring for Jack, who had to spend full time looking at the flashing lights; it was the only way of knowing that the computer was working. Seeking a way of easing the boredom, he remembered seeing in the parts bin a discarded radio which he salvaged and plugged into the wall socket adjacent to the computer. To Jack's surprise, all kinds of weird noises emanated from the loudspeaker, instead of soothing music. He soon realized that the churning BINAC generated those noises because as soon as it halted, the noises stopped. Jack did not realize it at the time, but he was the first to discover that a computer could be used to make music, although discordant in this particular case. He put the computer-generated tones to good use. Jack found that by turning the volume up he was able to walk around the building and yet be immediately aware of any computer stoppage.

The party to celebrate the completion of BINAC was an event that Eckert-Mauchly employees will remember for a lifetime. All were invited. It was held right at the BINAC test area one August evening. In addition to hors d'oeuvres and cocktails, the BINAC crew arranged a spectacular computer show. Someone had discovered that, by programming the right number of cycles, a predictable tone could be produced. So BINAC was outfitted with a loudspeaker attached to the high speed data bus and tunes were played for the first time by program control. The audience was delighted and it never occurred to anyone that the use of a complex digital computer to generate simple tones was ridiculous. It still seems to be great sport, even with multimillion dollar computers.

The crowning achievement of the evening came after a long, laborious arithmetic computation; the machine laid an egg! The engineers had programmed the machine to release a hard-boiled egg from its innards. Immediately afterwards, the voice of a screaming female could be heard, and the bulky form of our production manager, a fellow named Horvath, was seen chasing a good looking blonde around BINAC.

BINAC proved to be an excellent training vehicle, for we knew what had to be done to develop a reliable commercial computer. The clock rate of 4 MHz pushed the state of the art too far; 2 to 2.5 MHz would be more reasonable. It was also clear that the pulse formers had to be completely digital with no adjustments. Various other necessary improvements were noted by Pres, Jim, and Al.

The search for funding continued. To develop and produce commercial computers was going to take a lot of financing. Satisfying the payroll was a difficult matter; we even heard rumors that Frazer Welsh was asked not to cash his paycheck one week, but to hold it for the next. The matter seemed to resolve itself when it was announced that the American Totalizator Company was investing in the Eckert-Mauchly Computer Corporation. It seemed a natural marriage. American Totalizator owned the tote machines that handled betting at the race tracks. These were electromechanical devices which were relatively slow and unreliable, and it was envisioned that computers could do the job better. Before long we were introduced to the president of American Totalizator Company, Mr. H. L. Strauss. He was an impressive man, always immaculately dressed. He visited us on a frequent

Eckert-Mauchly Computer Corp. Engineering Group—1949. Row 1: Fran Morello, Bob Shaw, Pres Eckert, Brad Sheppard, Frazer Welsh, John Mauchly, Jim Weiner, Al Auerbach, Betty Snyder; Row 2: John Sims, Marv Jacoby, Paul Winsor, Gerry Smoliar, Art Gehring, Betty Jay, Ed Blumenthal, Bob Mock, Jean Bartik, Herman Lukoff, Bernie Gordon, Ned Schreiner; Row 3: George Gingrich, Marv Gottlieb, Lou Wilson, Doug Wendell, Charlie Michaels, Ben Stad, Si Levitt, Larry Jones.

basis, enjoying walking through the lab and talking to the engineers about their progress.

My electrostatic memory test rig was now wired to operate as a memory instead of being an open loop test device. It worked! I was able to select any of 1024 positions, push a button and enter a circle around a dot to represent a "1." Initially, the "1" was remembered for seconds. With some adjustments it became minutes, and with much sweat the information could be stored for hours. One advantage of the CRT memory was that it did not require an oscilloscope to see the stored data which was clearly visible on the face of the memory cathode ray tube. One morning I had entered my initials, H L, into the memory to initiate an endurance test. After several hours I went out for lunch. When I returned, I found Mr. Strauss looking inquiringly at the memory system. When I explained the operation of the memory system to him, he said he was honored that he should be so remembered. His first two initials were H L!

It was shortly after that, when driving to work one morning and listening to the news, that I heard a report that sent shivers through my body and changed the course of the infant computer industry. Mr. H. L. Strauss had been killed in a light plane crash. Our benefactor was gone. Henry Strauss was a one-man show and no one was left at American Totalizator who had the gumption to provide further financing. The problems of financing Eckert-Mauchly began all over again.

Electrostatic memory was developed to the point of being a working memory; however, there were many other concerns. The high voltages used in the circuitry caused peculiar problems. Silver used on contacts would migrate across the phenolic component mounting boards and cause short circuit "splats." Signal-to-noise ratios were marginal for some memory positions. We concluded that electrostatic memory was not reliable enough to use in a computer system. The results of our work culminated in a presentation by Pres at the IRE convention in March, 1949, and the publication of a paper in the Proceedings of the IRE of May, 1950.

Several other computer system developments in later years went on to use electrostatic memory, but true to our prediction, they were short lived. The electrostatic memories were replaced with ferrite magnetic cores as soon as they became available.

In June, 1949, I, along with several other engineers, received a curious letter. It was from a professional employment service that was empowered to seek out a man of my professional standing and ability. If I was interested in an opportunity for advancement, the agent was awaiting my telephone call.

I wasn't the least bit unhappy at Eckert-Mauchly. I had gotten several salary increases, and I was no longer a junior engineer, but still the letter was intriguing. A call to the agent disclosed that the client was Remington Rand Incorporated, located in Norwalk, Connecticut. It just so happened that I had planned a vacation trip through New England the first two weeks of July and would be in the vicinity on July fourth. I probably would not have gone out of my way for an interview, but the vacation trip made it convenient.

Shirley and I took off on July third and headed for Connecticut. Overnight lodging for tourists had not advanced to today's luxurious state, but we found a broken-down chicken coop that posed as a motel on the edge of Norwalk. The place was even furnished like a chicken coop, with the feather pillows providing further reminders. After a sleepless night we arose to a hot and steamy Fourth of July. I had to wear a business suit and tie, of course, for the interview with Mr. Draper which was scheduled for 10 a.m. at his home on the property of the local yacht club. The directions were perfect and I entered the club grounds with time to spare, until I went down the side road. Before I could realize my plight, I was embedded in sand. The car would go neither forward nor backward. The more I tried to move the car, the deeper it sank into the sand. What a predicament! I had to hoof the last few blocks to Draper's house. A ring of the doorbell brought to the front door a tall, distinguished looking gentleman, dripping wet in his bathing suit.

"Hi," he said, "I am Art Draper."

I introduced myself and told him my sad story. "No problem," said Draper, as he dripped into his car and drove us back to mine, now a foot deeper into the sand. He connected a set of snow chains between our cars and in seconds my car regained its natural height again. What a way to start an interview!

Upon returning to the house, Art Draper introduced us to the other dripping guests. I was the one who felt out of place in my business suit, but soon I started to drip too, from perspiration. Mr. Draper explained that Remington Rand had been in the business-machine field for many years, and was successfully growing under James H. Rand's leadership. Mr. Draper was aware of the ENIAC development and its implications. He was convinced that electromechanical calculators and tabulating machines were bound to be replaced by speedy electronic computers and was pushing Remington Rand in that direction. A magnificent new Laboratory for Advanced Research had been completed overlooking Long Island Sound, and General Leslie R. Groves of atomic bomb development fame had been brought in to direct it. Mr. Draper explained that all that was needed now were some engineers with computer expertise. Draper's choice was limited—there were only a couple dozen computer engineers in the world.

After a pleasant lunch, Draper took us on a tour of the Laboratory for Advanced Development, and then I was further interviewed by Joe Brustman, one of the chief engineers responsible for developing an electronic calculator. I bade the gentlemen from Remington Rand good day in the middle of the afternoon, and loosened my tie as I returned to the car. Remington's facilities and intentions were impressive, but I had already made up my mind before leaving Norwalk. Nothing could beat the opportunity I had in Philadelphia. Apparently the several other engineers from Eckert-Mauchly agreed.

Chapter 9

THE FIRST STANDARD OF EXCELLENCE – UNIVAC I

The main development effort on the UNIVAC I computer started in the summer of 1949 just as the BINAC project drew to a close. There had been some earlier studies. John Mauchly, Betty Snyder, and several others had worked toward optimizing the instruction code of the machine through trial programming. They had worked their way up to the C-10 version of the instruction code and that became the one incorporated into the design of the UNIVAC I computer. One of the convenient features of the code was the use of a mnemonic alphabetic character to represent an instruction. The UNIVAC I computer could directly interpret alphabetic characters. Thus an "A" instruction meant an addition. It was much easier for the programmer than attempting to write the binary equivalent which would have been necessary if the machine had been purely numeric. The chances of error were much less, too. Before long, we dubbed the machine's ability to handle alphabetic and numeric as having "alphameric" capability.

Pres Eckert and Frazer Welsh made a very important contribution to the C-10 code with the invention of the "R" order. It provided, for the first time, a means of recording where you were in the program by storing the control counter reading in memory. Thus you could easily return to the main program from a subroutine. When used with the transfer of control (U instruction), it provided a powerful means of nesting programs.

A group of logic designers, Bob Shaw, Betty Jean Bartik and Art Gehring, had worked on some preliminary designs. Gerry Smoliar had gotten a head start on the power supply design.

The design team for the UNIVAC I computer was assembled on the second floor of the building, close to the front office. It was a wide open area interrupted only by desks. Assignments were handed out by Pres and Jim. Al Auerbach was given responsibility for the arithmetic section with Paul Winsor, a newly hired junior engineer, assigned to work with him. Lou Wilson's job was to develop the control section. Gerry had the power supply while

Brad Sheppard and junior engineer Charlie Michaels were given the memory development responsibility.

My assignment was to develop the magnetic tape input/output control unit, an integrated part of the central processor. A junior engineer, Bernie Gordon, assisted me, and later, Tom Fitzgerald joined the activity. Bernie was a brilliant young lad fresh out of MIT and barely five feet tall. What he lacked in height, he made up in cleverness. He developed into one of the sharpest circuit designers at Eckert-Mauchly, and was consequently given some of the tough design jobs that stymied other engineers. Bernie had an undauntable spirit that kept him tangling with our chief engineer, Jim Weiner, to the amusement of the other engineers. Bernie was destined for greatness and, in his later years, became the president of several companies.

A group of engineers including Frazer Welsh, Ted Bonn, and Ned Schreiner handled the UNISERVO tape drive development. Mechanical design chores were handled by John Sims. In addition, technicians were assigned to each group. Pres and Jim covered all waterfronts and filled in where necessary. Altogether, there were approximately 12 engineers engaged in the design of the UNIVAC I system.

The atmosphere for development was encouraging. In 1949, a contract based on the sales literature had been negotiated with the National Bureau of Standards for three UNIVAC I systems. The contract price was $159,000 for the first system and approximately $250,000 for the others. They were to be delivered to the Bureau of the Census, the Air Controller's Office, and the Army Map Service, in sequence. Later the price for a typical system would be $1,000,000.

The performance goals for the UNIVAC I system were well formulated prior to the start of circuit design. It was to be a general purpose business computer, balanced between the handling of high speed input and output data and arithmetic computation. Slow input and output (I/O) operations were divorced from the mainframe. All I/O was to be handled via the high speed UNISERVO tape drives. Reduction to media handled by operators was to be done via offline magnetic tape controlled low speed devices.

High speed tape performance was planned at the unheard of rate of 12,500 characters per second, corresponding to a recording density of 128 pulses per inch. To raise the I/O rate further, backward and forward read was planned, as well as simultaneous reading, writing, and computing.

The UNIVAC I computer was to utilize an alphanumeric coded decimal internal code to facilitate the computer's use in the business world. A large (at that time) memory was provided: 12,000 characters (1,000 words). Perhaps one of the more revolutionary features planned was the large amount of checking to be employed. We knew that business would be slow to adopt the computer because of fear that the computer would make a mistake. There was always worry about the computer writing checks for $1,000,000 dollars instead of $100 and, indeed, with the reliability of the vacuum tube, that worry was justified.

Our logic designers spent much of their time devising means for detecting errors. While we did our utmost to improve hardware reliability, we couldn't prevent failures from occurring. So all effort was bent toward determining that, if an error did occur, it would be detected and the computer would be stopped. Thorough checking was employed. As it flowed through the system, each character, composed of six bits, carried along an additional bit, called a parity bit. At various crucial points, the bits were counted to ensure that there was always an odd number. If one bit of the character was lost, an error condition would be indicated. To check the arithmetic section of the machine, a duplicate arithmetic section was employed and both sections were continuously compared. Various other types of error checkers were placed at strategic points in the machine. Approximately 30% of the hardware in the system was devoted to error detection. This represented a high point in the history of computation, and commercial computers of today are still striving to achieve this level of checking.

Jim issued the design standards that everyone was to use. They were primarily the BINAC standards updated. Marginal conditions that existed on BINAC were improved or eliminated. The clock rate was reduced to 2.25 MHz, which gave us manageable pulse widths of nearly half a microsecond. The workhorse tube was changed from a miniature type to the more rugged octal based 25L6, used in every AC/DC radio. The standard logic gate using germanium diodes and a 25L6 amplifier tube was designed and promulgated to all engineers. Although use of the standard logic gate was mandated, there were many more nonstandard circuits required and these had to be designed by the engineer. The I/O controllers, on which I was working, required an extensive amount of custom circuit design because of the many interfaces and circuit speeds they had to accommodate.

Circuit designs were exacting. Each one had to be calculated to work under the "worst case" conditions with regard to component and voltage variations and timing tolerances. Jim reviewed all of my designs carefully at first, but less so after I had demonstrated my competence. I reviewed Bernie's designs, and we often collaborated. In fact, we jointly disclosed and had a patent issued on one circuit we called a "thyraflop." It was a circuit capable of being triggered by a narrow pulse and could produce delay times in the seconds.

Rough logic drawings with brief descriptions were issued by the logic designers. The engineers had to refine these logic drawings to greater accuracy, and verify that the designs were correct. The timing at each logic gate had to be examined in detail. It was important to confirm that all designs were correct while they still existed in paper form because changing them on paper was much easier than after they were implemented in hardware. Betty Jean Bartik and Art Gehring were the logic designers assigned to my portion of the machine and together they worked out the logic design of the I/O section. Then Art went on to other sections while I resolved the remaining details with Betty Jean. We were fairly confident that the design was solid.

Phase two consisted of replacing the logic elements with circuits. This entailed a large volume of work spread over many months. Our desks grew in height as the sheets of paper formed mountains. The problem of the paperwork jungle was alleviated somewhat when some bright soul thought of clamping all of the reference drawings on a tabletop board mounted on a movable cart. The tabletop could be tilted vertically or horizontally as needed, and the top pages flipped over and out of the way.

The next phase of the project consisted of laying out all of the circuits onto many chassis. John and Pres had given masterful thought to the chassis design. It was a long thin channel, wide enough for a tube and long enough to house fourteen of them. Low power and precision components were mounted on internal boards. Power resistors, dissipating watts, were mounted on external boards next to the hot tubes. Each chassis had eighty-seven silver-plated nubs on a rear phenolic strip for making connection with female contacts set in the backboard. Each terminal, component position, and tube socket had a geographical coordinate marking. Tracing paper, with an outline of the chassis, tube sockets, boards, and terminals, was given to each engineer so that he could fill in the components and show interwiring. Layout was a tedious job that needed constant checking for errors. Tony Occhiolini headed a group of layout draftsmen who did a tremendous job of keeping the drawings unsnarled.

Prior to the completion of our circuit designs, an estimate was made of the number of tubes in the system. It totaled over 5,000 tubes, a jolting increase over the 1,500 quoted in the early sales brochure. Engineering optimism was overwhelming in those days. John and Pres had a problem in figuring out the form of the cabinet to hold that number of chassis. If strung out in a straight line, the chassis in the end sections would be electrically too far from each other. The problem was solved by placing all of the chassis bays around the periphery of a rectangle forming a structure approximately 9 feet high, 10 feet wide, and 14 feet long. A small room was actually formed inside the arrangement. A door provided access to the inside area where the backboard wiring and main memory mercury tanks were to be located. Signal wires that had to traverse the distance between bays could do so across the roof of the room. The whole arrangement, while large by today's standards, was a great improvement over ENIAC.

Mercury tank memories can be seen through the entrance to the interior room of a UNIVAC I computer. Transparent plastic doors were used at times during the test period.

The advantages of working in a small company were prevalent. All of the mainframe engineers were within shouting distance of each other. If I needed another cycling unit signal, I would yell, "Al, I need a t46," or "Lou, feed me another Time-Out B." It was done as soon as said.

We toiled through the fall and winter of 1949 in the design phase. Enthusiasm was high and our working hours proved it. As spring of 1950 broke, the first signs of hardware started to appear. First, one bay was set up on the floor, then another, and another. Soon, the outlines of the mainframe were formed. The manufacturing team on the first floor did a great job of following our drawings.

My married life survived the design phase of the UNIVAC I computer; in fact, it thrived on it. We continued to live in the third floor apartment at my in-laws' house while Shirl kept busy at her drafting job at Frankford Arsenal's Gauge Laboratory. We were able to save much of our earnings, and eagerly looked forward to the day when we could plunk it down as a deposit on our own home. All of my radio equipment was packed in cardboard boxes and stored in my father-in-law's second-floor storage room. I was anxious to get it unpacked and put to use again, but that was impossible in the apartment.

A major portion of our free time, just about every Sunday, was spent in looking at houses. Shirl and I had the same thoughts about a home. We wanted it to be a single house with grass and trees surrounding it. This was looked upon as a form of heresy by our parents who were reminded of the misery of their earlier days in the "old country." They thought that row homes in the congested city offered security and luxury. Nevertheless, we knew what we wanted and continued the search. Each Sunday's expedition was plotted by reading the real estate section of the Saturday night edition of the newspaper. One good thing about this exercise was that we became very well calibrated on housing values; another benefit was that it provided endless activity and consequently saved on our entertainment expenses.

We found one nice little cottage on Veree Road in far out Northeast Philadelphia. My mother referred to it as "weary" road and objected strenously because it had a cesspool instead of a city sewer connection. The cesspool had me a little concerned too, and so our search continued. Eventually, we uncovered a new development of single houses being built in a closer-in section of Northeast Philadelphia. We fell in love with the houses and selected the model we liked, a four-bedroom, two-story brick colonial on a lot 80 by 120 feet. The price of $13,500 seemed astronomical and the mortgage a lifelong commitment, but it was exactly what we were looking for. In January, 1950, I signed on the dotted line and became the proud owner of a mudspot at 909 Glenview Street. Until the house was completed in October, Shirl and I were kept busy either checking on the construction progress or visiting department stores to get an idea of the kind of furnishings we would need. We did take time off to go to the zoo, museums, and swimming at Parvin Lake in southern New Jersey. Life was exciting and we were enjoying every bit of it.

Meanwhile, the cost of developing and producing the UNIVAC I computer was turning out to be more than anyone had ever dreamed. The money received from the government for the first three UNIVAC systems wasn't going to be enough to see us through. We knew that Eckert and Mauchly were secretly negotiating for further financing. Still, it came as a surprise in the spring of 1950 when they announced that Remington Rand Incorporated was buying the Eckert-Mauchly Computer Corporation. My first thought was that Remington Rand had to buy the company because it wasn't successful in hiring any of its engineers.

The principal impact the purchase of the company had on the employees was assurance that our jobs were now safe. For Eckert and Mauchly, it meant trading in their company ownership and accepting external control. I heard rumors that Eckert and Mauchly had also received an offer from IBM, but chose Remington Rand because it was a smaller company and presented the best opportunities for success. I often wonder what the company would be like today if an IBM offer had been accepted instead.

Shortly after the announcement, Remington Rand officials appeared on the scene and we soon got to recognize Jim Rand. It was no surprise when Art Draper, the man who had interviewed me the year before at Norwalk, Connecticut, also showed up. He remembered me quite well, probably from hauling me out of the sand. Art acted as the liaison officer between the Eckert-Mauchly Division and Remington Rand, making frequent trips between Philadelphia and Norwalk. He was a true gentleman and it was a pleasure to conduct business with him.

The only immediate action instituted as a result of being bought was a change to Remington Rand typewriters. Si Levitt, one of our mechanical engineers, had spent many months evaluating various manufacturers' typewriters. The din emanating from the banks of typewriters clanking away in the basement was always present. After tortuous testing, Si determined that the IBM typewriters were most rugged, and consequently they were adopted for use in the UNIPRINTER devices and supervisory control panel. Almost immediately after the acquisition, the nameplates were removed from the IBM typewriters and shortly thereafter, the typewriters were replaced by Remington Rand models.

Pres Eckert and John Mauchly were given a free hand in running the company. If there were changes, we engineers did not know about them.

As the summer of 1950 approached, we were into the full swing of testing. All the basic elements were on the floor, wired backboard and frame, plug-in chassis, one mercury memory tank, and the supervisory control panel. Testing was a rigorous process. Each path had to be checked for logic and electrical performance. With over 5,000 vacuum tubes in the machine, this constituted an exhaustive effort. In many cases, data flowing through the circuitry could vary, which greatly increased the number of logic combinations that had to be checked. To provide signals to do the checking, special test gear and temporary rigs were required. In my I/O portion of the system, I devised a black box that was made to look like a UNISERVO tape handler. It provided signals at a 12.5 KHz rate that simulated tape unit signals. Switches on the front panel controlled the bits that formed each character to provide changeable information. The tape simulator was an extremely useful device to have around, especially since the UNISERVO tape handlers were unproven devices and the touchiest part of the system.

Testing the design was like plodding through a battlefield. It was slow and each inch forward represented another logic circuit checked. Frequent logic or circuit errors were discovered and had to be corrected. In most cases it was not possible to go on to the next circuit unless the previous one was functional. Design changes were made on the spot or, in some cases, overnight. Technicians on the third shift took care of the longer, overnight changes. The first and second shifts were occupied by the testing crews. Because of the large number of logic circuits that had to be checked, test time became the critical path toward completion. All efforts were bent toward keeping power on so that the simultaneous testing of arithmetic, control, memory, and I/O could proceed. Yet, it was necessary to turn power off to plug in or remove a chassis from the machine, and feelings ran high when one group turned off power while another was in the middle of a critical experiment. Finally a scheme was devised to reduce the element of surprise. The person turning off power was required to sound a warning bell and wait for thirty seconds. If anyone wanted to object to turning off power, he had the thirty seconds to do so.

It was the first time in my life I had ever done shift work. Actually it wasn't too bad. I had all day to do the things I wanted to do before going to work at 4 p.m. Even though I got home after midnight, I had nearly a normal night's sleep. The second shift was actually pleasant during the summer months because it was possible to engage in daytime outdoor activities like gardening and swimming. Most evening activities had to be sacrificed, however.

Summer at 3747 Ridge Avenue tested everyone to his environmental limits. The location was at a low spot and did not get a whiff of breeze. Our UNIVAC I computer testing activities were on the second floor of the building, directly beneath an uninsulated, flat, black roof. The building was not air-conditioned; few were in those days. The UNIVAC I computer, by midsummer, had nearly all of its vacuum tubes plugged in, thus dissipating its maximum power. Approximately 40 kilowatts of electrical power went into just lighting the filaments in the tubes. Another 80 kilowatts were required by the power supply to feed the many plate and grid voltages. Of the total 120 kilowatts input, nearly all was dissipated as heat—heat that was dumped into our test area and made necessary a ventilation system to keep the components from disintegrating. A very large blower system hanging from the ceiling of the floor below the computer forced a hurricane of air through the system.

Normally, casework surrounding the computer deflected the heated air into the large plenum chamber on top of the computer and then through a large duct for discharge through a side window. Under test, however, the casework could not be installed, because it drastically curtailed the movement of chassis into and out of the computer. As a result, the large volume of computer-heated air added to the already hot room environment. Temperatures of 100° F to 120° F were common.

Survival became a prime objective. Neckties had long since disappeared. Second and third layers of clothing were discarded, to the point of impropriety and shorts and undershirts became the uniform of the day. Some of the engineers, forgetting how they were attired, wandered into the front office area. Shortly afterwards a notice was posted and a memo issued to everyone calling for proper dress in the front office where visitors would be shocked by our informal dress. We took the directive in good spirits.

ECKERT-MAUCHLY COMPUTER CORPORATION — MEMO

TO All Engineers — DATE August 11, 1949

FROM J. Presper Eckert, Jr. — FILE

SUBJECT

It would be appreciated if anyone who is not wearing trousers and shirt in the future refrain from entering the Foyer or Purchasing Department during business hours. Since they are very apt to have visitors in this section of the building, this does not create a good impression.

It was so hot during the summer and the 120 kilowatts of heat dumped into the test area by UNIVAC I computer led to various recourses including wearing shorts at work. It also led to this memorandum.

Our desks were near the computer where it was so blasted hot you could hardly stand it for any extended period. Fortunately, we were young and of the pre-air-conditioning era. There was a job to be done and we had to do it, regardless of conditions. One of the engineers, Ed Blumenthal, solved the problem. He had a half dozen soda bottles sitting on the edge of his desk and every once in a while, he reached for a soda bottle, placed it over the top of his head, and poured. The bottles were filled with water! We lost no one despite the intense thermal exposure although there was a good cause for some of us to be half baked.

Testing was proceeding reasonably well. The problems we had found in BINAC were not repeated in the UNIVAC I computer. Instead, new problems appeared, but they were minor and correctable, although they did add up to a sizable number. Bernie Victor's technicians did a magnificent job in keeping the hardware coordinated with the drawings.

As summer ended, everyone had checked out his portion of the system independently of the others. Now the task began of tying the major pieces together and coordinating them to act as a computer. This generated further restrictions on how many people could get at the computer at one time. Only one person could have control and this limited our progress.

Several UNISERVO tape handlers were now connected into my I/O controller. A whole new sphere of testing began as the UNISERVO tape handler crew entered the scene. The UNISERVO tape handler itself was a complex electromechanical device with many different types of circuits in it—circuits for switching the magnetic head from recording to playback, high power thyratrons for controlling the reel motors, and lower power circuits for logic and control. There were horrendous problems in keeping the higher power circuits from generating noises that entered the weak signal playback circuits. Hour after hour was spent in tracking down each point of noise entry. Corrective shielding and filters provided the answer in nearly all cases, but as the major sources of noise were removed, it became harder to find the minor sources. Every single one had to be located; otherwise, information could not be reliably read back from the tape. The going got tougher after a while because some of the sources were elusive and, in fact, took several years to find. After a whole sequence of adjusting recording currents and wave shapes, respectable playback signals were received at the I/O controller. Eventually it became possible to transfer a block of sixty 12-character words from the output mercury memory tank to magnetic tape, read it back through the input controller, and deposit the information into the input mercury memory tank. Larger and larger sections of the system were starting to function correctly. It was most heartening to reach this point.

Pres Eckert was working like a demon. Shift work didn't mean anything to Pres; he worked all shifts. He was there whenever anyone else was, working on the nagging problems of the moment. The only way his poor wife, Hester, got to see him was by coming in during the evening and idly standing by. She brought food and a hot thermos of coffee for him; otherwise Pres would be so immersed in a problem that he would never stop to eat. After a while, Pres's work habits developed into a peculiar cycle. Each day he worked a little later and consequently was forced to arrive a little later in the morning. As the days went by, his work period slipped later and later into the day and then the evening. Finally he had to take a day off so that he could get rephased and come in with everyone else in the morning.

Eckert was a genius, there was no question about that, but he had to think things out orally and in the presence of someone else. Sometimes it was a technician, or even the night watchman, but most of the time it was Frazer Welsh. Frazer was the only person who had the mental facility to keep up with Pres and generate real-time responses. The rest of us took hours to analyze what Pres had said. Pres Eckert and Frazer Welsh were a familiar pair who could often be observed discussing something in the most peculiar fashion. Pres's nervous energy was so great he couldn't sit in a chair or stand still while he was thinking. He usually crouched on top of a desk or else paced back and forth. In many of his discussions with Frazer, the pair started out at the computer test site, walked to the back of the second floor, then down a flight of steps to the first floor. After an hour or so, they would arrive back at the test site, having made a circular tour of the building, but completely oblivious to the fact that they had done so. The intensity of their discussion locked out all distractions.

By October, 1950, the mudhole at 909 Glenview Street had become a house. With Pres Eckert's father acting as our real estate agent, we went to settlement and became the proud owners of our first home. It was a joyful day for Shirley and me as we moved into our dream house. I took vacation that first week so I could stay home and get my workshop set up in the basement and my radio shack established in the smallest bedroom on the second floor. Everything went together perfectly because I had spent many months planning the event. By the end of the week, my amateur radio station was back on the air, nearly nine years after I ceased operation on Pearl Harbor Day.

Most of my radio equipment was decrepit by post-World War II standards, so I embarked on a program to modernize. I noticed an advertisement for an excellent receiver, a Collins 75A1, in QST, a ham radio journal. A quick telephone call persuaded the fellow to hold it for me and the following Saturday we headed for Washington, D.C. His place, a shack on the edge of the railroad tracks was difficult to find. He claimed he had just been discharged from service in North Africa and he had brought all of his radio gear back with him. I didn't ask any further questions although I could think of many. The receiver worked perfectly, so I paid him $175 and headed back to Philadelphia.

For a new transmitter I decided to buy a kit marketed by the E. F. Johnson Company. The Viking 2 was a very versatile phone-and-code, 120-watt unit that covered all of the major amateur bands. Putting it together was an excellent project for the winter months.

It felt great to be back into action again but along with it came the responsibilities of being a homeowner. Many hours were spent picking up stones, planting shrubs, and fertilizing the ground, but at this point in our lives, it was a pleasure.

During the winter months we became chummy with our neighbors. Although I did not enjoy card games, I indulged frequently at first because it was the social vehicle for getting to know our neighbors. Planning outdoor projects for next spring also occupied my winter evenings. I wanted to put up rose trellises, a grape arbor over the walk by the side of the house, and a backyard patio with a fireplace.

As 1951 began, the UNIVAC I system was basically functioning as a computer. We were coming down the home stretch at a hectic pace, working all hours of the day and night to get the system ready for acceptance. An entry in the engineering log book on January 15, 1951, at 2:00 a.m., gives some insight into the charged atmosphere.

> All hell has broken loose! The entire computer seems to be running and nothing seems to stop it except turning off DC power. +84 fuse in power supply just blew.
> There is a peculiar odor, smells as though it might be a selenium rectifier cooking.
> Could be that a rectifier is on its way out and is putting a large amount of hum on some voltage and this may be causing the strange symptoms described above.
> Replaced fuse, turned on power after several minutes, same symptoms.
> Computer is running in some strange manner. Time-out will not remain set. Most of the counters in the machine seem to be counting.

> At this point, +84 fuse in power supply again blew.
> Strange odor again present.
> Visually checked power supply rectifiers and filter electrolytic capacitors. All seems ok.
> (signed) L. D. Wilson

Although this problem had many complex symptoms, it was not atypical. The next morning a plug containing many control wires was found loose at the top of one of the bays.

Many of the error circuits that had been suppressed until now were turned on and, sure enough, the computer stopped quite frequently. We had to determine the cause of these errors, track them down, and correct them. Once we had solved these problems I was able to direct the UNISERVO tape handlers to read or write by entering the instructions into switches on the supervisory control panel. The instruction was in excess three binary coded decimal form, a code I eventually got to know as well as the English language. I also found out about the machine instruction cycle—alpha, beta, gamma and delta, which fetched the instruction and operand, performed the operation, and increased the control counter by one. Later, I could type in an instruction, enter it into memory, and then execute the instruction.

Al and some of the others had worked up a design verification routine for BINAC called "Old Faithful." It was designed to test every aspect of the arithmetic, memory, and control portion of the systems by using pseudo random numbers. It started with a number, performed an arithmetic computation with another number, then performed the reverse operation on the resultant to generate the original number. The starting number and ending number were compared for equality. All the arithmetic and central instructions were checked in this manner while sequencing through each memory location. The routine also tested for pattern sensitivity by providing variations in data. It has been previously noted that a marginal memory channel was sensitive to certain combinations of pulses. The design verification routine went through a sequence of improvements as the engineers would think of something else they had forgotten to check. Finally what emerged for the UNIVAC I computer was a new version of "Old Faithful" which thereafter was called "New Old Faithful" or "NOF." NOF was heard playing its singsong tune throughout the laboratory. Everyone became familiar with its melody, which took about three minutes to cycle before it started over again. If the tune stopped at any time, engineers busy at their desks would come running to the supervisory control panel to see which error light was lit. Then the detailed analysis began of examining the memory, registers, etc., to pinpoint the cause of the error. The number of stops steadily decreased until finally NOF would run for hours without errors.

To test the UNISERVO tape handlers and I/O controllers, another test routine was created called "Tape Test." It took a block of data in memory and wrote it in 60-word blocks throughout the 2,400 foot length of tape on the first UNISERVO tape handler. Then it read backward from the first UNISERVO tape handler while simultaneously recording on the second UNISERVO tape handler. Following that, the second UNISERVO tape handler was read backward while recording on the third UNISERVO tape handler. This process continued until the last UNISERVO tape handler in the string completed its recording. After rewinding the latter, the tapes on the first and last UNISERVO tape handlers were read forward and compared character by character for equality. It was a tough test. We knew that if the system could pass this test, it would be in good working condition.

NOF had long since been seesawing away while I was still struggling with "Tape Test." It was clear that the tape handlers were going to be the touchy part of the system. Before "Tape Test" would run, I had to concentrate on being able to read reliably from a single tape. Endless hours were spent peering into an oscilloscope to see what the tape signals looked like and trying to identify extraneous signals. One little pip consistently appeared which we affectionately called "Little Joe." It always followed a normal signal. The edge of the magnetic head was generating "Little Joe," and this edge had to be rounded off to eliminate the spurious signal.

Another phenomenon we degradingly called "crap in the gap" appeared, and had me baffled for a while. This had to do with an unerased signal in the space between blocks that sometimes got picked up. A change in blank-out timing and erase-head polarity corrected this situation.

Equalizing the signals from eight magnetic head channels, from each of the UNISERVO tape handlers with independent adjustments, into eight high gain adjustable amplifiers was a technique that had to be developed. A standardization process evolved around reading one magnetic tape with standard magnetic properties recorded with a fixed continuous pattern. The sense amplifiers' gains were set to a given value. Thereafter, each channel in each UNISERVO tape handler was adjusted to give the required output level when reading the standard tape. This tuneup process could take an hour, and had to be done frequently at first because personnel on the various shifts were tweaking the adjustments to get their marginal tape signals through.

During these later phases, Bernie Gordon, who had been working with me on the I/O section, was transferred over to assist Brad Sheppard in the mercury memory effort. Bernie was an excellent circuit design engineer and his assistance was needed there. Two junior engineers who had been hired earlier were brought in to help me. Eckert and Mauchly planned for the younger engineers to stay with the Univac systems in production while the experienced veterans were slated for new product development.

A software development group was building up a head of steam. Their activities up until this time had been confined to paper studies, but now that the computer was largely functional, they begged for time on the system, any time. Although we still had I/O problems to resolve, we thought it a good idea to give the central processing unit (CPU) as much of a workout as possible, so the programmers were given whatever time remained in the twenty-four hours after the two engineering shifts quit for the day. Invariably, the time slot occurred after midnight. The system was turned over to the programmers in an "as is" condition with no guarantees that it was in good running shape, or if it was, how long it would stay that way. The next morning there would be notes in the engineering log book about the troubles encountered. The exercises proved helpful to the engineering force but quite demoralizing to the programmers. There was many a midnight when they would arrive only to find the machine down or ailing. Some waited around all night hoping that the lone technician on the graveyard shift might miraculously bring the machine back up.

The software organization was called the Computation Analysis Laboratory (CAL). The director, Dr. Herbert F. Mitchell, Jr., assembled a very competent group of programmers. Dr. Mauchly had hired Dr. Grace M. Hopper, who later achieved fame in her own right. Both Herb Mitchell and Grace Hopper had developed programs for the Harvard MARK I system.

Programming for a computer was an art even though the C-10 code for the UNIVAC I system was considerably easier than programming a binary computer. Still, it was done in machine language, and required a high level of skill. It wasn't surprising when the more innovative people started thinking of easier ways of developing programs. I use the term "program" because software hadn't been invented yet; that came years later. Dr. Mauchly first suggested a shorthand way of writing a mathematical expression. It was called "short code" and used a

From left to right Dr. J.W. Mauchly, General Leslie R. Groves, head of the Remington Rand Laboratory for Advanced Research, and J. Presper Eckert examine a mercury memory tank tester.

2-digit code to express everything, including the subroutines for computing the standard mathematical functions. Short code was developed during the BINAC era but was completed and operational on the UNIVAC I system. It was still awkward to write formulas in this shorthand notation, and because the short code had to be interpreted by a program, it ran slowly.

Grace Hopper was dedicated to making the computer easier to use. She devised the first mathematical compiler, called A0, in 1952. The compiler was a program that translated a higher level language into a machine code program which could then be processed at high speed on the UNIVAC I computer. This was the beginning of the higher level language era.

This was followed in 1953 with the A2 compiler, an improved version of A0, containing some business functions. In 1955, Dr. Hopper released MATHEMATIC, the A3 compiler, and followed this in 1957 with FLOW-MATIC (B-0), the first English language data processing compiler. She subsequently played a major role in the development of COBOL, the standard business language employed by many computer users today.

About a month before the acceptance test, we were shaken by a disastrous event. An extensive wiring revision was planned for the supervisory control panel. As usual, all such changes were scheduled for the third shift when only a few technicians, and in this case, a young engineer, were present. Hundreds of wires from all bays of the machine were conveyed to the supervisory control panel via cables. These were unplugged at the back of the panel to permit the wiring change to take place. In the course of replacing the cables, the young engineer somehow got them reversed. In the loneliness of the early hours, all kinds of strange things can happen. In any event, when power was turned back on again, dozens of grasshopper fuses popped off in each bay. It took hours to assess the damage but it soon became evident that the damage was widespread and serious. Sabotage couldn't have done a better job. The weak link in the UNIVAC I computer circuitry was the solid-state germanium logic diodes, only a problem when subjected to unusual stress. In the direct coupled circuitry employed, shorting one line could cause chain reaction failures through the system. Protective crowbar rectifiers designed into the system allowed for the most probable lines to be shorted but it couldn't accommodate the large number of plugs that were switched.

Fortunately, blown diodes could be detected with an ohmmeter. Every engineer and technician went to work with an ohmmeter on each chassis in the machine. Each chassis was removed from the machine and meticulously checked for the functionality of all the diodes. Several days were lost in the process, but the computer was restored to its previous condition. One young engineer became several years older in that brief time span. The one place in the system where the plugs had not been coded to prevent this type of accident is where it occurred. We all learned a lesson in accident prevention and Murphy's law.

Terms for the acceptance test for the UNIVAC I computer were established some time before the end of March, 1951. The test itself was developed jointly by the National Bureau of Standards and The Bureau of the Census. Drs. Sam Alexander and J. L. McPherson and their staff visited us on several occasions to become familiar with the test programs we were using. Some of NOF and Tape Test were embedded in the acceptance test, which consisted of Part A and Part B. Part A was a test of the central computer and was divided into two sections. The first section tested every internal operation, 2,500 operations in 1.26 seconds and repeated this sequence 808 times (17 minutes). The second section of Part A included the solution of a heat distribution equation, a short routine involving the input/output device and a sorting routine. They were performed twice for each test and when added to the first section, made a total of 20 minutes for Part A.

Part A called for 18 test units to be completed within a prescribed time.

Part B tested the I/O capabilities of the UNIVAC I system. It also had two sections. The first recorded 2,000 blocks (1.4 million digits) on magnetic tape, then read it backwards on each UNISERVO tape handler, and compared it with the original data. This section took 12 minutes, after which the second section performed a writing and reading sequence over one spot on the tape for 700 passes (13 minutes). A perfect test unit took 25 minutes and was repeated 19 times to make up Test B.

The tests were jointly debugged of software errors and then were made available for our use in practice sessions. By the end of March we had developed enough confidence in the system to submit it for the formal acceptance test. On March 29th, Alexander, McPherson, and other officials appeared to witness the event. The test area had been cordoned off and only key people were admitted. Al and I were there ready to spring into immediate action should the computer so much as hiccup. Part A started. The officials kept a running log of each test unit as it was initiated and completed and 6.6 hours later, Part A was successfully completed.

The UNIVAC I computer just after it was turned over to the Bureau of the Census. It was operated at the Eckert-Mauchly plant for nearly a year.

The next morning Part B started. We knew if anything would fail the computer, that would be it. Failure consisted of exceeding the allowable downtime or failing to read/write the information correctly, in which case the test unit had to be rerun until it was

The UNITYPER I data entry device. It was many years before the rest of the world accepted the concept.

The UNIPRINTER output device was the first of the offline printers. Its speed was just 10 characters per second but it held the fort until the 600 line per minute high speed printer was delivered.

correct. Our UNISERVO tape handlers were tuned to as high a state of perfection as the art would permit but we were not sure that this was good enough. I hung on to the edge of my seat throughout the day. The atmosphere couldn't have been more charged. After 9.47 hours, Part B was successfully completed.

On that day, March 30, 1951, the UNIVAC I computer, Serial 1, belonged to the Bureau of the Census and was no longer our plaything. On that day, the computer industry was born.

Chapter 10

UNIVAC I COMPUTER AFTERMATH

The Bureau of the Census made a crucial decision. It decided to lease space from the Eckert-Mauchly Division of Remington Rand and keep the computer at its present site for an indefinite period. Pres Eckert had made this recommendation earlier. A contract was also written for Eckert-Mauchly personnel to maintain it during its stay. This decision was responsible for proving to the world that the computer was reliable enough for commercial use. It is my opinion that if the UNIVAC I computer had been removed from the watchful eyes of the Eckert-Mauchly engineering force, the whole computer industry would have been set back several years. Proof of this theory was substantiated by the events of the next two years.

All during the period of central processor development, another group worked on the first wave of peripheral devices. The UNITYPER I data entry device that keyed data onto magnetic tape was completed first but was of little interest to the Bureau of the Census. Their vast data files were contained on punched cards. Consequently, a card-to-tape converter device was developed for their use. The device was highly electromechanical and we had many challenging problems to overcome. However, it passed its acceptance test with 11 out of 14 good reels of tape produced. The acceptance test had required 10 good reels to be produced in 12 hours. The UNIPRINTER I output device, a typewriter that printed information contained on magnetic tape, also passed its acceptance test by printing a block of information (720 digits) 200 times in 6.16 hours. These peripheral devices would have to suffice for several years until the engineering forces could design the higher speed devices of the future.

The Bureau of the Census took over operation of the UNIVAC I computer with some caution at first. Three Eckert-Mauchly operators, Harold Sweeney, Dick Malaby, and Jim McGarvey had a slight amount of training in operating the system, and they trained the Bureau of the Census operators. Unfortunately, there still was no classification for "computer operator" in civil service, so the Census Bureau enlisted clerical personnel who were accustomed to handling punched card equipment. Their qualifications were minimal, and the first several months of operation amounted to a training period.

The UNIVAC I computer was scheduled for use 168 hours per week. Four eight-hour periods were set aside for maintenance by Eckert-Mauchly engineers, and these were fitted into the first and second shifts. Whatever time the Census Bureau did not use was absorbed by our programmers and this usually was the third shift. They considered themselves lucky to get that.

Shortly after the Census Bureau took over the computer, Jim Weiner approached me and asked, "Herm, how would you like to take the responsibility for all of the UNIVAC I systems, including maintenance of the Census Bureau machine?" Jim explained that he wanted to get the other members of the senior engineering crew into new development work. I thought about it carefully and decided it would be a great opportunity for me. Although I knew my section of the UNIVAC I computer thoroughly, I did not know too much about the rest of the machine and this would be a good chance to learn. It also meant a promotion to Project Engineer with many of the technicians and younger engineers working for me. Within a day I went back to Jim to say I'd be glad to accept. The responsibility for the continuing engineering, testing, and installation of the UNIVAC I computer for the next several years was in my hands.

Almost immediately, I had to place emphasis on testing the second UNIVAC I computer which was now ready for a concentrated effort. Serial 3 was just being assembled on the test floor, and would soon require testing manpower. Sandwiched in between these two systems, the preventive maintenance shifts had to be manned on the Census Bureau machine, and emergency maintenance also had to be provided on a priority basis. With computer time being priceless, an immediate response was required without regard to time of day or day of the week. The junior engineers remaining with the project knew less about the UNIVAC computer logic than I did. So until they were trained, I would have to handle the brunt of the emergency calls.

The UNIVAC I computer passed its acceptance test with flying colors but, deceptively enough, it was far from being reliable. A further shakedown was required and this occurred during the ensuing months. During the scheduled maintenance period, there were still many details that required attention. A peculiar new source of error from the UNISERVO tape handlers appeared during the acceptance test and this required more tests and study. The magnetic tape was somehow developing folds or crinkles which resulted in unrecoverable information. We did not understand what was happening, but knew that the success of the tape system was in jeopardy. With the Bureau of the Census engineers in attendance, we had to be careful that our deep concern was not conveyed to the customer. A "fold" in the tape sounded like a very serious matter, and so our engineers were instructed to refer to the specific malfunction as a "dolf" (fold spelled backwards). Somehow, it didn't sound so bad that way.

The resolution of this problem required many months of maintenance periods and many tests. Transparent plastic reels were designed so that we could observe the tape continuously. That was the key to seeing how a fold was being formed, and once the formation process was understood, the solution was evident. Cutting back on both the oil lubricant on the tape and the power into the reel motors drastically reduced the problem.

My indoctrination into providing emergency maintenance came very rapidly. During the first and second weekday shifts, there were usually sufficient Eckert-Mauchly personnel around to handle any problems on the Census Bureau machine so that emergency calls were generally only made after midnight and on weekends. My telephone number was prominently posted near the supervisory control panel, conveniently located for the operators. At first I received a few calls during the early morning hours of each night. The operator would describe the symptoms over the phone. We usually had to go over the problem several times until I was sufficiently awake and my brain was in gear. Most of the time during the learning period, it was operator error. Typically, I would say, "Libby, it sounds as if you have pushed the wrong button. You can't write on tape when the supervisory typewriter output switch is on." Libby would check and find this to be the case. Libby was one of my favorite Census Bureau operators. She tried hard, but with only a clerical background, she had a lot of learning to do. The other Census Bureau operators also had their egos deflated when they found that nearly all of the computer errors were due to faulty operator manipulation. After the first week, the number of operator errors decreased and true computer malfunctions started to register. Also, Census Bureau programmers became serious about getting their programs to run. Thus when the call came through at 1 a.m. the first day of the second week, I had no alternative. I stumbled into my clothes, started up the car and after a half hour drive, arrived at the computer site. For no apparent reason, a +79 volt fuse had blown in one of the bays. The fuse was replaced but the system refused to work. The input control unit register would not store information. I had to trace the signal through its logic path with an oscilloscope. An oscillating cathode follower was found to be the culprit and an engineering design change was created on the spot. At 5:15 a.m., I was back in bed for two hours of sleep before starting a normal day's work.

The next night was peaceful. I only received one or two calls, and the problems were resolved over the phone. The following night I was called in again at 5:20 a.m. This time the A register was not responding to instructions. Signal tracing led me through many different sections of the machine until the problem was finally traced to a loose plug at the top of bay D. When that problem was fixed, I could not read NOF from the instruction tape. Several more hours of diagnostic servicing led me to a 28D7 tube with an open heater. At 11 a.m., the Census Bureau machine resumed operations.

Saturday evening I was called in at 8 p.m. to fix a problem and I didn't get home until just after midnight. The following week the pattern continued. Either my sleep was disrupted several times during the night or I had to get up early to go in and get the system back into service.

After two weeks of such heroic effort, it was clear to me that I wasn't going to last much longer. My tail was dragging—something had to be done and I was responsible for doing it. The solution, of course, was to share this great potential for experience among my neophyte engineering crew. As Charlie Michaels hovered into view, I yelled, "Hey, Charlie, you know how the computer cycle works, don't you? Alpha, beta, gamma, delta."

"Yes," he hesitatingly replied.

"Great, you are now a Computer Maintenance Engineer," I stated with authority.

There was only one problem; Charlie did not have a telephone. He had moved several months ago to Rydal, a suburb of Philadelphia, during a period when the telephone company was experiencing a shortage of equipment. It would be another six months before the lines could be run to his house. "This is ridiculous," I said to myself. "The census for the whole United States is going to come to a halt because they can't get a telephone into Charlie's house. I can't let this happen." The solution came to me in a flash. Mobile radio telephones were available, and one could be installed in Charlie's car. But it would not be fair for him to bear the expense, so I would have to get the company to pay for it. Thus, I had my first encounter with the new Remington Rand general manager.

A week after the acceptance test, Art Draper had introduced us to Phil Vincent, who was brought in to be our full-time resident manager. Phil listened to my story and with no hesitation approved the expenditure. Within a few days the mobile telephone was installed in Charlie's car. Fortunately, he had a ranch style house so that he could park the car outside his open bedroom window and be able to hear the telephone buzzer. We also had to buy Charlie a battery charger to hook up to his car at night to keep his automobile battery fully charged. The system worked to perfection and satisfied a crucial need. Charlie never did disclose whether he answered the telephone by crawling through the bedroom window or by walking out the front door in his nightclothes.

Half a dozen other junior engineers were mobilized to provide emergency service. I used the sink or swim philosophy to train them. No one drowned, and they learned the logic of the UNIVAC I system mighty fast. I posted a schedule showing which week-day night, Saturday, or Sunday each engineer was on duty. What a relief! I could start to live again. Just one day in every six or seven did I have to stay within earshot of the telephone at all times.

Whatever extra time was taken by the junior crew in fixing the trouble was worth it, but it did lead to some embarrassing moments. Dick Walkling was called in one morning around 2 a.m. because the UNISERVO tape handlers would not move tape. At 8 a.m., when I came in on the normal day shift, there was Dick, bleary-eyed, still tracking the problem. He explained the symptoms to me and all the troubleshooting he had done. I bounded over to the input/output corner of the machine, opened the door and immediately found a UNISERVO tape handler center drive power amplifier tube with an open heater. It was not lit up like the surrounding tubes. Dick will probably remember that embarrassing episode as long as he lives. In spite of it, he turned out to be one of our better maintenance engineers.

I had become an expert on the UNIVAC I computer by this time, knowing its logic rather thoroughly. This was the first time any one person had had the chance to develop a total understanding. The designers of the other sections of the system knew their designs well but, unlike me, never worked on all portions of the system. The names of many of the logic gates became engraved in my memory for many years afterwards.

The emergency maintenance calls were occurring regularly at this point and engineers were putting in all kinds of extra hours without recognition or compensation. They were also expected to work their normal shift in testing the second and third UNIVAC computers. After several weeks of involvement in emergency service, the wear and tear started to show. I decided it was time to approach Phil Vincent again.

"Mr. Vincent, the engineers are providing service above and beyond the call of duty. They are giving up their sleep and their weekends to come in here and keep the Bureau of the Census on the air. Don't you think they should be paid for their effort?"

He understood the situation and said, "I am sure we can work something out."

We did. I don't remember the actual dollar value but it was a reasonable amount. The plan provided for a four-hour minimum compensation in fairness to the man who had to get up in the middle of the night just to replace a fuse. No one got rich on the extra payments but it did help maintain morale. I earned enough in that one summer to pay for a bedroom window air conditioner. That helped a bit in soothing my wife's ruffled feathers.

Betty Snyder approached me one morning after an all-night session on the computer and reported, "This is the third night in a row that my program bombs out at exactly the same point. The tape runs away when it is reading backward." I knew Betty very well and knew that she was a competent programmer. Just about all of the bomb out complaints I had heard from other programmers proved to be programmers' errors, but something told me this case was a little different. Since it was a Census Bureau maintenance period, I decided to investigate. Betty put the program on and sure enough, the failure occurred just as she described it. I turned on the oscilloscope and connected it to the SYI1 loop, a key circuit in the input controller. When Betty ran the problem again to the failure point, the pulse circulating in the SYI1 loop disappeared. That certainly would cause the tape to run away because further count of the incoming data would cease.

"Now, why would the pulse drop out of the loop?" I asked myself. To find out, I had to trap the instructions preceding the failure and keep repeating them. In the dim flash on the oscilloscope, I finally found a timing signal, t46, dropping to half amplitude. Now the picture started to fit together. The same timing signal, t46, was also used in the arithmetic unit. Betty's routine called for a read backward followed by several multiplication instructions. This sequence used t46 for both operations because of overlap between reading tape and multiplying and, consequently, caused an overload of the timing signal. Once the cause was discovered, I was able to redesign the logic circuit and effect a cure in short order. Betty was vindicated. It was amazing that this logic error had escaped detection for so long. I found out later that this was just the beginning, as other logic errors we had never dreamed of cropped up.

The scheduled maintenance periods were devoted to methodically measuring or adjusting the components that could deteriorate. We tested the tubes in each bay of the machine starting with bay A, progressing to B, and so on. The tube tester was specially designed to test tubes in the UNIVAC I computer with the replace point on the meter clearly marked. Another chore executed once a week was scanning through the power supply voltages to see if they were within tolerance limits. With approximately 60 different voltages emanating from 13 different power supplies, it was indeed a chore. Selenium rectifiers do age with time, and so the voltage adjustments were required. Automatic voltage monitoring was built into the system. The concept was excellent but the hardware components used in the implementation were far from it. Stepping switches which did the scanning were impossible to keep in adjustment for any length of time. Thereafter, the voltage monitor was turned on only during maintenance periods.

Reading and recording the automatic gain control (AGC) voltages at each mercury tank amplifier also became routine. The AGC voltage told us how much life was left in the amplifier tubes. An hour before turning the system back to Census Bureau, the engineering test routines NOF and Tape Test were run. These were the tools for determining that the system was in good operating shape.

Thursday, June 14, 1951, was a day of major importance—dedication day. Weeks before, workmen were busy erecting a glass windowed partition around the UNIVAC I system area, laying floor tiles over the rough wooden floor, and installing fluorescent lighting. The old place took on a new gleam.

On that eventful morning, sleek, chauffeur-driven, black limousines and official Army and Navy cars drove up to 3747 Ridge Avenue. Prominent among the high level officials were Albert M. Greenfield, president of the Philadelphia Chamber of Commerce; Charles Sawyer, U.S. Secretary of Commerce; Dr. Edward U. Condon, director of the National Bureau of Standards; Dr. Roy V. Peel, director of the Bureau of the Census; General Leslie R. Groves, director of research for Remington Rand; and James H. Rand, president of Remington Rand.

Pres Eckert explained the operation of the supervisory control panel to the distinguished visitors, and then the UNIVAC I computer was demonstrated. Following the exhibition, the visitors were driven off in the limousines to Alden Park Manor for a luncheon. After lunch, other invited guests were admitted to the first public showing of the UNIVAC I system. Subsequently, a letter signed by Vice Presidents Eckert, Eltgroth, and Vincent was sent to each employee thanking him for his part in the success of the program.

The UNIVAC I computer was clearly a technical success, but would it be a financial success? The first three systems had been sold to the government in 1948. Our marketing department was active, attempting to sell further UNIVAC I systems but no further sales had been made. Commercial companies, Prudential and A. C. Nielsen, interested earlier, had dropped out. Was this it, three sales to the government? There had been an early forecast that five systems would be sold. I had even heard some wild speculation that this country could support eight to ten systems. Of course, my test crew had a lot of work to do in completing the second and third systems but the future was certainly unclear.

The last half of 1951 was devoted to testing the other two machines and, of course, providing maintenance for the Census Bureau machine. The Census Bureau had brought a team of engineers aboard to be trained so that they could provide their own maintenance when the computer was eventually moved to Suitland, Maryland. Gordon Goldstein headed up the group which included Pete Simon and Bernie Stock. Gordon arranged for time on the system so that his engineers could get hands-on experience, but maintenance continued to be the responsibility of Eckert-Mauchly personnel.

Digital computers are peculiar in some respects. Every single one of the tens or hundreds of thousands of parts must function properly for the computer to work. This is unlike an automobile, which can deteriorate considerably and still run. The full significance of this was brought home with a problem that occurred on Serial 2. The test engineers had been plagued for months by intermittent errors, and no one was able to localize the difficulty. As soon as anyone started to pursue the problem it went away. For four months it remained elusive until it was finally brought to my attention. I worked on the problem very carefully, because I knew if I caused any disturbance, it would disappear. The problem yielded to my investigation. I was able to prove that a critical signal was not getting through a chassis connector contact. Upon examination of the chassis and backboard, I found that one female contact had not seated completely, and consequently, spread too much when the chassis was plugged in. I was impressed! One two cent connection was capable of reducing a half million dollar computer to the level of a village idiot. It did not seem fair that a two cent item should have all this power.

On occasion, the lack of casework fit gave us fits. A panel, called a kickplate, snapped into place above each top bay door and below the bottom bay door. The top kickplate provided access to all of the plugs carrying low speed signals at the top of each bay. All too frequently when someone opened a top bay door, the kickplate would be jarred loose and come tumbling down. Sometimes opening a middle or bottom door would trigger the fall of a kickplate. Why the several-pound plate never hit anyone on the head I will never know, but there were some close calls. Invariably the cry for John Sims would be heard throughout the floor.

John would arrive and tighten the catch tension, and the kickplate would then hold its position for many months.

John had been released from the UNIVAC I computer project months earlier. He was working on the advanced development phases of magnetic printing, and it was hoped that the concepts would lead to the future high speed printer. John had constructed a test vehicle, and much to the delight of his audience, he proved its capability by printing $5 bills. Fortunately or unfortunately as the case may be, the ink was black instead of green.

One of the serious problems that plagued us was leaks in the mercury tanks. It was a most disastrous and unpredictable type of failure. Test crews arriving in the morning would get a report that all of the channels in a mercury tank were bad. The crew did not have to look too much farther to find mercury all over the floor and subfloor. Anyone who has played with mercury knows how difficult it can be to pick up, especially if it has fallen into cracks. The technicians spent considerable amounts of time rolling the little mercury balls into each other to make larger balls which could then be rolled onto a sheet of paper and scooped up. We were not concerned about any dangers in handling mercury although we knew it was poisonous if swallowed. The mercury scare had not yet been invented.

The reason for the spill was quite subtle. A quartz crystal would develop a crack because of a stress created during assembly. When the tank was filled with mercury, the cracked crystal could not be detected. It functioned normally. Over a period of time, mercury or its vapor penetrated the crack and amalgamated with the solder holding the crystal to the termination. The solder/mercury combination had no strength, permitting the crystal to become displaced, and then mercury seeped through the crack and leaked out of the tank. Our mercury tank development and manufacturing group devoted a large effort to clearing up the problem, but it was particularly difficult. It was never really eliminated, but it was reduced to a low level of occurrence.

A major event occurred early in December. The AIEE-IRE Computer Conference had become an established annual affair and this year it was being held at home base—Philadelphia. With the first commercial computer now in the hands of a customer, it was appropriate that a paper should be presented. It was written by Eckert, Weiner, Welsh, and Mitchell, and gave an excellent overview of the system. It also included the performance record for the previous six months. Unscheduled maintenance time varied from six to twenty-five percent for the 168 hour week, which wasn't considered too bad for a new system.

Approximately 900 people attended the conference; 400 of them boarded special buses and took advantage of the opportunity to see the UNIVAC I computer in operation at 3747 Ridge Avenue. The UNIVAC I computer was now well into the public arena.

Another encouraging event was the sale of several more UNIVAC I computers to government agencies. Serial 4 was sold to the Atomic Energy Commission (AEC) for installation at New York University, and Serial 5 to the AEC, University of California at Livermore, California. Somewhat later the David Taylor Model Basin signed up for Serial 6. Our marketing organization, seeing a glimmer of light at the end of the tunnel, planned to install Serial 7 when it became available at the Remington Rand Sales Office in New York City. The marketing department thought they had to have their own dedicated system if inroads were to be made in the commercial market.

The picture was starting to look a little brighter as far as the future was concerned, and management planned accordingly. The traditional Remington Rand approach was to have organizationally separate development and manufacturing divisions. Because it worked well for typewriters, the same thinking tended to continue for the computer operation. The fact that there was a difference between typewriters and complex digital computers didn't seem to frighten anyone but me. The engineering activity needed room for expansion anyway, because 3747 Ridge Avenue was occupied with further UNIVAC I computer production. A suitable home was found at 23rd Street and Allegheny Avenue, not too far away. The building, a sizable two-story affair, was to be occupied by engineering personnel, leaving me and my crew to continue with the UNIVAC I computers. Pres and Jim were anxious to get serious work started on the offline peripherals which were vitally needed if we were going to crack the commercial market.

At the head of the list of priorities was a high speed impact printer. Next came a reliable punched-card-to-tape converter device. The card-to-tape device for the Census Bureau needed considerable improvement. Finally, a more reliable, lower cost UNITYPER/VERIFIER data entry device was needed to replace the original UNITYPER I data entry device.

All of these projects were initiated. Earl Masterson, a highly innovative and competent electromechanical designer, headed up the high speed printer project. Ed Blumenthal was placed in charge of the card-to-tape converter and Lou Wilson tackled the UNITYPER II data entry device. Pres Eckert and Jim, of course, multiplexed through all of the projects. My contact with the development projects during the next year and a half was minimal because of my continuing assignment on UNIVAC I computers.

Early in 1952 there was an announcement from Remington Rand headquarters that was to have a profound impact for many years to come; Remington Rand had acquired Engineering Research Associates (ERA). ERA, located in St. Paul, Minnesota, started up during the World War II years as a government contractor. They had done some work with digital circuits and after the war entered the computer field. Because of their military contracts, they were oriented toward large scale scientific application. ERA, in fact, had delivered to the U.S. Navy in 1950 a large scale scientific computer using rotating magnetic drum storage. It was later named the ERA 1101 computer.

No one was quite sure why ERA was acquired. Some guessed that ERA's scientific leaning complemented Eckert-Mauchly's commercial bent. Others theorized that if one computer company was good, two were better. To others it was a mystery.

There was no immediate impact of the ERA acquisition. ERA and Eckert-Mauchly were handled as two entirely separate companies, and to my knowledge, no communication took place between them. The conflict was to come later.

Something else was brewing—Bernie Victor and several other technicians were asked to transfer to the Remington Rand factories in New York State. I could only reach one conclusion: serious thought was being given to moving UNIVAC I computer production to the upstate factories. This I found untenable. Somehow or other I had to convince people that the UNIVAC I computer activity had to stay right here in Philadelphia, next to the engineering department. What the manufacturing organization did not realize was that changes were still being made on a weekly basis, even though UNIVAC I was in production. Problems that had not shown up on the Census Bureau machine appeared on Serial 2. Serial 3 had a new set of problems. Even Serials 4 and 5 had problems that had not been disclosed previously. Systems availability was clearly in need of improvement and this would take more investigation and redesign. I had a deep conviction that the commercial success of the UNIVAC I computer depended upon manufacturing staying in Philadelphia. I used every argument I could think of, spoke to every official who would listen, and wrote strong memos decrying the "bend it until it fits" techniques employed at Remington Rand's New York State typewriter factories. I must have made a dent in their thinking because shortly thereafter, plans were announced to continue UNIVAC I computer production at a new site in Philadelphia. The new site was the fourth floor of the immense Pep Boys building at 31st Street and Allegheny Avenue. Serial 8 was to be the last one produced at 3747 Ridge Avenue. Actually, overlapping operations lasted nearly a year so that there would be no large break in delivery schedules.

The announcement also placed the production responsibility with the Remington Rand Manufacturing Division. All of the test technicians were transferred to that organization, but I objected to that arrangement for the engineering staff. I had strong feelings about continuing to report to the engineering side of Eckert-Mauchly. The problem was amicably resolved by placing my engineering team in the engineering organization but putting them on loan to the Remington Rand Manufacturing Division, who paid our salaries.

Our first installation of the UNIVAC I computer was due in March, 1952, at the Air Controller's Office in the basement of the Pentagon. A small, but powerful, installation crew was selected from my junior engineering group, with Dale Davidson heading it up. One of the members of the group was a bright young lad, Oliver Aberth. Ollie had an analytical mind, and every computer malfunction was a crossword puzzle challenge to him. The last thing he wanted to do was grab an oscilloscope and start brute force signal tracing. Instead, he gathered all of his information from the supervisory control panel. He devised all sorts of diagnostic tests, and using that data was able to pinpoint the trouble within a logic gate. His technique was sophisticated and scientific. The irony of this situation was that a technician with much less understanding of the machine could correct the trouble in a fraction of the time merely by plugging a spare chassis into the suspect area.

Something peculiar was happening. Dr. Mauchly had not been seen for some time. The unofficial word was that he had an office in town, but strong rumors had it that Dr. Mauchly's clearance was revoked and he was not permitted entry to 3747 Ridge Avenue because of the government business now being conducted on the premises. The picture was very muddy but a piecemeal story was gradually put together. This was the era of the "red herring." A person who knew anyone with leftist leanings was instantly barred from many activities. There was no recourse; an individual could do nothing to clear his name even if he was innocent. Mauchly apparently had a secretary who was somewhat radical in her thinking. That was enough. Mauchly, one of the inventors of the computer, was barred from entering the doors of his own company.

We had been living in our house for two years, so Shirley and I decided it was about time for open house. I invited all of my good friends from Eckert-Mauchly. The appointed evening arrived, and so did the guests, except for Jim Weiner and Bernie Gordon. They came a little later carrying a box and in the box was a most adorable collie puppy with a ribbon around its neck. By unanimous agreement the pup was given the name Luke. Luke was a thoroughbred collie and had the papers to prove it. All I had to do was fill in his full name, Sir Luke O' Glenview, on the form and send it in to the American Kennel Club. We put down lots of newspapers in the kitchen that night.

Along with about a dozen other members, I belonged to the Beacon Radio Amateurs, a club started in the mid-1930's by a group of radio amateurs who met in each other's homes in the north Philadelphia area. Often the meetings got boring and members were always on the lookout for ways to liven things up. Sometimes guest speakers were invited, and occasionally we found a good film. The club members knew that I was involved in "new fangled" computers and asked me to give a talk on computers. "I'll do one better than that," I said, "You are all invited to attend a demonstration of a UNIVAC computer for our next club meeting."

A week before the meeting, I went to work and created a file on magnetic tape of each club member's call letters, name, address, and telephone number, except for one member whom I was going to treat in a special way. Then I wrote a simple sort routine. The demonstration consisted of having a member type his call letters on the keyboard, after which the tape would run through a search to find the right record, rewind the tape, and print out the member's name, address, and telephone number.

The night for the radio club meeting arrived. The subject must have been of interest because all twelve members appeared promptly at 8 p.m. at the plant entrance. After registering with the guard, I led them to a UNIVAC I computer test site. For the first forty-five minutes I gave a simple explanation of how a computer functioned and how the supervisory control panel interfaced with the computer. Then I loaded my instruction tape into the memory and asked Harold to type in his call letters. He responded by slowly hitting the keys W3ETA and then struck the execute button, following my instruction. Immediately the tape on UNISERVO 2 tape handler started spinning and lights on the supervisory control panel flashed at a merry rate. Within seconds the typewriter spewed out: W3ETA, Harold Fox, 7610 N. Second St., Melrose Park, Pa. ME5-0692, while the tape rewound. The group had never seen a computer before and were truly amazed. There was an undercurrent that it was a trick.

The next club member, Mort, typed in his call letters and within seconds the computer responded with W3DYL, Mort Eisenberg, 1928 W. Airdrie St., Phila., RA5-0295. Again the computer was right. Several other club members went through the same procedure. Now that confidence had been established as to the computer's credibility, I asked Nate to do likewise. Nate pecked away at his call letters, reels spun, lights flashed and the computer responded with "LID." That did it! The club members couldn't stop laughing for five minutes. In amateur radio parlance, a LID is the worst kind of operator. No other word could be more degrading. The members clamored to know how the computer could be smart enough to know that Nate was a LID. It was clear that UNIVAC I computer had just earned their esteem because of its wisdom. Of course, I later apologized to Nate for making him the butt of a joke, and he took it very graciously.

Shirley and I planned to start our family after we were comfortably settled in our own home. The time had arrived and with engineering precision, son Arthur was born June 12, 1952. Anyone who has ever had a child knows what an impact it has on your mode of living. It was probably a more traumatic experience than getting married. The first months were the roughest, but by the time Arthur was three months old, things were a little easier. In fact, I started my backyard patio project. An idea that appeared in *Better Homes & Gardens* looked intriguing, using broken up pieces of paving instead of expensive flagstone.

I counted on starting work on the project one Saturday morning but Shirley told me she wanted to go in town for the day and I would also have to baby-sit. "No problem," I said, "I'll just put the baby carriage near me while I am working, and if Arthur cries, I'll stop and take care of him. It is a beautiful summer day and there should be no difficulty." With that, Shirley was off and I was on my own.

I had no sooner laid the first cement piece in place when the wail of a baby pierced my ears. Arthur had just been fed, watered, and changed, so I was sure he didn't need anything. I rocked the carriage. It soothed him and in ten minutes he was sound asleep. I got a good half hour's work accomplished when baby cries again filled the air. It worked the first time, so I rocked the carriage again and in five minutes Arthur was happily snoring. I had discovered the means for quieting a baby, something mothers have known for thousands of years. After another half hour nap, Art woke up again unhappy. What was I going to do, stand here all day rocking the carriage? I could see that if I wasn't getting anything done, Shirley wouldn't either for the next year. So I started thinking. If rocking the carriage keeps the baby happy, why don't I build an electric baby carriage rocker? 'Tis often said that necessity is the mother of invention, and in this case I could see that the whole day would be wasted unless I got that automated rocker put together fast.

One advantage of being an amateur radio operator was that in my workshop I had a large junk box filled with parts. Design started immediately. The optimum motion for pulling down on the carriage handle seemed to be sinusoidal travel of two inches in a two second period. The amount of pull needed was quite small, about a pound, because of the carriage spring suspension. Some rapid calculations showed that a very small motor, less than a thirtieth of a horsepower, would do because of the high gear ratio required to get down to one revolution every two seconds. It didn't take more than an hour to throw the contraption together. The motor and gear box was mounted on a two by four piece of wood. A flattened piece of lead pipe was screwed to the wooden base just to give it enough weight; otherwise the motor would be moving up and down instead of the carriage. Then a half inch wide canvas strap was hooked over the center of the carriage handle and run down to the gear box crank shaft.

With Arthur still yelling his head off, I put the contraption in place and applied power to the motor. It worked precisely as I expected. The carriage rocked back and forth exactly as I would have done it. Arthur didn't know he was being jostled by a robot instead of his DaDa and promptly lapsed into euphoria. When

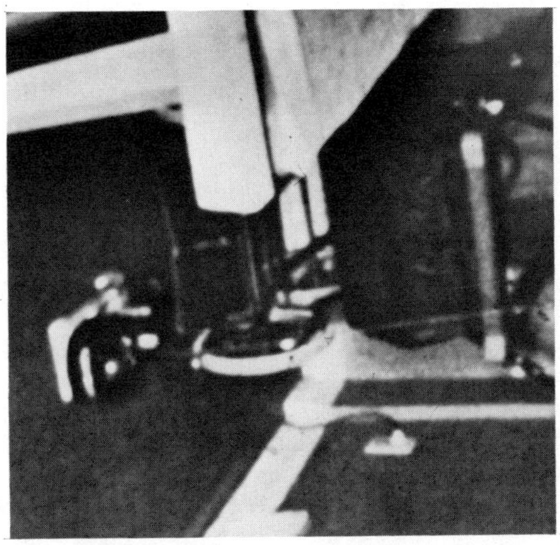

The Bubelator was very successful in keeping my four children happy while I was able to concentrate on other things.

Shirley came home, the rocker was still going strong. She couldn't believe what she saw. The following week Shirley had the chance to try the rocker while I was at work. She reported phenomenal results and soon used it all the time.

Arthur's nickname was Bub, and as using the rocker made Arthur very happy, we referred to the rocker as a Bub-elator, which became its official name. We did have a concern though. Could use of the Bubelator cause any long term, harmful effects on the child? We consulted our pediatrician, who was amused by the whole thing. He assured us that if used normally and only when needed, there would be none. We often wondered about his advice, though; he always carried dog biscuits in his jacket pocket and would take an occasional bite on one. However, the Bubelator worked such wonders that we were inclined to make good use of it.

A thought occurred to me; I hadn't seen anything like the Bubelator on the market. One would think that with millions of babies being born each year, Bubelators would be in every home, especially as it seemed like a nice gift item in the $10 to $15 range. Maybe I had invented something new! There was only one way to find out—file a disclosure and have a patent search made. A call to my old buddy, Jack Trachtman, got the search started. Jack warned me that the search could amount to $100, but by this time I was enthusiastic enough to go ahead.

All during the time the search was going on, I thought of how to design the Bubelator for lowest cost. I wrote to many motor and gear manufacturers and received large quantity quotes. Sand proved to be a much cheaper weight than lead. An inexpensive molded plastic form could contain the Bubelator and an adjustable plastic or canvas strap could make it readily connectable to any carriage handle. I even thought of an extra cost option, a microphone that picked up the baby's cries, turned on the Bubelator automatically, and then turned it off after a few minutes.

Four weeks and $85 later, I received a packet from Jack. In it was a listing of dozens and dozens of carriage rockers that had been invented starting in 1892. It was unbelievable! There were spring driven rockers, electric motor driven—just about every variety you could think of. It was quite clear that my invention had been invented dozens of times before. Jack verified that there was almost no chance of getting a patent on my design. Furthermore, all of the patents had expired years ago and were in public domain. Yet none of these was on the market. I couldn't sell the patent rights I did not have, so the only choice remaining was to manufacture the Bubelator myself, but I really couldn't consider that a serious prospect. Computer development was my profession.

The original Bubelator saw my four children happily through babyhood. As the last child outgrew babyhood, the gears finally wore out and Bubelator was put to rest. I still think, even today, that it was a great idea, but my need is over.

With our home and family launched, it was now time to get serious about Shirley earning her amateur radio license. She wanted to get it so we could share a common hobby. She had the determination; I made the time available to teach her. Each evening we sat down and practiced the continental Morse code and then followed it with radio theory. We worked slowly and methodically over a period of many months. The payoff was still a distance off.

Art Draper had the brilliant idea of using the UNIVAC I computer to predict the 1952 election. He asked Dr. Mauchly whether the idea was feasible. Dr. Mauchly consulted with Dr. Max Woodbury, a statistician at the University of Pennsylvania, who verified that it was. Dr. Woodbury was retained as a consultant and he and Dr. Mauchly started preparing for the event.

The feat to be attempted was a good match for a computer. The machine's ability to gobble up vast amounts of data and provide rapid computation made it a natural. Today's sophisticated reader who sees this being done routinely at all elections must remember that this was the first time such a thing was attempted. Newsmen on the radio and TV networks had worked up their own methods of early election prediction, but it was all done manually and at high risk. The early prediction based on actual early returns should not be confused with the opinion polls of Gallup and Roper. In this election the opinion polls were forecasting a fairly close race between Eisenhower and Stevenson.

The software development activity at Eckert-Mauchly started at least four months before the election, and before it was over, nearly the whole group was involved on a day-and-night basis. Responsible members met with CBS news officials, including Charles Collingwood and Walter Cronkite, who shared their experience gained from previous elections. The algorithm that they embedded in the software recognized that the early returns from eight key states were the barometer. The key states were New York, Pennsylvania, Massachusetts, Ohio, Illinois, Minnesota, Texas, and California. Up until this time, Ohio had missed selecting a winner only two times since 1896, and California had always been in the winner's column. Breakdowns were even provided for key districts. Early return voting records for these states and districts were available from the previous three elections, and this information was entered onto magnetic tape via the

UNITYPER device. The results of the 1944 and 1948 elections for each state were also recorded in the data base. This material included the total popular and electoral vote for each candidate, broken down on an hourly basis. Various other factors and trends that the statisticians deemed important were cranked into the program.

CBS was to call at least once each hour during election night, reporting to the UNIVAC computer via teletypewriter from New York the latest returns from around the country along with the percentage of districts reporting. Immediately the UNIVAC computer was to respond with an analysis and a prediction of the total popular and electoral votes for each candidate. As the next hour's returns were fed to the computer, it would modify its earlier estimate, if necessary, and also announce the percentage of change in the earlier prediction. These percentages should lessen as the night wore on.

Walter Cronkite was to serve as anchor man at election headquarters in New York, and Charles Collingwood had the assignment of working primarily with the Univac people. A TV broadcast was to originate each hour from the Eckert-Mauchly plant in Philadelphia. Between broadcasts, results would be sent to CBS headquarters via teletypewriter.

There were other necessary preliminary arrangements. In order to televise the hourly computed results, the supervisory control typewriter font had to be greatly increased in size so that it could be seen by the camera. Fortunately, having the Typewriter Division of Remington Rand available facilitated matters. CBS also wanted to have a dummy supervisory control panel located at its New York headquarters for use as a backdrop while reporting between the hourly Philadelphia TV pickups. A supervisory control panel for one of the next systems was commandeered for the cause. However, someone thought it would look better if lights flashed on the panel rather than just having it sit there looking stupid. The technicians quickly wired up a group of incandescent bulbs to Christmas tree light flashers, then off to CBS headquarters in New York went the supervisory control panel. There were undoubtedly millions of people watching CBS-TV on election night who thought that the flashing light control panel was the UNIVAC I computer!

Having the UNIVAC system up and running was my responsibility. I knew that my career would reach an abrupt turning point if the computer should break down at that crucial moment of prediction. Therefore I couldn't take any chances. I had to mobilize all my resources and leave no stone unturned. The Serial 5 system, destined for the AEC/University of California at Livermore, California, was close to completion and in good running shape. Just in case Serial 5 should develop problems, arrangements were made to have Serial 4 and the Census Bureau system as backup, ready to take over at a moment's notice. In addition, I planned to have a team of the most capable engineers and technicians in attendance. The Serial 4 machine was to be used in any event for the preprocessing of data. Its function was to validate the data on the magnetic tape and produce an output tape for initiating the prediction run on the Serial 5 machine.

A day before the event, the CBS-TV crew arrived to install the camera, lights, monitors, teletype, and microwave relay equipment. They went about their job in the most professional manner and had the equipment installed in a very short period. Having the TV crew crawling all over the place created an air of excitement. The Eckert-Mauchly programmers worked through the night as usual, never satisfied with what they had. They, along with everyone else, were quite worried about the computer prediction. The computer industry could be set back several years if the UNIVAC computer should goof; egg is not easy to clean off the face of a computer.

Election evening arrived. We couldn't hold it back any longer although the programmers would have liked to do so. Serial 5 test site was alive with lights and people. Chief operator Harold Sweeney was at the supervisory control panel, and other operators were poised at a bank of four UNITYPER data entry devices. Everything was in a charged state of readiness. Soon

The operators at these UNITYPER devices entered the election data on to magnetic tape as it was received from CBS headquarters in New York City. The data was then processed by the UNIVAC I computer.

The UNIVAC I computer on the evening of the 1952 Presidential Election. This was the first use of a computer to predict any election. Art Draper is facing the TV cameras.

some of the very early scattered returns started coming in. The UNITYPER operators went to work. The volume of information sent via the teletypewriters started to pick up. The operators worked faster and produced some reels of tape from their UNITYPER devices that were then brought over to the computer. Harold Sweeney started flipping the control panel switches like a maestro. The UNIVAC system was now digesting the data fed in.

At 8:30 p.m., the supervisory control printer started clanking away in its big bold type and what it printed was:

IT'S AWFULLY EARLY, BUT I'LL GO OUT ON A LIMB

UNIVAC PREDICTS--with 3,398,745 votes in--

	STEVENSON	EISENHOWER
STATES	5	43
ELECTORAL	93	438
POPULAR	18,986,436	32,915,049

THE CHANCES ARE NOW 00 to 1 IN FAVOR OF THE ELECTION OF EISENHOWER.

Our election officials, Herb Mitchel, Max Woodbury, Art Draper, and Phil Vincent looked on in disbelief. The computer called for an Eisenhower victory by an overwhelming landslide. The odds by which he would win exceeded the two digits allowed in the program; thus the printout showed 00 to 1 instead of 100 to 1. The officials put their heads together and said "We can't let this go out. The risk is too great." It was beyond their comprehension that with so few votes counted the machine could predict with such a degree of certainty that the odds would be greater than 100 to 1. Only scattered returns were in and those from Eastern states only. Frenzied activity started. Woodbury and Mitchell figured out which constants would have to be changed in the program to water down the results. A run took place with the factor changed but the results still indicated landslide. Again the factor was adjusted and the results were still overwhelming. Finally a third try produced the mitigated results that were nationally televised to the public at 9:15 p.m. The revised prediction still showed an Eisenhower win by 8 to 7 odds but the public did not hear of the earlier landslide prediction which turned out to be amazingly accurate—and with just 3,400,000 votes in. The final count was 442 vs 89 electoral votes. Art Draper later went on TV to explain what had happened after it became apparent that a landslide was developing.

There are several Eckert-Mauchly officials who are still kicking themselves today for not letting the first UNIVAC computer prediction be aired. On the other hand, it makes a greater story telling it as it actually happened. There isn't a major election now that doesn't use a computer. The programs have been pruned and tuned to provide even greater accuracy. The use of the UNIVAC I computer on that first election prediction, I am sure, opened the doors to undreamed of applications.

The UNIVAC I computer, Serial 5, ran the election prediction without a flaw, and my employment at Eckert-Mauchly was assured for a while longer.

For its first six months of operation, the Bureau of the Census computer log disclosed an average of 21% of the time devoted to preventive maintenance and 17% to unscheduled downtime, which provided an availability of 62%. Because there were no other operating computers for comparison, it was hard to tell whether to be happy or unhappy about the computer's performance. A 50% availability, I believe, was considered acceptable at that time. However, I was convinced that the UNIVAC I computer had to do much better than that if it was going to be a commercial success. Therefore, I launched a program to improve its availability.

Just turning the system off over a weekend proved to be a horror. The Census Bureau machine did not suffer from the weekend syndrome because it was operated around the clock, seven days a week, but the other machines did. I decided to find out why the computers displayed the human trait of hating to go back to work on Monday morning. In 90% of the cases, heaters in the vacuum tubes were found to be open. In fact, rather than diagnosing problems each Monday morning, we walked around the machine looking carefully for vacuum tubes that were not lit. But why did the tube heaters fail at a much greater rate over the weekend when they were not operating instead of during the week when they were on? Two theories for failure prevailed. One had to do with thermal stressing and the other with the high starting current a cold tube can draw. The high current could create a large magnetic field that would tend to throw the heater wires apart. Following on the track of the latter theory, I ran some simple experiments to show that starting currents were eight to ten times the normal running current. That surge could be causing the problem.

A solution involved installing a high power resistor in the line powering the tube heaters. The resistor was adjusted to limit the starting current to no more than a factor of two over the running current. After five to ten seconds, the resistor was shorted out so that full heater voltage was available. This hookup was left operational for several weeks to permit an evaluation of the effectiveness of "slow turn-on." The results were evident after several weekends. Only one or two tubes suffered weekend mortality instead of the usual half dozen. Slow turn-on had proven itself. Consequently, it was put through on a change order for all future installations.

Tape read errors were a weak link in the system that contributed greatly to lost time. The UNIVAC I computer was designed so that it came to a halt when a tape read error occurred. The inexperienced operator rewound all tapes and started the run over again. A more experienced operator was able to try a reread via a cumbersome manipulation of the supervisory control switches. He had to insert the read backward instruction in binary coded decimal form into the switches, execute the instruction, and then insert a read forward instruction in the same manner. If the latter operation was successful, he could then return to continuous operation. Out of desperation, and against regulations, some of the sharper CAL operators found that they could adjust the gain of the tape amplifiers a little higher or lower and the error would disappear. This gave me an idea. Why not provide a switch on the supervisory control panel that could provide easy control of the tape amplifier gain?

The details were worked out; instead of the tape amplifier gain being raised and lowered, the tripping level into the input buffers was varied. It had the same effect but was easier to implement.

The design was tested on the Census Bureau machine with remarkable results. Now, 90% of the tape errors were rereadable. Weak recordings were resurrected by flipping to "high gain." At other times, noise pulses were dropped below the level of recognition on "low gain." The high-low gain switch made a profound improvement in "good" time.

There were still too many opportunities for foul-ups to occur. Rereading the tape first at normal gain, then at high gain, and, if required, at low gain, called for six manual insertions of the instruction into switches. It was too easy to goof. Operators were losing their place on the tape and reading the wrong block of information. I could see that automating the reread would be an immense benefit, and it became one of my next projects.

Fortunately, Jim and Pres had the vision to allow for some spare chassis in the machine. The design required a full chassis' worth of components. I knew the input control section thoroughly so it was easy for me to tap in at the proper places. Despite my expertise and confidence, the "automatic reread" required debugging, but it finally worked as planned. When a tape error was detected, automatic reread took over. It went through all the sequences that the operator previously had had to do manually, only without fouling up. Automatic reread made another great contribution to improving the UNIVAC computer's "good" time.

A mysterious malady was also contributing to unavailability. We called the disease "sleeping sickness." As long as a 25L6 tube continued to receive impulses, it functioned normally; however, if the tube was left in the non-conducting state for any extended period, it showed great reluctance to turn back on. We also found these tubes to have a high reverse grid current. The first pulse arriving after a long off period would usually be obliterated. The problem was clearly due to the tube itself and not our design. Discussions were held with our vendor, the General Electric Tube Division, who theorized that cathode material was being boiled off to contaminate the grid of the tube. The solution, as they saw it, was to protect the grid wires by gold plating them, and a batch of gold plated grid tubes were made for our evaluation. That solved our problem.

Spring 1953 saw the opening of our new manufacturing facilities at 31st Street and Allegheny Avenue. John Beach was appointed manager of the facility, reporting to Remington Rand Manufacturing management, first to Bev Bond and later to B. F. Anderson. The Remington manufacturing managers had a traditional hard-line approach to manufacturing and had always manufactured a stable product in the past. It was difficult for them to cope with manufacturing a product that kept changing, but John learned fast.

John made a personal campaign of introducing me to the virtues of alcohol after he heard I was a non-drinker. At our first luncheon John said, "I am going to order a hopped-up milk shake for you." I must confess the brandy alexander did taste good. For the remainder of my stay at 31st Street, Johnny Beach kept feeding me brandy alexanders. If he could see me now with a manhattan in my hand on ceremonious occasions, I am sure he would be proud of me.

I settled down into the 31st Street building with my engineering crew. Meanwhile, the high speed printer and card-to-tape projects were moving into high gear at the engineering building. In fact, they needed more engineering manpower. At a meeting with Jim Weiner, John Beach, and Phil Vincent, we decided to send some of my key UNIVAC I computer engineers to work on the new projects. This would serve two purposes, supplying needed engineering manpower and having them fully trained to assist with getting the product into production.

Unfortunately, I had nothing to do with the development of the high speed printer and card-to-tape converter projects, but I did hear of their trials and tribulations. They were as momentous in their development as the UNIVAC I computer, but in a smaller way. Maybe Earl Masterson, the project leader, will become motivated some day to record the magic moments in the high speed printer development. These two products unquestionably led to the successfull commercialization of the UNIVAC I system.

Finally it happened. The commercial breakthrough we were all looking for occurred—the General Electric Company signed up for a UNIVAC I system in 1953. All sales prior to that time had been to government agencies. A number of large companies were considering the UNIVAC I computer but no one wanted to be first; GE's plunge into computers opened the door for other commercial sales. GE got Serial 8, and others were sold in rapid succession to Metropolitan Life, U.S. Steel, E. I. DuPont, and Franklin Life. the UNIVAC I computer was on its way to becoming a success. It appeared that the computer industry was here to stay.

A major improvement was scheduled for Serial 9, the first system under test at 31st Street. Water cooling was being substituted for air cooling. This would greatly simplify the installation of a system at the customer's site, because the old air ducts had been large, cumbersome, and difficult to install. The heat dumped into the room during tests was unbearable. In the winter the situation was reversed; on several occasions when the air filters were left out for cleaning, the test crew was greeted with a flurry of snowflakes when they opened the bay doors. In fact, drapes had to be installed around the machine under test to keep the cold air from spreading all over the surrounding area. All of these inconveniences were to be eliminated by piping chilled water into heat exchangers in the base of the computer. The new cooling system was a big improvement but it introduced its own problem, condensation. Leakage in the casework and open bay doors permitted the humid air in the room to enter the system and form condensate. Keeping the condensate from developing in the first place required some careful juggling of environmental conditions. Preventing the condensate from creating damage required a little more work.

Meanwhile, Shirley's study for her FCC amateur radio license came to fruition in March, 1953, when she passed the novice class test and received the call letters WN3VNN. I was very pleased with her accomplishment especially as women amateur radio operators were few and far between. She started pounding the telegraph key each evening making contacts with other novice amateurs. The objective of the novice license is to get people on the air and painlessly build up their code speed ability to thirteen words per minute by communicating with other novice amateurs. She made many contacts on the novice band including several

A portion of a UNIVAC I computer being hauled up the side of the Metropolitan Life Insurance Company in New York City. It was too big to be moved through the doorways.

with a Hatfield, Pa., woman, who is now a lifelong friend. The woman used amateur radio to keep in touch with her husband, the skipper of a Sun Oil tanker. We continued code practice and study of radio theory each evening until Shirley was ready for the general class test. A trip to the FCC office at the Customs House verified her capability and in early September, the "N" for novice dropped out of her call letters and she became W3VNN, a full fledged ham. The world was at her call!

One of the first things I did then was build a small, remote control box and place it near the kitchen sink. A switch on the box could turn on and off my transmitter and receiver located in the second floor shack. The equipment was always left pretuned to 29132 KHz and in the squelched (quiet) position. Each day at 5 p.m., Shirley flipped the equipment on and listened for me from my mobile unit in the car while she got dinner under way. We could chitchat back and forth over the ten mile trip home with relative ease as it was an unused frequency. Occasionally other amateurs, hearing us, joined in the conversation. Several times fellows in England broke in and wanted to know what was cooking for dinner. The real advantage of the radio link was that I could give Shirl all the news of the day while riding home, thus leaving me time to read the newspaper in peace after dinner.

By late 1953, the 31st Street building was humming with activity. Many test sites were occupied with UNIVAC I computers at various stages of construction and test. The engineering center at 23rd Street was also bustling with energy. A sizable number of new engineers had been hired for the major product developments, and a few were working on advanced technology involving magnetics, spurred on by Pres Eckert. Now there were 273 people in the engineering department.

Pres and Jim had a few people working on possible enhancements to the UNIVAC I computer. I don't know whether the stimulus for this work came from our local management or from our marketing organization in the wake of IBM's announcement of its 702 system for commercial use. Various packages were put together based on Marketing input and studies made by our designers. The basic circuits were to remain the same but the enhancements considered were such improvements as ferrite core storage and changes in the instruction code. Development and manufacturing costs were estimated for the modifications, which were then forwarded to Remington Rand headquarters. These costs were in addition to those needed to keep the solid-state computer project going. We never received an approval for the project.

The transistor was invented in 1948, but it remained a laboratory curiosity for many years. The point contact type, prevalent in the early 1950's, left much to be desired. Pres knew that the vacuum tube had to be replaced by some kind of solid-state device. Research work had been taking place in the lab to develop a high speed magnetic amplifier; these amplifiers had been used for years, but at very low frequencies. Bob Torrey, Ted Bonn, and others found that winding miniature cores of thin permalloy metal provided the basis for amplifiers that would work at 1 MHz with up to seven loads. A significant number of patents were issued for these new developments and the term FERRACTOR™ was derived as the official name for the magnetic amplifier.

I can remember the day that Pres Eckert gathered all of the engineering personnel together at Alden Park Manor to discuss future plans for the company. He stated that the transistor was not yet a practical alternative; therefore, we would be casting our lot with the magnetic amplifier. Several weeks later, a week long course in magnetics was organized and all engineers were requested to attend so they could be updated on the new magnetic amplifier technology.

For a moment, let me backtrack in time. Toward the end of 1950, we found that the UNIVAC I computer logic was in final form and the logic designers were available for new assignments. One of the directions that Eckert and Mauchly wanted to pursue was the development of a systems architecture utilizing electrostatic memory. Art Gehring, Betty Jean Bartik, and Bill Schmitt were engaged in that project. The approach was revolutionary considering that this type of memory was random access compared to the previous serial organizations. The architecture utilized multiple registers and microprogramming with writable control store. This was a major innovation, and the first use of microprogramming in this country. Unfortunately the electrostatic memory itself never proved reliable enough to be committed as a product, so the whole project was dropped after a year. It is regrettable, though, that the world has never known of this historic venture.

Following that, design was initiated on a small business-oriented tabulator with improved calculating capability. It was called the UNIVAC Calculating Tabulator (UCT) and was initially thought of as a plugboard machine. Engineering ingenuity upgraded the machine with a drum memory and it was designated the 409-3, an improvement over the UNIVAC 60 and 120 tabulators under design at the Remington Rand, Norwalk,

Connecticut laboratory. Marketing, fearful of the loss of the plugboard, decided not to back the development; thus the 409-3 computer was shelved in late 1952.

As the magnetic amplifier evolved into a promising hardware element, desire arose to utilize it in a product. The first test came with a small desk calculator built as a prototype unit at the Norwalk lab in 1954. The calculator worked, but it was never put into production.

The Philadelphia lab, meanwhile, took the 409-3 system design off the shelf and redesigned it to utilize the magnetic amplifier. In keeping with the magnetic technology, a very high speed drum was proposed for the memory. Early in 1954, the Air Force developed an interest in the all solid-state computer concept. A contract was signed to deliver such a system to their research facility at Cambridge, Massachusetts. The 409-3 computer became the Air Force computer. An engineering team was established and the project was launched. The Air Force computer was completed in March, 1956, and the commercial version with input/output devices finished its testing in early fall, 1957. It was called the UNIVAC Solid-State Computer. Unfortunately,

This all solid-state computer (except for a dozen tubes in the center) used high frequency magnetic amplifiers and was first developed for the Air Force. It later became the commercial UNIVAC Solid-State Computer. The very high speed drum main memory is visible as the black object on the lower shelf.

this computer got caught in the rivalry that had developed between the St. Paul and Philadelphia divisions. A UNIVAC File Computer, developed by St. Paul and in roughly the same price range as the UNIVAC Solid-State Computer, was already being marketed. There was great concern that the "Solid-State" would interfere with the "File Computer" sales. Consequently, the "Solid-State" was held back from the marketplace and not delivered in this country until the summer of 1959, although it was marketed in Europe several years earlier.

The late entry of the UNIVAC Solid-State Computer resulted in a shortened life span for the project, although 500 systems in various forms were sold. By 1960, it was clear that the transistor was here to stay, and magnetic amplifier technology would not survive.

The prototype high speed printer was brought to a successful stage of operation early in 1954. It was interesting to watch each new viewer's face as he saw the printer spew out paper at a fantastic rate with sounds like the popping of a Gatling machine gun in the background. A thousand and one problems had been overcome to produce the essential ingredient for a commercial system. Immediately behind the prototype followed a second high speed printer being completed by the engineering crew. This was the only way to have a high speed printer in time for the General Electric installation. As an expedient, the development engineers were sent to install the high speed printer at Appliance Park in Louisville, Kentucky, as we did not have time to train our regular installation crew.

I arranged to take a week's vacation during the summer of 1954, specifically to head south and inspect the General Electric installation. The Skyline Drive was beautiful and so was our high speed printer. G.E. had planned the UNIVAC I computer installation to be a gorgeous showplace, and it was. Those were the days when having a computer was a status symbol. The computer gleamed in its multicolored environment behind a glass observation wall. Gigantic potted plants and ferns dotted the area, and we wondered a bit about what all the excess plant-generated oxygen might do. Shirley and I headed back to Philadelphia, happy at having seen the UNIVAC I computer housed in all of its glory.

My engineers, now trained on the prototype high speed printer and card-to-tape machines, came back to the manufacturing building to assist in getting these units into production. Again, many latent design errors cropped up for the first time as the production units rolled down the line, but my trained crew was able to devise the fixes required. Production of the UNIVAC I computer and subsystems was at an all time high. The pace was hectic.

The need for marketing an improved UNIVAC I computer waxed stronger and forced a management decision. The Remington Rand organization had some peculiarities which resulted in a strange turn of events. The Philadelphia operation reported to the vice president of engineering, while the St. Paul operation reported to the vice president of marketing. The separation of the two organizations may have been one factor that led to the St. Paul operation also putting in a bid to do the UNIVAC II design. The St. Paul bid was considerably lower than ours, and they were awarded the job even though they had no familiarity with the UNIVAC I design.

Some time during late 1954 or early 1955, I was requested to go to St. Paul for several days to answer questions regarding the UNIVAC I computer design. I was instructed to meet with Mr. William C. Norris, who would set up the meeting. I had never traveled by airplane and this was not the time to try to overcome my aerophobia, so I paid the penalty by boarding the train at North Philadelphia station on Sunday evening just after dinner. The clickety-clack of the endless track contributed to one long sleepless night. At 7 the next morning the train pulled into Chicago right on schedule. A taxi trip across town brought me to the Burlington Railroad station and at 9 a.m. the train's wheels started churning. It was an icy winter day, which became even more evident as the train proceeded north along the Mississippi River. The scenery was beautiful. A layer of snow covered the countryside and icicles dangled from the trees. A little later I was amused to see a few automobiles traveling on the frozen river. However, it was an all-day, rather boring trip, lasting until late in the afternoon when the train pulled into the Twin Cities.

The next morning I took a taxi to the Minnehaha Street building and asked to see Mr. Norris. He was warm, friendly, and anxious to do business. He reiterated the purpose of my visit and the importance of the work, then introduced me to a number of the top technical personnel including Arnold Cohen, Jack Hill and Frank Mullaney. For the remaining two days I met with engineers assigned to the UNIVAC II computer project. They went over their plans to replace the 1,000-word mercury tank memory with a 2,000-word ferrite core memory. This would provide a good speed-up factor by greatly reducing the access time. The alpha control cycle would be eliminated to save another 40 microseconds and the magnetic tape recording density was to be doubled, thus providing an improvement in I/O performance. A new type of magnetron counter tube was to be employed in the input/output control sections to reduce the tube count. What was presented looked reasonable. The St. Paul engineering group had received all the UNIVAC I computer drawings sent from Philadelphia a month before, but there were very few questions about the computer or its design philosophy. The two days of meetings were concluded. I boarded the train on Thursday morning, and retraced the path I had taken several days before. It was another long, uninteresting train ride, and my last one. Whatever the evils of air transportation were, I decided I would have to accommodate them.

The year 1955 was a momentous one for Remington Rand. It merged into the Sperry Rand Corporation, and we became Remington Rand Univac, Division of Sperry Rand Corporation. At my level, I was not privy to the considerations that entered into the merger. All I knew about it was what I read in the newspapers and business magazines. Most of the employees felt that acquiring more resources was a good thing for our money-gobbling computer business.

I got to know Harry Vickers, president of the Sperry Rand Corporation, rather well. He was a fellow amateur radio operator, so we had a common bond. Whenever he visited our company premises, he would wander off into the laboratory with me and look at some of the latest oscilloscopes and test equipment. When we attended corporate functions (not many for me), we would manage to get together and discuss amateur radio. He told me about his three stations, one at his home near Detroit, another at his camp in Maine, and the third on Long Island. He also related the problems he was having with his Collins kilowatt transmitter. I offered to fix it if the Collins engineer couldn't. At several functions I was given the seat next to Mr. Vickers. I got the impression that he was much more at ease in the laboratory than in the business world.

At that time, General Douglas MacArthur was chairman of the board of directors for Sperry Rand. Of course, it was only fitting that the board of directors get a first-hand view of the newly formed Remington Rand Univac Division, so arrangements were made for a visit to the UNIVAC I computer factory. On the appointed day, long black limousines pulled up in front of the Pep Boys Building at 31st Street and discharged their passengers. Everything at the manufacturing plant had been spruced up days in advance. It was like getting ready for captain's inspection on Saturday morning in the Navy. The distinguished visitors were met by John Beach and brought up to the production floor. I recognized MacArthur immediately, although with some shock; he was a wizened old man. I remembered his wartime

General Douglas MacArthur, chairman of the board, Sperry Rand Corporation, visits the Philadelphia operations shortly after the Sperry-Remington Rand merger. Philip S. Vincent is on the right.

photographs, always beautifully posed with corncob pipe in mouth, jutting jaw, and determination in his face. It was a real disappointment to see him in civilian clothes, an ordinary mortal, looking like any ordinary man. MacArthur hung back from the group that had gathered around a UNIVAC I computer test site listening to a lecture. He seemed to be disinterested and alone throughout the visit. In an hour they were gone.

My time to move on had arrived. Jim Weiner called to say that I was needed for a new computer development that was just getting started at the 23rd Street engineering building. I was ready for a change after initially babysitting with the UNIVAC I computer, then seeing it grow from adolescence to maturity over a four year period. I felt good about my accomplishments. Over one hundred change orders had been put through to correct latent defects. It made a big difference in the reliability and availability of the system. Well maintained UNIVAC I systems in the field were now providing 90% "good" time. The four years' experience in maintaining, manufacturing, and installing UNIVAC I computers had a profound effect on my design philosophy that was to follow me for the rest of my life. I can't stress too strongly the importance of including the field and factory requirements in the design. Many engineers are oblivious to these problems, and it is too bad that each designer can't spend at least six months to a year living with the real world, as I did.

Up until the first half of the 1950s, the computer field was dominated by Remington Rand Univac, although much activity in computer development was taking place in the industry. After ENIAC was completed, a group from The Moore School left to join Dr. Von Neumann in a computer development at the Institute for Advanced Study at Princeton, N.J. They built a very fast scientifically oriented computer using binary parallel arithmetic and random access electrostatic memory. This development spawned a whole series of similar computers at important universities and research laboratories across the country; ORDVAC and ILLIAC at the University of Illinois, JOHNIAC at The Rand Corporation, and MANIAC at Los Alamos.

MIT started its own development in 1947 with WHIRLWIND I. It was a very fast machine oriented toward real-time operation. Most notably, WHIRLWIND was the first computer to make use of coincident current magnetic cores for memory, a major innovation that was to stay with the computer industry for many years.

The National Bureau of Standards was anxious to explore computer usage, and ordered a system that RAYTHEON had under development. The progress on RAYDAC was slow, and eventually just one system was delivered. NBS decided it couldn't wait, and undertook its own development of SEAC on the East Coast and SWAC on the West Coast. The computer was a binary serial device using mercury delay lines for memory. It became operational in May, 1950.

All of the developments mentioned above were laboratory devices designed by the user and not commercially marketed. In the commercial area, a number of companies were formed to exploit the market for a small computing system using magnetic drum for memory. These systems were less expensive than the UNIVAC I computer and also much inferior in performance. Computer Research Corporation brought out the CRC 102A. Electronic Computer Corporation built the ELECOM 100 and later the ELECOM 120 and 125. Electro Data Corporation delivered the DATATRON in 1953. Burroughs produced its first entry, the small E101. None of these systems made a significant dent in the marketplace until IBM announced its card handling 650 system in 1953. The 650 used a high speed drum to boost performance, and proved quite popular, with over 1,000 of the systems sold.

The sleeping giant, IBM, was stirring. It cooperated with Dr. Aiken between 1939 and 1944 in building the MARK I electromechanical calculator at Harvard University. Later, at its headquarters in New York, IBM completed a monstrous electromechanical machine in January, 1948, that employed 13,000 tubes and 23,000 relays. It was during the Korean War in 1950 that IBM announced an all-electronic computer called the Defense Calculator. The name later was changed to the IBM 701. It was a scientifically oriented machine that used Williams tube (electrostatic) memory. The system was first delivered early in 1953, with 18 more delivered in the following three years. The scientific line was continued with IBM 704 in 1956.

In general, two approaches seemed to be evolving: computers that were oriented toward solving scientific problems and computers that were oriented toward handling commercial business needs. The latter were called data processors, and the scientific machines became known as "number crunchers" because of their enormous ability to handle complex and voluminous figures rapidly; but they had little ability to handle the tremendous volume input/output data required by the commercial users.

Competition for IBM's scientific line was provided by the Engineering Research Associates' 1101 computer. It used a large drum for memory, which greatly limited its performance. Yet it was the first in the marketplace in 1950. An improved version, the UNIVAC 1103 computer, was brought out in 1953. It used coincident current magnetic core storage, making it 2,000 times faster than the ERA 1101 computer.

IBM turned to the commercial data processing field with its 702 system. It was a character-oriented machine using 10,000 characters of Williams tube memory. It was scheduled for delivery in early 1955, but because of its many deficiencies, it was withdrawn from the marketplace and replaced with the IBM 705. Only a few 702's were delivered because the 705 was available a year after the first 702 delivery. The UNIVAC I computer system had been delivered more than four years earlier.

The UNIVAC I computer became a legend. It had checking features built into it that today's systems are just approaching. A total of forty-six UNIVAC I systems were produced. The number could have been much greater if Remington Rand had emphasized leasing in addition to purchase, but the cash and aggressiveness weren't there to finance it. UNIVAC I computers remained in operation through the 60s, with the last one deactivated in 1969, twenty years after it was designed. The first generation of computers was over.

Chapter 11

AHEAD OF ITS TIME—LARC

In 1954, the University of California, Radiation Laboratory (UCRL), now the Lawrence Livermore Laboratory, at Livermore, California, decided that more computing power was needed to solve some of the very complex nuclear physics problems encountered while operating the laboratory for the Atomic Energy Commission. UCRL already had a complex of several computer systems including a UNIVAC I computer, but the total computing power was insufficient. They estimated they would need a system having one hundred times the computing power of any existing system. Because nothing of this sort existed, they realized they would have to contract for its development. The request for proposals was released but there seemed to be discrepancies in who received it. Our St. Paul operation was a recipient but the Philadelphia operation was unaware of its existence. In fact, St. Paul worked on a reply to the proposal for six months before Pres Eckert heard about it. Pres was furious. He was most anxious that Philadelphia get a crack at the coveted prize, and wanted to enter the race. Pres's strong desire gave our corporate management a headache. It meant that the Philadelphia operation would be competing against the St. Paul operation, something that wasn't looked upon very favorably. The battle raged at corporate headquarters with Pres presenting a very compelling case. He emerged the victor. Only the Philadelphia operation would be allowed to bid on "LARC" (Livermore Automatic Research Computer), with St. Paul acting as support.

Pres was most eager to get the award, because he thought that the company had to develop solid-state technologies for the next commercial large scale systems following the UNIVAC I computer. Magnetic amplifiers which had just been developed for the Air Force computer would be satisfactory for the medium to smaller systems. The FERRACTOR magnetic amplifiers in these systems took one kilowatt of clock power, a limiting factor. Also, at 1.5 microseconds propagation time per stage, they were not particularly fast.

What followed in the next ten days was a heroic and frenzied effort to get a proposal together. All the brains in the Philadelphia operation were mustered for this one event. Art Gehring, Al Tonik, Lloyd Stowe, and several others wrestled with the architectural concepts. Josh Gray, I, and other circuit experts grappled with the hardware elements. Some ideas were hastily put together that would permit a basic instruction to be executed in four microseconds, the speed considered necessary to meet Livermore's requirements.

The FERRACTOR magnetic amplifiers that we had developed for use in the Air Force magnetic computer were not fast enough. Extrapolation showed that if the magnetic amplifier cores were made smaller, they would operate at higher speeds. Brainstorming with these devices, our engineers conjectured several unusual circuits. One of them was called "coil gating." Many high speed magnetic cores were arranged in a serial array. A pulse could pass through the array depending on the saturated or unsaturated state of each core. A saturated core exhibited a low impedance to the pulse while an unsaturated condition looked like an open circuit. Another winding on the core controlled whether the core was saturated or not. This type of logic element used many magnetic amplifiers and few transistors. That was the objective, because transistors were still expensive and not fast enough. The total component count to do the LARC job was estimated to be 10,000 magnetic cores and 5,000 transistors.

The architectural concepts included a faster arithmetic unit logic, instruction overlap, and a separate small processor to handle the input/output devices. The Air Force magnetic computer was envisioned as the small processor.

Armed with these ideas, Pres Eckert presented the Remington Rand Univac Division proposal to UCRL in April, 1955. St. Paul representatives accompanied Pres on the trip, but acted only in a supporting role. IBM had presented their proposal the previous day.

Before letting the contract, Dr. Edward Teller, head of the AEC/UCRL laboratory, and his staff decided to get a first-hand exposure to the advanced technology effort and facilities of Remington Rand Univac, and therefore scheduled a visit to the 23rd Street engineering laboratory during Easter week.

Dr. Josh Gray and his assistant, Bill Winter, had been experimenting for weeks on high speed circuits and how to achieve them. Means of getting higher speed from the best available transistors were being investigated. Various magnetic circuits were being used in combination with transistor switches including "coil gating." Pres worked closely with Josh during this early development phase. Dr. Teller couldn't help but be impressed when he was shown all of these circuit developments and many other new technological projects that were under way in printers, tape units, and magnetic drums.

For weeks after that visit, Pres and Jim worked with groups of key people in studying how the 100 times computer power could be obtained. I was recalled from the manufacturing building to participate in the study. Art Gehring, Lloyd Stowe, and others delved into further arithmetic unit studies. Josh Gray and I became engrossed in the circuit design considerations.

On September 9, 1955, the contract was awarded to Remington Rand Univac for the design, construction, delivery, and installation of a LARC computer system. The contract price was $2,850,000. Pres wasn't sure that we could develop a LARC for that amount of money, but the feeling existed that in any event Remington Rand Univac had to develop advanced solid-state technology for its future product line. If there was any overrun, the costs would be borne by Remington Rand Univac. Specifications for LARC were to be mutually developed by UCRL and Remington Rand Univac over the next six month period.

At this point, Jim Weiner, our chief engineer, appointed me project coordinator for the LARC. It was my responsibility to get a mutually agreeable set of specifications formulated. UCRL created a team of people with whom we were to negotiate. The team included Dr. Sidney Fernbach, head of the computation lab; Kent Elsworth, one of the most active participants; and, on the engineering side, Jim Norton, Lou Nofrey, and Jim Moore.

Over the next six months, the UCRL and Remington Rand Univac negotiating teams worked out the details of the specifications. Our team usually consisted of Jim Weiner, Pres Eckert, Art Gehring, Al Tonik, and me. Meetings were held every three weeks, alternating between Philadelphia and Livermore. Air travel at that time was provided by propeller-driven DC6s and DC7s, a far cry from the speed and convenience of today's jets. Our negotiating team would board a plane in Philadelphia, and have breakfast, lunch, and dinner, and 12 hours later, we would land in San Francisco, after stops in Chicago and Denver. The propeller-driven planes flew at 15,000 feet and consequently were subjected to continuous turbulence as they bounced from one cloud to the next. I developed motion sickness on several occasions, and usually felt uncomfortable, ill at ease, and worn out by the time we landed. It was a long flight that I had to make five times in the last half of 1955.

The lengthy travel did have its positive side. We managed to see something of San Francisco and its surroundings. The Claremont Hotel in Berkeley served as our base and it was delightful, as was the whole Bay Area. We succumbed to some of the attractions and better restaurants, such as The Hungry i, Ernie's, Trader Vic's, Fisherman's Wharf, and Chinatown.

The basic architecture of LARC was evolved by December although many engineering details were left to be pinned down. I spent a full week at Livermore closeted with Lou Nofrey and Kent Elsworth to complete most of these details. Some of the issues had to be approved by Remington Rand Univac management; consequently, it wasn't until March, 1956, that the final and complete specifications were issued. The official starting date for the LARC computer program was September, 1955, with completion by February, 1958.

The architecture for LARC was spelled out in the specifications, and contained many dazzling concepts. It had to, in order to achieve the factor of 100 times computer power. Two independent computers were contained in the basic system. One was an input/output processor (IOP) designed primarily to provide flexible, parallel, and coordinated control of the input/output equipment. The second was a computing unit (CU) designed to perform the arithmetic functions of the system. The basic concept was to separate the CU from the overhead of handling input/output chores and let it concentrate on arithmetic computation for which it was especially adapted. If increased computing capacity was required, the basic system could be readily expanded to include a second CU. The CU was a parallel (12 digits, 60 bit) computer capable of both fixed and floating point arithmetic operations, an addition in 4 microseconds or a multiplication in 8 microseconds. The internal code was a modified 5-bit, biquinary coded decimal system. Except for certain intercommunication facilities, the CU and the IOP operated independently.

A high speed magnetic core memory was shared by the CUs and IOP. The memory was divided into units, each capable of storing 2,500 words. Operating independently and in parallel with other units, each unit of the memory contained all the necessary switches, read/write regenerate circuits, and buffer storage. The main memory could be expanded to a maximum of 39 units, equivalent to 97,500 words. Eight memory units were used in the basic system on a multiplexed high speed bus to provide an effective rate of one word every 0.5 microsecond.

The high speed main memory was backed up by a magnetic drum file memory. Up to 24 magnetic drums could be included in a system. Each drum was capable of storing 250,000 words. A continuous data transfer rate of 2,500 words every 83 milliseconds was called for by interlacing the sequential operation of two drums. The drums featured a new air-floated, read/write head assembly to achieve high reliability.

The computing system included a complete complement of input/output equipment including UNIVAC II type magnetic tape units, online high speed printers, as well as keyboards and printers on the control consoles. As optional equipment, the system could have a card reader and a Charactron-type cathode ray tube device for direct viewing or photographic recording.

Another striking feature in the specifications was the large number (26 expandable to 99) of high speed registers that could be used for arithmetic computation and indexing the memory addresses. These registers had to operate in 1.0 microsecond.

With the architecture fairly well established by the specifications, the next step was implementation, devising the detailed logic and circuits. The critical path was contained in the arithmetic unit. Basic machine timing was determined by the multiplication instruction; it required eleven additions of partial products, several cycles devoted to the generation of multiples of the multiplicand, and a few more cycles for handling the sign and transferring the results to a register. Sixteen operations had to be accomplished in 8 microseconds; thus the basic clock rate was 2 MHz. Information had to enter the arithmetic circuits every 0.5 microsecond.

Our logic designers working on the arithmetic unit estimated that it would take a maximum of nine levels of logic. Allowing for tolerances and pulse reshaping, we computed a maximum propagation time per logic stage of 40 nanoseconds. That's when our problems began. No circuits were fast enough. Coil gating fell by the wayside; it was not capable of that kind of performance. Available transistors in late 1955, as typified by the CK762, were in the 1 to 5 MHz range. It was becoming clear that we were going to have to eke every bit of speed out of transistors and forget about using magnetics. Every trick in the book for speeding up a transistor circuit would have to be investigated. One trick considered was operating in the avalanche negative resistance region. This did indeed provide a very fast transistor turn-on, but, alas, it could only be operated at a low repetition rate. The effort to find a fast transistor circuit was paramount. Toward the end of 1955 we started hearing rumors about Philco's development of a new high speed transistor, something called a surface barrier transistor (SBT). Meanwhile, I decided to visit several of the most advanced development laboratories on the East Coast to see if they were doing any work in high speed logic. A visit to MIT was promising. I was introduced to a young engineer by the name of Ken Olsen (now president of Digital Equipment Corporation) who had obtained some of the new surface barrier transistors from Philco and was using them in lab experiments. He verified that the transistors were fast, ten to thirty times faster than contemporary transistors. Philco called them 30 MHz units.

Pres set up a number of technical exchange meetings with Philco. We soon met Cy Warshaw, head of the Philco marketing department, and a number of the key technical people. Before long, a few prototype SBTs found their way into our lab and now we faced the task of optimizing circuits around the device.

By January, 1956, sufficient logic was completed to enable a new component count, assuming all transistors rather than a magnetic amplifier mixture. With some safety factor, the count was 35,000 transistors and the cost of the system was double the contract price. It was also obvious that an Air Force magnetic computer would not suffice as the IOP. A more capable processor would have to be designed.

The large increase in cost of the LARC system was a factor that led the company to sign a contract with the David Taylor Model Basin for the delivery of a second LARC. Most of the estimated costs were allocated for development rather than reproduction; therefore, dividing the development cost between two customers would alleviate matters.

Considering the huge quantity of logic elements in the system, it was evident that a large logic design effort was required. We did not have anywhere near the number of logic designers required to meet the schedule. There was only one solution; we would have to find more. But where? Computer logic wasn't taught in colleges; logicians evolved through on-the-job training. Our dilemma was solved by setting up an in-house training course. For the next few months, Lloyd Stowe was the instructor for the intensive course. Art Gehring and Lloyd interviewed many new math major graduates and selected ten for the course, including two women fresh out of Chestnut Hill Academy. Months later, ten promising logic designers emerged, and they were immediately assigned to the LARC computer program.

Logic and circuits were only part of the required development. Many other phases had to be worked on in parallel, such as packaging and power supplies, ferrite core memory, drum mass storage, and various other input/output devices, including the Charactron. The project needed a leader, and Jim and Pres asked me to be that leader, as I was already thoroughly immersed in the project. So in March, 1956, I became the engineering director of the LARC computer program.

Chuan Chu became my boss. Chuan had joined Remington Rand Univac in 1955 after working on a computer project at the

Argonne labs for a number of years. I remembered Chuan from The Moore School. While I was in the Navy, he had joined the ENIAC project to design the square rooter, and then had worked on the magnetic tape input devices while we were both members of the EDVAC project. He and I developed an excellent working relationship. I pursued the technical progress while he concentrated on overall administration. At times, others were not so fortunate in getting along with Chuan.

Interesting and strange things were happening at 23rd Street. On several occasions, we noticed Phil Vincent trudging back to his office with muddy boots. Also, a large map of greater Philadelphia appeared on his office wall with red pinheads splattered across it. Finally, Phil disclosed his clandestine project; he was looking for land in the suburbs to be the eventual home for Remington Rand Univac. The pinheads on the map represented where each professional currently lived. The objective was to find land closest to the center of the population density. Because most of the employees lived in the northern or western part of Philadelphia, Phil was concentrating his search in the northwestern suburbs. He found a cornfield in Whitpain Township that was readily accessible and looked particularly interesting. But there were two problems; zoning was one, and the other was that the widow owner wanted to remain in her farmhouse in the middle of the 87 acres of rolling countryside.

The first problem to be overcome was getting the zoning changed. Phil turned to Army Adams, our public relations expert, to develop a presentation for the Whitpain Township commissioners which would convince them of the benefits to be achieved in allowing Remington Rand Univac to utilize the site. The township zoning meeting was held one evening at the Center Square Fire House. Army's presentation was a winner. Remington Rand Univac was depicted as a light industry that would generate no noise and no pollution. The employees were on a high level, and the tax benefits to the community would be substantial. The presentation was so effective that before the meeting was over, there was practically a stampede to change the zoning. Shortly afterwards, Remington Rand Univac became the owner of 87 acres of our future home.

Adjusting to the widow's enclave gave us more of a problem than we had envisioned. A few years later when we were comfortably settled in our new home, employees started to complain about mysterious deposits appearing on their automobiles while in the parking lot. No one was immune. Spotted around the top surfaces of the cars were stripes three eighths of an inch long that hardened like epoxy within hours and could not be washed off.

Scraping the material off with a fingernail was the only reasonable way to remove it. Complaints increased until the company had to investigate. For a while the incinerator system was under suspicion but it was soon absolved. In desperation, some of the material was sent to an analytical laboratory. The report came back—bee excrement! The widow was in the beehive business. When I got home that evening, I soaked my fingernails in warm water for an hour but somehow the thoughts of Mrs. Myers' revenge remained with me for years. A settlement was reached with the lady and we no longer had that problem.

However, the move to our ultimate home in Whitpain Township was a long way off. There were more immediate housing problems. The 23rd Street engineering building was bursting at the seams, and it was obvious that the LARC wouldn't fit there. The manufacturing building at 31st Street was in a similar state. Furthermore, the plan to begin UNIVAC II computer production (under development in St. Paul) would only make matters worse.

March, 1956, was an eventful month. Both the engineering and manufacturing activities moved into a new location at 19th Street and Allegheny Avenue. Although it was new for us, it was actually the immense, old, former Exide Storage Battery building. The acid fumes had left their disfiguring marks but the refurbishing crew did a remarkable job of restoring the interior. Not much could be done about the exterior. The Pennsylvania Railroad passed by one side of the building and the Reading Railroad on the other. With the windows open in the summer, living with dust, dirt, and noise became a part of our daily lives.

Manufacturing occupied the first four floors, with Engineering taking over the fifth and sixth floors. In addition, there was the annex, Building 1A, which was a large shed. It was a perfect spot for setting up our drum mass storage operation. The drums were heavy, the machining equipment was heavy, and the plating lab required drainage and sources of water and other chemicals. The solid ground floor of the annex lent itself to the drum preparation and plating operation.

I, for one, was glad to see the engineering and manufacturing operations together again, even if the building did leave something to be desired. I have always had the strong conviction that very close association between engineering and manufacturing is essential, particularly where high technology is involved.

Moving the engineering laboratory was surprisingly easy. We left work at the end of the day Friday and reported into the new building on Monday morning for a stay that was to last five years. The acid scarred walls became homier each day.

Even before the LARC specifications became firm, it was evident that more manpower was going to be needed in all areas. A successful recruiting campaign was mounted. Many new people were brought into Remington Rand Univac over a period of a year to staff the various departments that had been set up. Lou Wilson headed the CU development; Francis Lee, the IOP; Bill Schmitt, logic design; Al Tonik, IOP programming; Bill Bartik, core memory; and Walt Thomas, drum storage. High speed logic circuit development was the responsibility of Dr. Noah Prywes, a very clever but peppery individual.

The most pressing problem to be solved was what to use for the basic logic circuit. The SBT opened a whole new field of circuit exploration for us. Every configuration that we could think of was evaluated. Each had its pluses and minuses, thus creating a dilemma. In April 1956, I presented to Pres, Jim, and Chuan my recommendations based upon a figure of merit calculation that took into account output drives, propagation time, logic complexity, and cost. The winner, an inverter, we called the 1C circuit. It used high speed diodes for logic, a resistor, capacitor coupling network, and an SBT amplifier to produce a 3-volt signal swing. The circuit could meet our speed requirements if we were careful about the packaging. But the problem that emerged was that the SBT just barely had enough current gain (beta) to drive three loads. In fact, many SBTs in a lot did not have the basic capability without including safety factors. It took many more months of work in our lab, meetings with Philco, and measurement of SBT lot characteristics to reach a compromise solution. The transistors would have to be graded and selected for each position, depending upon loading conditions. As much as we hated the idea of selecting transistors, there was no alternative; thus, five color-coded categories were established.

Limited output from the 1C circuit posed a problem, especially with the 60-bit parallel organization. Other circuits had to be devised so that a practical fan-out could be achieved. The 1E circuit provided a partial solution. With its one-third current level, nine of them could be driven with one 1C circuit. A high power amplifier was also devised to drive thirty-two loads. The latter circuits paid the price by operating at a slower speed. The crucial, clocked-pulse former circuit, which retimed and reshaped the signals after each nine levels of logic manipulation, also evolved after a strenuous design period.

I found another use for the surface barrier transistor. I was anxious to see what kind of wonderful things I could do with it in my radio hobby. The opportunity was there because of the overflowing bin of reject transistors that did not have enough current amplification to be useful. Even though these transistors couldn't amplify very well, there was no reason why they could not oscillate to generate a radio frequency. My thoughts turned to using the SBT to build a high frequency walkie-talkie for the 28 MHz amateur band. This was an ideal chance to build a really small walkie-talkie because the transistors required only a few lightweight penlite dry cells to operate.

I was spurred on by memories of an episode in my earlier years. I had built a vacuum tube radio transceiver that fastened to the handlebars of my bicycle. Vacuum tubes took a lot of current to light their heaters and high voltages for circuit operation. To provide this source of power, I used a surplus police dynamotor mounted over the rear wheel carrier and an automobile storage battery placed in a small cart which tagged along behind the bicycle. It converted the 6 volts of the battery to 200 volts direct current. The mobile unit on the bicycle worked! I was able to contact Camden, New Jersey from Fairmount Park in central Philadelphia, but it was an all uphill operation. There had to be an easier way. The transistor was it.

With the SBTs, I built the radio into a small plastic case with a dangling wire several feet long to act as an antenna. The workbench checkout went fine and the moment came for an

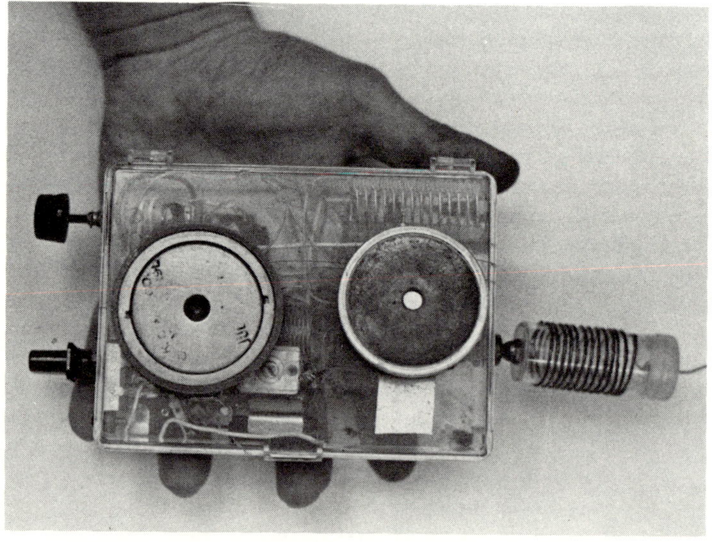

Here is where two of the LARC reject surface barrier transistors were used, in my 28 MHz walkie talkie.

actual field test. I sent Shirley out into the street with the walkie-talkie in hand while I operated the home base station. The test, in her cruise around the neighborhood, was very successful despite the stares of several neighbors and a string of dogs that followed her. The transmitter produced only 20 milliwatts output but it was enough to be effective. The transistor era had arrived.

The time had also arrived to test the basic circuit designs with a test vehicle. A section of the arithmetic unit utilizing several thousand transistors was chosen. Circuits were laid out in conventional printed circuit board fashion and then hastily constructed. The results were nearly a disaster, with horrible ringing and noises on signal lines. It was clear that we were going to have to devote a huge effort to packaging, noise considerations, transmission line problems, and minimizing lead lengths, if LARC was to meet its goals.

Up on the sixth floor, Bill Bartik and his crew were finding that building a 4 microsecond ferrite core memory also had seemingly insurmountable problems. The state of the art at the time was 12-microsecond memory, although rumors of 8 microsecond activity were prevalent. Bill found that the available cores wouldn't switch fast enough. A program was initiated to develop a smaller diameter core (30 x 50 mil) that would switch faster. Another serious problem he ran into was the unavailability of a transistor that was fast enough, yet capable of driving heavy currents. As a result, brute force solutions were tried. High current, slow transistors used as X-Y drivers were turned on and off rapidly by pulsed power supplies. The power supplies had to put out a kilowatt of pulsed power with a rise time of 0.25 microseconds. Even the high current diodes used in the X-Y memory selection did not exist. Sperry Semiconductors, a division of the corporation, was called upon to solve this problem. We thought we had an answer for producing a 4-microsecond memory but it wasn't cheap. Several years later the components would be available to greatly simplify the job.

In Building 1A, Walt Thomas had his hands full planning the mass storage drum system. It had all kinds of new challenges, including developing the drum surface and magnetic plating techniques, the 6-channel magnetic head flying in its own air stream, a reliable head stepping mechanism, and a means of high density recording at a low error rate. The annex took on an intriguing appearance after the large vats and overhead cranes were installed. Some of the lathes were gigantic, commensurate with their ability to handle the 24" diameter drums. The annex was an impressive place to visit but wearing one's best clothes wasn't advisable. Fortunately, the drum mass storage system was a peripheral device and could be developed in parallel and independent of the mainframes. The amount of pioneering that the drum file group had ahead of them was great because nearly every aspect of the development required solving new problems.

As we looked further into the designs, we found we were uncovering more problems than we were solving. The volume of work yet to be accomplished was enormous. Everyone was working hard; I couldn't have asked more of them. As for me, I was spending every working hour providing technical direction. There was no time to spend on paperwork and reports. Those I took home with me each night. The after-hours chores continued to grow and before long, most of my Saturdays and Sundays were committed for the five-year period that the LARC computer was being developed. Saturday became a normal workday for all of the technical people on the project. I acquired an administrative assistant named Z. Z. Li to help with some of the chores. He was of great assistance in keeping my accounting records straight. ZZ's agility with an abacus was simply amazing, and he never had to worry about the battery running low.

Pres Eckert was spending a large percentage of his time in the lab buzzing from one technical problem to the next. We needed his innovative thinking. Completion would have been impossible without his constant prodding and questioning.

Late in 1956, we started looking at the packaging problems, as the transistor count was still edging upward daily. From the test vehicle experience, we knew that the success of the LARC computer was dependent on keeping the lead lengths short and controlling the noise factors. We became fanatic on the subject. How to package the large number of logic gates in the IOP and CU became a prime consideration. Ideally, the mainframe should have been a cube to reduce the longer interconnecting lead lengths. This would have required long printed circuit (PC) cards and a solution to the problem of how to get all of the logic leads through a connector. (Today we face the same problem of being able to perform an enormous amount of logic on a large scale integrated circuit chip, but not having enough pins to bring the signals in and out.) The limiting factor was truly the connector. How small could the connector pins be made? How closely could they be spaced and yet maintain the ultimate in reliability? Allowing for hundreds of insertions of each PC card, almost one million connections, and the very low voltage signals, reliability became the major consideration. Again we consulted with the oracles at Bell Labs and verified that there was only one proven path that would meet our reliability objectives, the use of gold as the contact material. Gold is not subject to atmospheric corrosion, has a very low contact resistance, but suffers from being a soft metal. The problem encountered was how to keep gold on the contacts without having it wear off with the hundreds of insertions. Our packaging engineer, Leon Schwartz, wrestled with these problems.

We finally decided on a PC card 3½" wide and 9" long. It was big enough to house five logic circuits on the top half, five on the bottom and a molded female connector at the end of the card. The molded male connector on the backboard (½"x3½") had to contain 84 pins to utilize effectively the logic circuits on each PC card. Connections to a male connector would have to utilize taper pins; there was no other choice that would permit high density wiring.

Once the hardware concepts started taking form, the circuit design group tackled the problems of minimizing crosstalk and stray capacitances. Exhaustive tests were run on the logic circuits to determine worst case conditions for lead lengths and proximity of wires causing crosstalk. In order to reduce congestion and stray capacitance on the backboard, we had to think in terms of using very fine steelcore copper wire (size 30) with a thin teflon insulation. But getting a good mechanical and electrical connection to the fine wire engendered another research project. One scheme for minimizing the crosstalk used twisted-pair transmission wires for all leads greater than 18 inches. To terminate the twisted-pair ground wires, we envisioned a network of taper-pin ground straps covering the complete backboard at half inch intervals. It would also act as a ground plane.

All the rules of wiring, algorithms, and physical coordinates developed by the circuits group were fed to Lloyd Stowe's activity to be ground into the computer-aided design programs. This was the first use of such an automated backboard wiring system, and there was widespread apprehension over its viability.

Even with the small diameter taper-pins and wire, a lab mockup showed that the density of wires was going to be fierce. Even if we were able to wire the backboard initially, how would we get into it later to make the inevitable changes? This proved to be one of our bigger worries. However, we knew that nearly all problems could be resolved if we were willing to put the time, effort, and money into it. At no time had management given any indication to me that they would consider turning back on the LARC computer program even in light of the continual increase in the amount of development effort required. We were spurred on by the knowledge that IBM had received a contract from the AEC installation at Los Alamos for the development of a similar capability superpower computer called "STRETCH." Continuation of the program became a matter of honor and reputation.

In the midst of designing the LARC computer, I started hearing some rumbles of problems on the UNIVAC II computer design effort being carried on at St. Paul. I had had no contact with the project since my visit with Bill Norris in early 1955, so the rumors were news to me. After several more smoke signals, Jim Weiner approached me with a bundle of UNIVAC II computer drawings and asked me to review the design and write a report to Bill Norris. I looked them over carefully and sat back aghast, wondering how I was going to tell Bill Norris that the design was a disaster with many fundamental errors. I finally decided to take each design fault (there were thirty) and explain the difficulties in a long memo. The memo was sent in February, 1957.

Summer 1957 came and so did Jim, to say that there wasn't much choice, a team of Philadelphia people with UNIVAC I computer experience would have to go to St. Paul to take over the UNIVAC II computer design responsibility. The UNIVAC II computer project was in serious trouble and our position in the marketplace was in jeopardy. Management considered the product so important that extraordinary measures were to be taken at the expense of anything else, even the LARC computer. Fortunately, only Lou Wilson and I were siphoned off from the LARC program. We were managers; the detailed design work would go on anyway. Test technicians, including Bernie Victor and Ed Loss, were snatched from the UNIVAC I computer production floor. Engineers Art Gehring and Pete Simon who had UNIVAC I computer experience but had somehow escaped the clutches of the LARC computer were also commandeered. Jim gave me the responsibility for leading the redesign effort.

We had no idea how long we would have to spend in St. Paul and couldn't know until we arrived and assessed the magnitude of the job. Those of us with families, of course, expressed concern. The immediate plans were to fly out on Monday morning and back on Friday night for as long as was necessary.

Monday morning, two weeks before July 4th, our team took off for St. Paul. Jim Weiner was with us for the first few days to be certain that the redesign effort was kicked off properly and that we had all that was needed. When we arrived, we found that Bill Norris had resigned some weeks earlier. Local rumors had it that he was forming another company, Control Data Corporation.

The St. Paul operation was in the process of moving some of its activities, including the UNIVAC II computer, from Minnehaha Street to a brand new building on 7th Street in south St. Paul. A large room in the beautiful new building was used as the center for our activities. We clearly were in charge, with the St. Paul engineers assisting. The relationship between the two groups was good and, indeed, lasting friendships developed. Everyone, especially the Philadelphia group, realized the seriousness of the situation and wanted to get the job done as quickly as possible.

I made assignments. Each engineer was given drawings so he could review the sections with which he was most familiar. Art Gehring was the logician at large. Everyone went to Art to resolve logic design dilemmas. By the end of the first week, it was evident that several months of redesign effort was required.

We returned to Philadelphia for the weekend, and gave our wives the bad news; we would have to be away from home for many months. No one enjoyed this idea, but the job had to be done. However, Shirley insisted on moving to St. Paul with all three children to be near me. Arthur was now five years old, Barry two, and daughter Carol was the new member of the family. She was just six months old and a major user of the DyDee Service. Shirley said, "When you come home next weekend, be prepared to drive back to Minnesota with the three kids, diapers, and everything else we need."

When I returned to St. Paul on Monday morning, I found that nearly all of the men had been handed similar ultimatums from their wives; consequently the evenings that week were spent looking for places to live. I needed a furnished apartment with a short term lease that was big enough for my family. The other fellows didn't have children and were able to find accommodations at Sibley Manor, an apartment complex very close to the new plant. I looked and looked but couldn't find anything to meet my needs. When the end of the week rolled around and I still had not located a suitable temporary home, out of desperation I reserved a room at the Paul Bunyan Motel on Snelling Avenue on the north side of St. Paul.

I returned home Friday night at the end of the second week, which was the beginning of the three-day 4th of July weekend. Shirley had everything packed—linens, tricycles, clothing, dishes, medicines, and all else needed for survival. She even had the rental company primed to connect a small trailer to my station wagon the first thing Saturday morning. Saturday was a busy day. The trailer was packed, items needed for the trip put behind the front seat, and a blanket spread across the back of the wagon so the kids could play and sleep. We closed down the house, said goodbye to the family, and retired at a respectable hour.

Early Sunday morning, Shirley and I packed the kids into the car, said goodbye to Glenview Street, and headed out the

Pennsylvania Turnpike. I remember the day very well because it was so hot and humid. The radio reported temperatures of 100°. Carol's clothing was reduced to diapers, rubber panties and a light gown to keep her comfortable. Anyone who has travelled with young children can appreciate the problems we had, and they lasted for two and a half days.

To save time, Shirley packed food for several days. The baby's bottle was warmed by a small sterno stove which was set up on the back platform. Diapers were changed and thrown into the pail without a slackening of the car's pace. In fact, Shirley complained bitterly the next day because she wanted to see Chicago as we passed through it, but the entire time was occupied with changing diapers and feeding the baby. By the time she was finished, we were north of Chicago.

After noon on Tuesday, we reached the Twin Cities. We unpacked just the essentials because I planned to keep looking for a furnished apartment or house. Life for all five of us in that one motel room was rugged. Fortunately, youth was on our side and we managed.

The next morning I resumed my work, leaving Shirley confined to the motel room with the three kids. How she maintained her sanity during the days that followed, I'll never know. Our first weekend in Minnesota was, of course, spent searching for a home, but we had no luck.

Meanwhile, back in Philadelphia, the LARC computer program was suffering from lack of coordination, and management decided to transfer someone from St. Paul to temporarily take over my position on the LARC computer program.

The person named was Stretch Renacker. After meeting him for the first time, it was apparent where his nickname originated—he was tall. The plans were to have Stretch stay in Philadelphia for as long as I was required in St. Paul. In a flash, we both found the answer to our housing problem. Why not swap houses? Stretch was also married, and had four children. At the end of the second week of our stay at the Paul Bunyan, I gave him my house key, and he gave me his, as his van left for Philadelphia. Someone later suggested that it would have been a lot easier if we had left our wives, kids, and belongings right where they were and just he and I swapped places. I'm not sure our wives would have appreciated that, however.

Stretch's house was architecturally unusual, but ideal for our purposes. I believe he called it the MIT design. Stretch's informal mode of living was symbolized by five half-consumed containers of ice cream, all vanilla, which were left for our use.

Now that my family was comfortably settled, I could fully concentrate on the UNIVAC II computer redesign. The effort was going well but it was painstaking. Each circuit had to be scrutinized and redesigned according to the proven UNIVAC I computer design rules. From the corrected circuits evolved chassis that had to be tested; Glen Turner had that responsibility. Fortunately, none of the arithmetic section was involved in the updating. Also, the ferrite core memory which replaced the mercury tanks seemed in good shape. The redesign was basically confined to the I/O and control sections, the sections I knew well.

Lou Wilson finished his review of the control section after several weeks and returned to Philadelphia, as he was no longer needed. The rest of us still had a long way to go.

One St. Paul fellow assigned to work with us was a technician who arrived by way of the customer engineering path. This chap was most unusual looking—he had large ears and a long, drawn face. He spoke with a West Virginia hillbilly accent and used corresponding colloquialisms. But, despite his deceptive appearance, he exhibited signs of genius and had a photographic memory. Engineers soon found out about it. Instead of looking things up in the reference documentation, it was quicker to ask, "George, where is gate 201 located?", or "Where does timing signal t5 originate?" George always flashed back the correct answer. He was a constant amazement to the engineers. Despite his humble beginnings and lack of formal training, George Cogar was destined for greatness. Years later he helped found Mohawk Data Sciences, and more recently, his own company, the Cogar Corporation. George's elevation to the ranks of millionaires is a Horatio Alger story.

There were four UNIVAC II computers on the production floor beneath us. As soon as a chassis redesign was completed and verified, it was rushed to the production floor to be incorporated into the production units. The UNIVAC II computer was already two years late in delivery, and management was most anxious to have the production units follow right behind the engineering prototype.

The place to be in the Twin Cities in the summertime is near a lake, and we were. Stretch's house was located at Lake Johanna in a beautiful setting with a small beach and dock just two blocks away. As members of the community, we had beach privileges and used them. One warm and sunny Saturday afternoon, Shirley and I were at the water's edge chatting with a neighbor. Art had just walked onto the dock which jutted forty feet out into the water. Barry was already out at the far end of the dock. We were engrossed in conversation, not paying much attention to our boys. The next moment I looked at the end of the dock, and Barry was gone. Instantly, I yelled, "Where's Barry?" Art screamed and pointed straight down to the water below. Barry was floundering, his head under the water. He was only two years old, and couldn't swim. The energy burst I developed in covering the forty feet to get to him was astounding. When I did reach him, he was still conscious. Immediately I placed him on the dock and jumped up beside him. I held him in the air, upside down, and pounded his back to get the water to drain out of his lungs. The emergency treatment worked and he started breathing normally. Shirley and I had our wits scared out of us. We nearly lost one of our children. Thereafter, we were much more careful and Barry, of course, was afraid to go near the water.

I was impressed by the warmth and friendliness of our midwestern neighbors who did their best to make us feel at home. Shirley was frequently invited to neighbors' coffee klatches.

Naturally, I had my amateur radio gear with me as part of the survival package trailered to Minnesota. With a temporary antenna strung up in the trees, I was able to reach Philadelphia with little difficulty. Weekend schedules were kept with my good Beacon Radio Club friend, Morrie Krathen (W3CSS), in Huntingdon Valley, Pennsylvania. Morrie was kind enough to patch us through the telephone line so that we could talk to members of our family in Philadelphia and tell them the latest happenings.

The end of the design phase occurred in September and now the remaining work revolved around proving it out on the test floor. Tests moved along as predicted and I could see that my services would not be required much longer, so I made arrangements to leave. The fundamental parts of the redesign were working properly, but there was still much to do in the way of details before any UNIVAC II computers could be delivered. I appointed Pete Simon to handle the clean-up work and remain in St. Paul until deliveries started. Pete didn't realize what a winter in Minnesota was like, but he found out, because the first UNIVAC II computer was not delivered until the spring of 1958. I think he is still in the defrosting process.

On October 15th, just as the season's first snow was falling in St. Paul, I took off with my family for Philadelphia. I was anxious to get back and resume leadership of the LARC computer program, and from what I had heard, my services were vitally needed. We returned home in just two days, a half day less than it took to drive out. Stretch timed his departure with mine.

Shirley and I still look back upon our St. Paul experience with many fond memories, despite the hardships along the way. It was an experience that we wouldn't have wanted to miss.

As for the UNIVAC II computer, our rescue effort was late. Consequently, only twenty-seven of the systems were produced. However, users of UNIVAC II computers were highly pleased with the system. It lived up to its specifications, and provided a significant improvement over the UNIVAC I computer performance. There was much sentiment expressed over the final shutdown of each UNIVAC II system but the cost of electricity to keep the vacuum tube system going was an ever-increasing problem. As late as 1970, there were still four UNIVAC II computers in operation, and the last one was not shut down until spring of 1978.

When I returned to the LARC computer project in October, 1957, it seemed as though I had never left. All of the problems were still there—some more, some less. It was obvious that we were not going to make the contractual completion date. The improbability of completion on time had to have been evident to Livermore also, because my monthly report accurately reflected the status. We at the project level were not aware of any consideration toward relaxing the specifications to meet the delivery date. Meeting the specifications became an unchallenged religious pursuit. Recently, I learned that Pres Eckert and Jim Weiner had visited UCRL in an attempt to negotiate a specification change but UCRL was insistent that the original specifications be maintained, even if delivery was late.

Dr. Thornton C. Fry was now vice president of all Remington Rand Univac development, at both Philadelphia and St. Paul. Dr. Fry, of *Probability and its Engineering Uses* fame, launched into his second career after retiring from the Bell Telephone Laboratories. He had a proven technical background, and soon developed an excellent rapport with Eckert. He also brought with him some of the personnel policies successfully practiced at the Bell Labs, including the octile rating system. Perhaps it was our implementation method that was at fault, or maybe it was the top management's decision to cut back expenses that led to some questioning of Dr. Fry's methods. A layoff occurred just as I returned to Philadelphia and it caused predictable morale problems. In any event, Dr. Fry attempted to steer us on a successful course.

One of the nice things that happened to me in the midst of the black days in the LARC computer program was a feature article that LOOK Magazine did on young people in the computer industry. It appeared in the November 26, 1957, issue, and was entitled "Youth Masters the Big Brains." Prominently featured in the article were writeups on Knaplund, Haddad, and Boehm of IBM, and Jim McGarvey and me of Remington Rand Univac. The article discussed the youth of the personnel in the industry and portrayed a glowing account of the enchanting world of computers. It pointed out that Pres Eckert was the ripe age of twenty-four when development of the ENIAC computer started. Computers were the work of the younger generation. Interviewing for the article provided me with one of the few respites during the whole LARC computer program.

Sometime in the midst of the LARC program I noticed some strange "twinges" in my stomach. As the punishing days progressed, the twinges developed into pains. Soon it became downright unbearable. A barium milkshake confirmed it; I had developed a duodenal ulcer. As soon as our chief purchasing agent heard of it he accosted me with, "Herman, you are a failure. You stopped at an ulcer when you could have had a heart attack!" His ideas of success and mine were not the same. It took a lot of milk, tranquilizers, and most of all, completion of LARC, to cure my ulcers.

Finally, an encouraging sign appeared. Marketing decided to investigate the possibility of additional LARC computer sales. Lou Wilson, who by this time was very well acquainted with the LARC computer, transferred to the marketing organization to head up the effort. Noah Prywes took over as manager of the CU development. Noah had been doing a fine job with many of the tough circuit designs. He accomplished the impossible even though he occasionally gave me a rough time. Noah was completing the A and B register design, a particularly difficult task involving small, fast-switching, tape-wound cores selected by diodes. Twenty-six of these 60-bit registers used in the basic system had a 1-microsecond cycle. The A and B register design appeared promising.

Logic design proceeded nicely now that all of the critical circuits had been defined. There were indications, however, that the final number of transistors was going to be twice the number we estimated in January, 1956.

Al Tonik's programming/systems group also made good progress. The means of communication between the CU, IOP, and memory was worked out in good detail and programming the I/O functions was underway. The IOP design group was also doing an excellent job solving its problems in developing multitudinous circuits for printers, tape, and drum controllers.

Although there were a few optimistic signs, there wasn't the slightest chance that we could meet the early 1958 delivery date. Mr. Norton and representatives of UCRL came to Philadelphia on December 13, 1957, to discuss with Remington Rand Univac management the status of the project and delivery date. It was not possible to pinpoint a delivery date in view of the unknowns still remaining. UCRL continued to emphasize the importance of meeting the performance requirements even though the schedule had to be sacrificed. Their concern was if we were doing everything in our power to keep the delay to a minimum. Dr. Fry was also concerned from another point of view; it was costing the company a bundle of money for each day that we were late. He instituted measures which he thought appropriate—super-expediter sessions.

Each Monday morning a meeting lasting several hours was held in the large conference room. A representative from each of the LARC computer activities, called a super-expediter, had to present the status, accomplishments of the preceding week, problems, and what actions were being taken to solve the problems. Dr. Fry personally sat in on the sessions for many weeks until he was satisfied that the effort could carry on by itself. In some of those cases involving logistics and material procurement, the sessions did help. For technical problems, it did not help; but at least Dr. Fry developed a deeper appreciation of the problems.

In January, 1958, Jim Weiner wrote a long letter of explanation to Jim Norton at UCRL detailing each one of the technical problems and its contribution in weeks and months to the delay in the LARC program. Jim covered eighteen fundamental issues but I can think of another half a dozen that he did not list. In part, his letter stated, "The principal causes for delay were the interplay between logic and circuit design, the non-availability of satisfactory standard components, and the increased size of the equipment." Jim Weiner's letter summed it up very well.

Two of the developments, power supplies and the Charactron display, were subcontracted. Stromberg Carlson designed the Charactron system for us and that went very well. Power supplies, the last thing designed and the first needed, did not go quite so well. Power supply requirements couldn't be computed until all of the logic circuit requirements were summed up. The original estimates of 10 KW became more like 70 KW and the number of supplies required for the memory wouldn't fit in the space available. When the first power supplies arrived from the NJE Corporation, they "sang" at a 400 Hz rate equivalent to their operating frequency. The supplies actually generated an acoustic whistle that could be heard all through the lab and exceeded the LARC computer noise specification. NJE investigated our complaint and found that there was nothing they could do about it; they stated it was a natural phenomenon caused by magnetostriction. To resolve the dispute, an acoustic consultant was hired. He confirmed NJE's position but also made a significant suggestion: a half-inch thick sheet of plexiglas makes an effective 400Hz acoustic filter. The idea worked! Plexiglas doors were put on all power supply racks to reduce the noise to a tolerable level.

Front view of the LARC Computing Unit showing printed circuit boards under test. The general purpose registers plugged into the space on the left.

Other measures for electrical noise reduction evolved. To insure low resistance throughout the ground system, all structural members carrying ground currents were gold-plated, a thin, flash coating to be true, but it added to the cost. Afterwards, we estimated the gold content used in the connectors, ground strips, bus bars, and structural members amounted to $20,000 based on 1957 dollars.

To keep the DC voltage and clock distribution line impedances low, a wide strip transmission line system was developed that covered the backboard at six inch intervals. With this added obstruction, the concern began to grow that perhaps the backboard could not be wired. This worry soon became a black cloud that hung over the organization, upsetting morale. Several of the engineers expressed their belief that "the machine cannot be built," or used even stronger words. One top level engineer asked to be transferred out of the LARC computer program as a result of his conviction.

View of backboard wiring of LARC Computing Unit. Printed circuit board connectors are completely obscured by the pile up of wiring. Power and clock strip transmission lines appear as vertical strips.

I, for one, never lost confidence that the machine could be built, although I will admit I did have concerns. A few meetings with Leon Schwartz helped resolve some of the problems. Special tools had to be devised for wiring the backboard. With a density of 6,000 taper-pin terminated wires per square foot, the pile up of wiring could amount to several inches. How could anyone work through that mess? Leon came through with a whole set of tools that made the operation seem like a surgical supply house. There were five separate tools, each approximately 3/16 inch in diameter and a foot long, capable of penetrating the mass of wiring without causing damage. Included in the tool kit were a taper-pin extractor, taper-pin inserter, wire gripper, wire cutter, and a borescope. The last one was an interesting tool. It permitted a wireman to look into the far end of the column and see what was happening at the connector. The borescope was initially developed to allow gunsmiths to examine the inner depths of a gun barrel. Several surgical instruments, like the cystoscope,

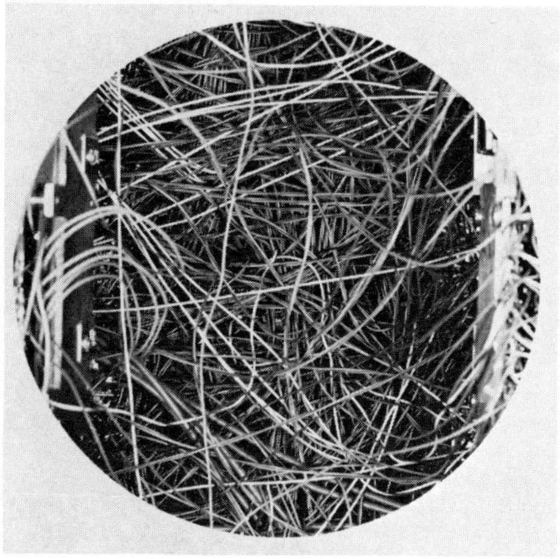

A closer view of the backboard wiring. It was dense enough to frighten anyone.

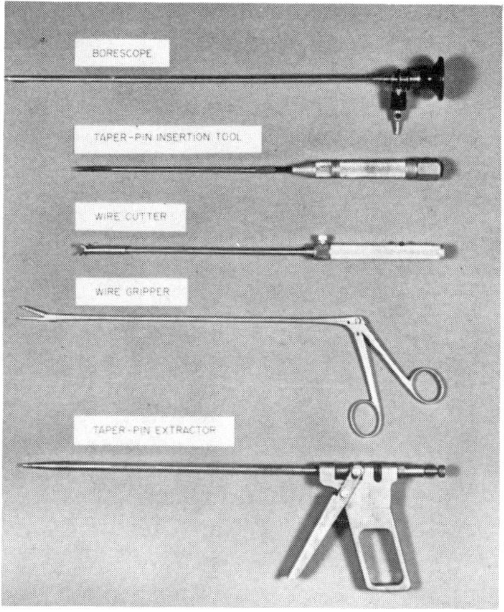

Special tools had to be developed to work with the dense wiring.

were considered, but the borescope served our needs best. Leon also developed a color-coded overlay which was put on the connector so the taper-pin holes could be identified more easily.

Construction of the LARC mainframes, started in the summer of 1958, was delayed mainly because of connector delivery problems. When a good batch finally did arrive, the wiremen started their chores, following the tabulated printout. All two inch wires went in first, then four inch wires. These were followed by increasing lengths until all the longer twisted-pair wires were inserted. I kept the wiremen isolated from the skeptical engineers. I did not want the wiremen to know that the job could not be done, and they, not knowing it, went ahead and completed the wiring.

While the backboards were being wired, thousands of PC cards were being constructed. This was a feat in itself, considering that the correctly color-coded surface barrier transistors had to appear in the right position in each card. After months of negotiation with Philco, we were able to get deliveries of transistors that would just barely permit us to squeak by. The price averaged $5.00 each; some were more, some were less depending on the current gain. Multiplying this figure by the final estimate of 57,000 SBTs used in a LARC computer showed where a large percentage of the reproduction cost was concentrated. Think of how simple and inexpensive the equivalent logic circuit is today. For 16¢, four 10-nanosecond circuits can be obtained in one integrated circuit package. This amounts to factors of 1/150th of the cost, four times the speed and three times the drive capability. Of course, I had no knowledge of the revolution to come in semiconductors. If I had, I might have thought, for a few milliseconds at least, of putting off the development of the LARC computer. Such a decision would not have been wise because technology had been changing rapidly since the birth of the computer, and if we had waited for the latest in technology, computer development never would have been started. As far as I was concerned, we had the fastest logic circuit in the world and it would build the fastest computer possible.

A contract was let to the General Atronic Corporation in Philadelphia to develop a PC card tester. They responded with a very clever scheme for dynamically testing each logic circuit under its loaded condition. The tester worked well, and provided assurance that we were starting the final systems test with known, good components.

In September, 1958, my able financial assistant, ZZ Li, and I constructed a total cost analysis for LARC from inception to completion. The costs were staggering—close to nineteen million dollars! I believe management considered approaching UCRL and DTMB for contract renegotiation but I was not aware of any final action. I received every encouragement to finish the project as soon as possible.

The pressure was on, even more than before. Everyone was working long hours, day and night, Saturdays and Sundays. Vacations were frowned upon and taken only by those who were weak in spirit. Holidays were non-existent. By the time mainframe testing began toward the end of 1958, the test crews had worked continuously through Christmas, New Year's, Easter, and July 4th holidays. The strain on the LARC development personnel and on their personal lives can never be fully described.

Dr. Noah Prywes, manager of the CU development, to whom I owe so much, decided to retire to academic pursuits at the University of Pennsylvania. Dr. Les Spandorfer, who had recently come aboard from the University, was plugged in to fill the gap. Les did an admirable job of taking over command.

The year 1959 saw us coming down the homestretch. All parts of the LARC computer system were assembled in one large room at the back of the fourth floor. New elements were being added weekly—memory units, tape handlers, printer, drum file units, etc. The people working on each of the major mainframe activities (CU, IOP, memory) engaged in independent testing of their own units. As always, testing was slow and methodical, and despite the extensive prior checking of logic designs, errors were found. Fixes were readily devised, and the special tools were used to wire them into the backboard.

It gave me great delight to walk onto the test floor each day and see how many more of the gold-plated PC cards were plugged into the frame. Insertion of the PC cards progressed rapidly. It reminded me of building a house; the framework is thrown up in a week and then it takes a year to finish the rest of it. So it was with the computer after the PC cards were inserted.

As a contractual requirement, we had to train a group of UCRL engineers in the intricacies of the LARC computer. Lou Nofrey, the chief engineering delegate, and I agreed that experience on the test floor was one good way of accomplishing this, so UCRL members were interspersed into our test shifts. One of the UCRL engineers assigned to CU test was a handsome, mild-mannered young fellow named Jim Moore. In addition, our crew included the two women logic designers, Mary Ann Breslin and Mary Lou Cush, and a strapping six foot four inch young engineering graduate from Purdue University, Don Neddenriep.

In work with the computer, not all paths proved to be logical; some were organizational and others emotional. Jim Moore

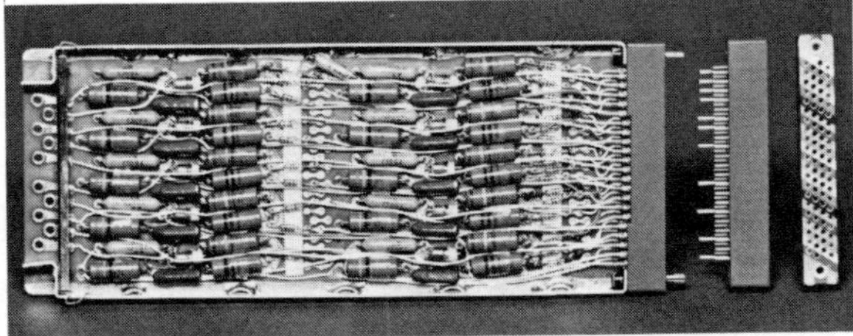

The printed circuit board contained up to 10 logic circuits. At the right the 84 holes for the taper pins are visible on the back of the connector.

One of the general register plug-in chassis. Tape wound cores in the white packages provided 0.5 microsecond access time. Two of these chassis formed the basic 26 registers.

wooed and won Mary Lou, and carried her off to the Livermore Valley when the LARC computer was delivered. Don Neddenriep later became a vice president of engineering and my boss. Mary Ann Breslin stayed with the company, and ultimately became a manager. She recently joined one of the mini-computer companies in a high level capacity.

During 1959, a few interesting organizational changes occurred. Jim Weiner decided to cast his future with a high flying venture in the aerospace industry on the West Coast. Chuan Chu was appointed to take his position, and I received the title of Chief Engineer of the LARC computer program. It was a promotion in title only; my responsibilities were the same. There was also a top level change. The "Bell Telephone administration" was out and the "IBM administration" was in. Dr. Fry started on his second retirement, and former IBM executives took over management—Dause L. Bibby at the Remington Rand presidential level, Jay W. Schnackel as the Remington Rand Univac Division general manager, and William J. Suchors as coordinating director of engineering.

I had frequent meetings with Bill Suchors; getting the LARC computer completed was high on his priority list. Bill, although not an engineer, was understanding and helpful. The new management wanted the LARC computer to look like the aristocrat that its performance implied and they insisted that the renowned industrial designers, Sundberg and Ferrar, do the casework styling. The consultants were called in to do "their thing" and they did. The designs were beautiful, and set the "square corner" trend in computer styling for years to come.

Toward early fall of 1959, the mainframe units had each gone through a first round of testing, and the results were encouraging. The test floor was now bulging with equipment. Two memory cabinets, each containing four units of 2,500 words, were operational and strung out twenty feet in length, more than half of it power supply. The CU and IOP cabinets ran parallel to the memories, and a roof covered all four cabinets. Cables interconnecting all four cabinets were sequestered in the roof. Two rows of six drum files in their handsome cabinets were a feast for hungry computer engineering eyes. Watching the magnetic head assemblies skit along the top surface of the large drums in their daily workout was another pleasure. The action at the consoles was a delight to observe as engineers and programmers moved back and forth; it reminded me of a department store the day after Thanksgiving.

Al Tonik's programmers were in the hot spot now. Getting that executive routine up and running in the IOP was a miraculous piece of work. I worried about using software to take over the former responsibilities of hardware, but Al and his crew proved very competent. Once the basic IOP executive routine was running, tests of the sophisticated concepts of communications between CU, IOP, and memory were launched.

In anticipation of the successful completion of the LARC, we thought it time to start telling the world of our accomplishment. The opportunity came with the presentation of two sets of papers at the Eastern Joint Computer Conference held in December, 1959, in Boston. Pres Eckert presented a paper co-authored by Chuan Chu, Al Tonik, and Bill Schmitt on the overall architectural concepts, and I presented a paper co-authored with Les Spandorfer and Francis Lee on the hardware design of the LARC computer. I had a feeling of euphoria after the presentation. The path for the previous four years had been such a rocky one. Pres, Al and I gave a similar presentation to the Philadelphia section

The prototype LARC drum file used a stepping head that floated on an airstream over a magnetically plated drum. It produced a 500,000 character/second data rate.

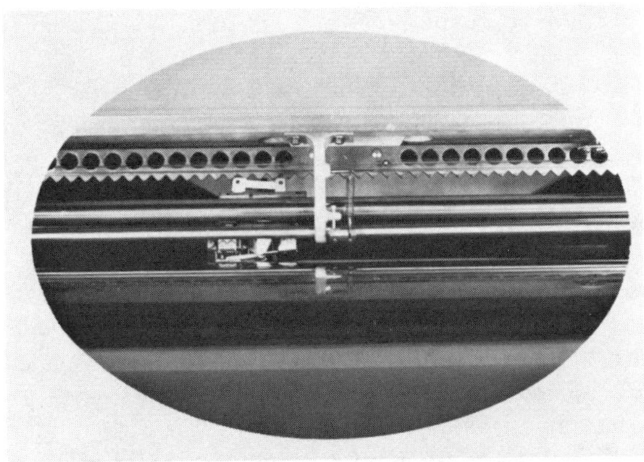

A close up of the stepping head flying on the drum surface. The stepping time to the next track was 50 milliseconds. Reading of a track on one drum was overlapped with stepping the head on another.

One of the ferrite core memory cabinets. It contained four independent 4 microsecond, 2,500 word units that were overlapped in operation and multiplexed onto a high speed bus.

meeting of the IRE at the University of Pennsylvania in January, 1960.

There was nothing left to do now but finish the LARC computer, and that we did in the spring of 1960. Of course, the LARC computer, had to pass an acceptance test before it could be shipped, and Lou Nofrey was insistent that we live up to the letter of the contract, and demonstrate the system operating at a room temperature of 110° F. Plumbers were called in to rig the steam pipes into heat exchangers, and on the scheduled day, the steam was turned on. The LARC computer continued on its merry way despite the heat, gobbling up test routines. After Lou's engineers made a few more tests and inspections, the engineering portion of the test was passed.

The performance test was a much more formal affair with 288 15-minute units of test routines to be run in two sixteen-hour periods, with the computer completely turned off for seven hours between the two periods. UCRL provided the test routines and they were designed to give every element of the system a rough time. Dr. Fernbach, Jim Norton, and several others arrived from

UCRL for the great event. The LARC computer ran through the test like a real champion and easily met the allowable downtime and error criteria. That was it! The LARC computer was ready to be dismantled for shipment.

A team of Remington Rand Univac installation people was organized under Bill Simon to go with the computer for whatever period was required to install it. A week later I stood on Allegheny Avenue opposite the plant as the first gigantic moving van pulled out of the loading dock with a big blue banner "Remington Rand Univac-LARC" emblazoned on its side. Four other huge vans followed in succession. I watched as the procession of five trucks slowly disappeared down Allegheny Avenue. I felt a tear drop on my cheek. It was appropriate—I had previously given the blood and sweat. An enormous feeling of relief came over me, even though the second LARC computer for the Navy awaited completion. It would be easy.

Bill Suchors was overjoyed with the completion of the LARC computer, and offered Shirley and me a bonus vacation trip to Florida. I politely turned it down, explaining that so many others had worked so hard on the project that it would be unfair for me to benefit. Shortly after that, Shirley and I did take a vacation, our first in four years, a cruise in the Caribbean. With my responsibilities completed, I was able to relax and truly enjoy the vacation.

LARC, 100 times faster than its predecessors, as installed at the Lawrence Radiation Laboratory, Livermore, California.

History has confirmed that the LARC computer was a fantastic technical achievement. It met every single one of its specifications that had been set years before. An addition that consumed 525 microseconds on the UNIVAC I computer took only 4 microseconds on the LARC computer, a factor of 130 times faster. The architecture for accomplishing all of this was revolutionary. Many of the concepts have been carried forward into today's computer systems.

Some of the most significant innovations included a separate programmed processor dedicated to handling the input/output functions. This permitted the computing unit to handle the arithmetic computation, for which it was optimized, at maximum efficiency. If necessary, a second computing unit could be added for additional capability.

Several techniques ensured high performance in the computing unit. Overlapping, or pipelining, of the instructions was implemented to the degree that at any time, four instructions were in various phases of execution. A minimum of twenty-six fast registers was included to reduce the number of references to main storage. The registers could be used interchangeably as interim storage or as memory address modifying index registers. Eight main storage units containing 2,500 words of sixty bits each were independently accessible so that data could be loaded from I/O devices, programs made available to the I/O processor to control the I/O devices, and data and instructions made available to the computing unit for computation. All of this was accomplished by high speed multiplexing the storage units and mainframes onto one common bus.

The high data rate (500,000 characters/second) stepping-head drum mass storage subsystem, employing a minimum of twelve drums, was programmed to provide a continuous flow of data to and from the main storage units. This minimized the time that the computing unit had to wait for information. Another intriguing output device was the electronic page recorder. It recorded the information from a special cathode ray tube on 35mm microfilm. The electronic page recorder operated at a speed of 2,000 characters per second or plotted 1,000 by 1,000 points per second. This broke the bottleneck in getting high volume output.

The technique for passing information back and forth between the CU and IOP was to go through memory locations known as mailboxes. LARC also had one of the first operating systems. It was called L'OPERA, and handled the job queues in the CU. The list of innovations goes on and on.

The two LARC computers served valiantly for their owners until late 1968-1969, when they were retired from service. The systems were in continuous use during the intervening period with excellent uptime. Not once did Remington Rand Univac receive a call for assistance from either customer. Typical problems run on the Navy's LARC computer included a three-dimensional, potential flow program, a 500 by 500 full matrix times a vector of order 500, accomplished in 10 seconds. It was also used to solve large scale reactor simulation problems.

The unsuccessful part of the LARC computer was, of course, financial. It was a terrible loss to the company at a crucial time. The computer operations had lost money for years, and the stockholders were getting impatient. Harry Vickers was committed to turning the corner. There was some small consolation, however. Our competitor's STRETCH system did not meet its performance goals, budget, or delivery schedule.

The LARC computer did not have to be a business failure. Lou Wilson, who spent several years in the marketing operation investigating the potential for further LARC computer sales, reported he was confident that an additional eight to ten systems could have been sold. Actually, an abortive attempt at a sales campaign was mounted. Full page advertisements were taken in the Wall Street Journal and the New York Times. A group of aerospace executives was flown in from the West Coast to see the LARC computer. However, by the time the computer was delivered, the Remington Rand Univac management had had such a bellyfull of past grief that they were in no mood to move forward. A decision was reached to carry many of the LARC concepts forward into a new system known as the UNIVAC III computer.

The lessons we learned from the LARC computer program were: first, don't take a fixed-price contract for a development of unknown dimensions; and second, don't push the state of the art beyond the "knee" of the technology curve. If we had stopped at the optimum point, the LARC computer could have been delivered years sooner, at a fraction of the development cost, but it would have missed its performance objectives by a long shot.

Chapter 12

GLORY AND HEARTACHE

The completion of the LARC computer in 1960 signified the end of the pioneering era. The time had arrived for the computer industry to operate on a businesslike basis if it was going to survive, and Remington Rand Univac now bent all its efforts in this direction. We had blazed a trail of technological innovation for the past sixteen years. We had created many dazzling new concepts, but innovation, by itself, did not guarantee success. That was more elusive. However, the sagas of the ENIAC, EDVAC, BINAC, UNIVAC I, and LARC will be fondly remembered by a few pioneers.

It is impossible to recreate today the spirit that existed on those early projects. Maybe it was the small company environment, or maybe it was the challenge of entering into uncharted territory, of doing the impossible. Maybe it was the individuals involved, Pres Eckert and John Mauchly. Maybe it was because I was involved in everything, logic, circuits, test, and machine code programming. Whatever it was, and it was probably all these things, I look back with longing and a feeling of great personal satisfaction.

The final chapter of my story will not dwell on each subsequent computer system development, but instead, focus on some of the highlights of the period from the completion of LARC until the present.

Activities at the Philadelphia operations in early 1960 were split into two parts, the LARC computer, and the other commercial systems including the UNIVAC Solid-State Computer (USSC) and the new UNIVAC III computer. I was chief engineer of the LARC computer program, and Ev Minnett was chief engineer of the other. Ev had a falling out with Chu which resulted in my appointment to the position of chief engineer for the Philadelphia engineering operations. Grace Hopper continued as chief engineer of Automatic Programming.

All of the problems were now mine to worry about. One of the first had to do with the USSC that our upstate factory at Ilion, New York, was trying to produce. The manufacturing people were having fits attempting to get the system on the test floor to work properly. The central processor checked out satisfactorily but as soon as the peripheral devices (card reader, card punch, and printer) were added, everything went wrong, even though the peripheral devices themselves passed all of the tests. The manufacturing people claimed the designs were faulty. My newly acquired engineering group countercharged that the factory didn't know how to put things together properly and, in addition, were making unauthorized changes. Meanwhile, there was no output from the factory.

The dispute had to be settled, and this I did by assigning a group of engineers, under Charlie Michaels' direction, to stay at the factory until all of the problems were resolved. After the first week I visited the factory to find out what progress was being made. The problems encountered were subtle indeed. They were due to electrical noise. Sometimes the noise was there to be seen on an oscilloscope; but most of the time it was fleeting and not discernible. Then I realized that few, if any, of our engineers knew anything about noise or how to design to prevent noise from interfering with the operation of digital circuits. It was the kind of know-how that was not taught in college.

To fill the gap, I wrote a primer on the *Fundamentals of Noise Elimination in Digital Computer Circuits.* It was a thorough treatise on the subject, and if used as a design guide it would provide high assurance that the problems of the USSC would not recur. The document, printed as a 30-page booklet with a decorative blue cover, was issued to all engineers, and became the bible on noise control for many years. A subsequent tutorial booklet *Fundamentals of the Use of Electro Mechanical Contacts in Digital Computer Circuits* followed. The work dealt mainly with methods for de-bouncing contacts. I look back upon those publications with a feeling of accomplishment.

The lease on our business property was due to expire, so Remington Rand Univac made commitments to construct an entirely new, custom-designed engineering center on the acreage purchased in 1956 in Whitpain Township. The news gave joy to all of the development personnel, for it was to be our own home, modern, air conditioned, and without the grime of the previous locations. Actually, it didn't make much difference to the old timers; we thrived on the grime, but having a modern building would be a significant factor in attracting new personnel.

The new Univac Engineering Center (UEC) was opened in January 1961. Sitting on a hilltop in the rolling countryside, the white brick building made an impressive picture amidst the corn fields. The employees were delighted with their new surroundings.

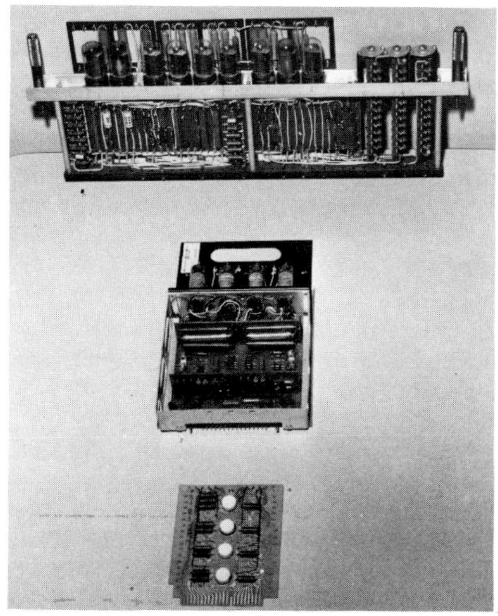

Top: A UNIVAC I computer chassis; Middle: A UNIVAC II computer chassis; Bottom: Printed circuit card from the UNIVAC Solid-State Computer. The magnetic amplifiers are contained in the four round white packages.

The UNIVAC Solid-State Computer with J. Presper Eckert and Dr. Grace Hopper at the controls. Over 500 of these systems were sold.

I was lucky to get an office on "walnut" row along with Chuan Chu, Grace Hopper, Pres Eckert, and several others. The offices came completely decorated with a different color motif assigned to each. Grace's office was next to mine. Various rumblings emanating from her office disclosed that she was mighty unhappy about the color of her couch. One afternoon I had to go to a meeting that lasted several hours and when I returned, Grace's couch was in my office, and mine was in hers. She didn't say a word to me about the change, nor I to her. I understood that beneath that tough COBOL exterior beat the heart of a woman. We continued to be the best of friends.

In April, 1961, another sweeping reorganization occurred. H. Burke Horton was named director, Engineering and Manufacturing Centers, reporting to Jay Schnackel, vice president and general manager of the division. Chuan was moved up to a staff position reporting to Horton at corporate headquarters in New York City. I was promoted to manager of the new Univac Engineering Center. My new responsibilities included the welfare of some 500 people in the engineering department as well as administration of an $11,500,000 budget.

I had mixed feelings about the position, happy to be rewarded, but concerned about advancing further into management. I never wanted to get too far away from the technical end of the business where my strength was. On the other hand, I felt I could do a competent job. Above all else, I knew I had good common sense, the ability to ferret out the important issues and dismiss the unimportant ones. One of my first steps was appointing Charlie Michaels chief engineer of computer systems development and Ted Bonn chief engineer of peripherals and research. With two competent chief engineers, I could relax for the first time, albeit with a feeling of uneasiness.

The high point of this period was exemplified by the staff meetings which Burke Horton held at Rockledge, an estate in South Norwalk, Connecticut. It was an aristocratic mansion of days gone by, complete with Victorian furniture that gave me the willies. A typical staff meeting was attended by Bob McDonald, general manager of the St. Paul operation; George Stephenson, manager of the Norwalk Center; Ken Snover, from the Ilion/Utica manufacturing facility; George Tranfield, Philadelphia manufacturing; and me from the Philadelphia Engineering Center. When I reflect on the divergent career paths of these people, I can't help but smile. Bob McDonald is now president of Sperry Rand Corporation. Burke Horton worked his way out of the company through successive reorganizations. George Stephenson became head of the maintenance services before he retired. Tranfield and Snover are no longer with the company. And I'm writing this book.

Dedication of the new Center on October 11, 1961, was a glamorous affair. All of the top corporate officials were there as well as Lt. Gov. John Morgan Davis, who cut the metallic computer tape in front of the building signifying the start of activities.

The following evening was even more auspicious. Remington Rand Univac and the University of Pennsylvania sponsored a dinner at the University's museum for the fifteenth anniversary of the ENIAC. Listening to Eckert and Mauchly retelling the wonders of ENIAC with the five thousand year old mummies surrounding us seemed somewhat incongruous, but it was a scene I shall remember forever.

Our New York City corporate office was drab compared to the pleasant surroundings of the Whitpain Township Center, which was soon being called the "Country Club." However, we were paying the price for the new facility. Bill Suchors would take me to the engineering area to show me engineers who were sitting motionless, staring into space. "How can you tell whether those engineers are working or not?" Bill would ask. It always bothered him that there was no visible way of knowing.

One of the staff program managers from New York, Dr. Werner Leutert, was determined to expose the alleged laxity at the Center. On a day that I was scheduled to attend a meeting in New York, Leutert stationed himself at the employees' entrance and counted personnel arriving late. For some reason my meeting was cancelled. I went into the office that morning and found Leutert counting heads. He was chagrined when he saw me but I let him finish his survey. When it was done, he confronted me with the evidence. "Yes, Werner," I said, "I agree there are people who arrive late, but there are also people who leave late." I insisted that we both stand at the exit at departure time and make another survey. My hunch paid off. There were substantially more people who left late than arrived late. I never heard anything further from Leutert.

All of our programs had to be approved by the corporate office, and getting a program approved was a major victory. There was no doubt in my mind that the Center could be more efficient if we could develop more of an engineering work backlog. Projects have a way of occupying time until the next project comes along. Also, an engineer may be held up in his work for extended periods and he could use that time to work gainfully on a fill-in project. I had in mind scheduling more projects than we had allowed for in our budget, but I never could get our controller, Rocky Laginestra, to consider it. I guess the concept was too advanced for its time.

The new Center was a good 50% farther from my home than 19th Street, and during the bad winter weather, the forty-five minute trip could easily double. Also, there was strong legislation afoot to turn our quiet street, at the end of the block, into the "Northeast Freeway." These factors, coupled with the need for more room because of an impending fourth offspring, led Shirley and me to look for a new home closer to the Center. We started on the old familiar pattern, using our weekends to search for a new home. Housing values had changed drastically since 1950; we had to get recalibrated.

I kept returning to the Dresher-Fort Washington area. One development was just starting up and two of the sample houses were completed. The development appealed to me because of its natural beauty and elevation; you could see for miles. This latter quality was important for good radio propagation. Further, the builder was a visionary, and would allow all kinds of buyer changes. We signed up for a two story colonial house which was quickly transformed into a contemporary one. For a while I questioned my own sanity at paying $36,000 for a house, but inflation in later years has mitigated that feeling.

In February, 1962, Shirley and I moved with the three children and infant, Andrew, into our new home with the same exhilarating feeling we had experienced the first time. Predictably, during the first two weeks in our new home, I used my vacation to construct the workshop in the basement and the combination radio shack-den on the first floor. The shack was a laundry room in the sample house, but Shirley thought it would be better for me to spend my time on the first floor instead of the basement. That's one of the advantages of having a wife interested in the same hobby.

My amateur radio activities had taken second and third priority during the LARC computer project, as had almost everything else. I had much catching up to do. The state of the art in amateur radio communications had changed drastically. Amplitude modulation had been completely replaced by single sideband (SSB) transmissions. I acquired a used SSB transmitter, rebuilt my old Collins receiver, and designed and built a 1,500-watt amplifier. By the time spring arrived, my plans were already made to put a sixty foot tower in the back yard to support the antenna system. The tower was erected on the first mild day, and the following weekend saw the motor and rotary beam antennas in place.

The results were fantastic. I was able to talk to other radio amateurs practically anywhere in the world. Searching for new countries to contact became my avocation, rather than "rag chewing." Soon I was up to 150 countries and going strong. What made it even more challenging was having my good friend and fellow member of the Beacon Radio Amateurs, Herb Strauss, W3FLY, move into a home two blocks away. Herb and I entered a competition to see who would first make DX Century Club honor role (a coveted award for contacting more than 300 countries). This pursuit was to last for many years.

We suffered a great loss in mid-1962. Eternally youthful looking and brilliant Frazer Welsh was piloting his plane near his summer home at Lake Sunapee, New Hampshire. As he approached the airport for landing, the light plane was caught in a gust of wind and crashed to earth, killing Frazer. Everyone was stunned. The greatest loss was to Pres Eckert who sorely missed Frazer's keen mind and their ongoing verbal rapport. For years afterwards Pres would wander through the laboratories looking for someone with the mental capacity to test his ideas on, but there was no one. In fact, some of the technical personnel, would rapidly disappear when they heard that Eckert was headed in their direction.

Pres Eckert questioned every approach, and gave the technical leaders cause to think twice. One phenomenon frustrated Pres. He never seemed to be able to interface with a project at the right time to inject his ideas. Either he was too early, when everything was in a state of flux and nothing was decided, or else the project's direction had already been decided, and there was no possibility of considering other approaches. The time in between, when he could influence a project, he called the "magic microsecond." He was never able to find that magic microsecond.

My role as manager of the UEC was not particularly exciting. The old stimulus was gone, even though a high performance UNIVAC III system was developed and delivered to the field, and further USSC enhancements were completed. This position probably marked the peak of my management career, if peak is measured in the traditional sense. In any event, it was short-lived. Along came another reorganization, and I found myself reporting to Lou Chaloux, formerly the staff quality assurance manager. Chaloux seemed like a reasonable person on the surface, but deep down he had a distrust of the engineering force which may have originated with some of the USSC problems. Although I had no problems in getting along with Lou, my chief engineer, Charlie Michaels, did, and he left the company. An exodus of other top technical people included Ted Bonn, Chuan Chu, and Earl Masterson. They all headed for Honeywell, on the upsurge at the time.

Morale in general was failing, with only two small systems projects active. One, called Apollo, provided a spurt. It was a contract signed with the Air Force in late 1963 to deliver 150 systems to Air Force bases around the world. Apollo became the commercial UNIVAC 1050 system shortly thereafter.

A major breakthrough in resolving the animosity between the Philadelphia and St. Paul engineering activities occurred in October, 1964, when Dr. Val Herzfeld of the St. Paul operations was placed in charge of both facilities. Val called me into his office to inform me that Harry Martell was appointed manager of engineering, and I was to have a staff position. I was crushed! After eighteen years of being on the front line, I was to be retired to staff service. The thought temporarily paralyzed me. One minute I had five hundred people to do my bidding, and the next I had no one but myself. The first time anyone moves back into a staff position, the shock is overwhelming. After the second, third, or fourth time, it isn't so bad. I made up my mind to do the best I could for Val. It was a great opportunity for me to put into practice some of my thoughts on how to improve Sperry Univac.

Previously I had written many memos to my various bosses on improvements that should be made in our mode of operation, policies, and procedures, but nothing ever came of them. This was my chance to bring them out of mothballs. Many of the policies I established with Val's approval during that period became the cornerstone for Sperry Univac's engineering operations.

Marketing sold Sperry Univac products. Engineering designed Sperry Univac products. But whether or not Marketing was selling what Engineering had designed was coincidental in some cases. Consequently, there was a lot of anguish when Marketing discovered what the product really was. I established a procedure under which the groups worked together formally to describe products, in which both were knowledgeable, in detail. The formal Product Description was, in essence, a contract between Marketing and Engineering and has become a sacrosanct document within Sperry Univac.

Design reviews were not novel, yet we had not been using them in Sperry Univac. Our engineers did not like them, but I was convinced they were beneficial. We began using such reviews, and they did pinpoint occasional blindspots.

I also directed the standards activities. Getting agreement from Marketing, Engineering, Product Planning, and Customer Engineering on a set of environmental specifications that all Univac products had to meet was a major task, but I was actually enjoying the work. The challenge was in getting things done, even though I had no power to direct anyone. I found that I could do it.

Belief in advanced technology was always one of my characteristics, and I took every opportunity to push in that direction. One of the new technologies I kept my eye on was thin-film, plated-wire memory. Our research group had developed it, mostly under government contract funding. Plated-wire memory looked like a real winner to me, with many potential advantages over the ferrite core memory. Ferrite core stacks were tedious to build, with the inside diameter of each core being only thirty thousandths of an inch. There were thousands in an array, and each had to have at least three fine wires threaded through it. Plated wire, on the other hand, was made with a continuous thin magnetic film plated on the wire, and required no threading. The advantages in manufacturing a continuously plated wire were also potentially great because the quality of the wire could be monitored while it was being produced. The biggest advantage of all was in plated-wire performance. The amount of magnetic material on the plated-wire was a fraction of the amount in a ferrite core; consequently the memory position could be switched in a much shorter time. Without half trying, the first plated-wire products completed a read cycle in 600 nanoseconds, several times less than the prevalent ferrite cores. Further, there was promise of reducing the thin film on the plated-wire to provide 100 nanosecond performance.

A by-product of the smaller amount of magnetic material required for plated-wire was the lower power it took for switching. Also, when the memory was resting between chores, it took no power, an advantage of magnetic devices. Plated-wire had another uncanny asset; it had nondestructive readout. A bit could be read out of a plated-wire cell an infinite number of times without destroying its contents. Ferrite core information was destroyed after each read out, and consequently an additional cycle had to be added to restore the information after each read cycle. I was convinced that plated-wire was a more superior memory than core, but it was dying on the vine in research.

Rather than see a good technology expire, I approached Val, and attempted to sell him on utilizing it in our systems product line. Val said "Fine, if you can convince Glen Turner." Glen was responsible for memory development at our St. Paul operation. I made a special trip to sell Glen on the wisdom of using plated-wire memory in the next development. He was convinced, and the first use of plated-wire was scheduled for our new small 9200 system then under development.

In retrospect, I believe going to plated-wire had all the earmarks of a good decision, but the full potential was never achieved. The rest of the computer industry did not adopt plated-wire, probably because of the high development cost, electing instead to force more performance out of the conventional ferrite core memory. This left Sperry Univac alone in the plated-wire field, without benefit of contributions from the industry. We had a difficult time. I felt bad that plated-wire memory wasn't a bigger success, but it did give us some advantage over our competitors' memory systems.

March, 1966, was a vintage month for the company and me. Val Herzfeld approached me to say, "Herm, I want you to take over as director of engineering." I was overjoyed. Everything was headed in the right direction. I could sense that Sperry Univac was now on the move. The 1108 computers were rolling out of the factory, and the small 9200 system was about to be announced. Now was the time to invest in Sperry Rand stock. I bought one hundred shares at 19⅞. My optimism was confirmed by the end of the month when Sperry Univac made a profit for the first time in its history. We had turned the corner after a twenty year struggle, and the management team that did it was Sperry Univac's own. Earlier regimes of management from Bell Telephone, IBM, and GE had been unsuccessful. It was a great feeling to know that we were now making money. It was also great to be back with my group managers and friends again, operating as a team.

In June, as I had anticipated, the Sperry Rand stock was up to 26⅛. I sold the stock, realizing a net profit of $578. The men who reported to me had undoubtedly contributed to this profit, and I believed that they should share in it; so, I divided the profit into six parts and gave each one of the managers a check for $62 with a little note explaining my feelings. I hope they didn't think I was insane.

My happy days were brought to an abrupt halt in August, 1967, by a family tragedy. My sister Fran's fifteen year old daughter, a vivacious, beautiful girl, was struck by a car while crossing a street in Atlantic City. As soon as I heard, Shirley and I took off for the Atlantic City Hospital. We got there in time for word from the brain surgeon; there was no hope. Three days later, the machines were turned off and Terri died, leaving my sister to grieve for years afterwards. My niece's death was an omen of events to come.

Company policy required that its top management personnel be examined by a physician each year. I had been taking the exam for a number of years with no more negative report than "Lose ten pounds." Two months after my niece's death, I reported for the physical. The exam ran true to form, only this time the report in the mail, a couple of weeks later, contained a message of some urgency. It said, "You should see a qualified physician as soon as possible. Your white cell count (WBC) is high." The report showed my WBC to be 27,000 compared to

10,000 the year before. I did not think too much of it, knowing that infections can raise the WBC. My family physician arranged for an appointment with Dr. Edward T. McGehee, a hematologist of some renown at Chestnut Hill Hospital. Dr. McGehee, a friendly man with a sense of humor and a southern drawl, took more blood samples and then placed me on the table.

"Now I am going to take a sample from your blood factory," he said, as he gave me a local anesthetic near the breast bone. I could feel the pressure of the drilling but didn't feel any pain. "Come back in a week."

I wasn't too concerned during the week, but Shirley was mightily concerned, and insisted on accompanying me to Dr. McGehee's office. Dr. McGehee was not one to beat around the bush. He looked me right in the eye and said, "Mr. Lukoff, I regret to tell you that you have leukemia."

I couldn't believe my ears. It wasn't true! I was condemned to die in the prime of my life! Minutes later the hammer stopped hitting me in the head long enough for me to hear him say, "However, if you have to get leukemia, at least you have the right kind, chronic lymphatic leukemia. Some of my patients have had it for ten, fifteen, even twenty years. Each case is different though, and it is impossible to predict how long anyone will live. For now, I am not going to prescribe anything for you except a visit to my office every six weeks so that we can follow the changes in your blood chemistry. Later, if your white cell count gets high, you will have to take a 'lil ol' pill' once a day. I don't want to give you the Chlorambucil until you really need it." His voice was reassuring amidst the overtones of disaster.

We left, with Shirley driving. I was shaking too much. That night was hell. We couldn't sleep. I just lay there shaken; I cried. So did Shirley. How did I get it? The thought raced through my mind of the x-ray treatments for acne I had received as a kid. I was sure they were responsible, but there was no way of undoing what was done. I had to think of what to do next, of providing for Shirley and our four children, of what to do and say at work. We stayed up all night discussing these crucial subjects.

From all outward appearances I looked fine. No one could tell my white cell count was high by looking at me. Dr. McGehee pointed out that the lymph nodes in my neck and under my arm pits were swollen. I could feel the lumps but they were not visible. I decided that as long as I looked and acted healthy, there was no reason for anyone at work to know of my illness. Pity was the last thing I wanted.

The next day at work was a complete loss; I couldn't think or work. The night was a repeat of the first night, no sleep, just trembling and feeling sorry for myself at being terminated at the age of forty-four. I kept thinking of my father who died at forty-seven, which seemed so young. My mind kept going through the same repetitious routine. I didn't want to die yet! I had too much to live for. Why me? Was I having a nightmare? Was it real? It was an endless rut that wasn't easy to break out of.

By the third night, Shirley had made a fundamental decision. She was going to prepare herself to go back to work so that she could take over the job of supplying the family's needs when I was no longer around. She decided that becoming a computer programmer would pay a higher salary than her former profession, drafting. With four children to send to college, this was a major consideration. Consequently, she signed up for a course in computer programming at the local community college. Going back to school full time isn't easy for a woman in her forties, with four children and a big house to take care of. I felt sorry for her and the job she was tackling. Our kids had no idea of the problem. They thought that Mom just had academic interest in finally getting that degree.

Each night was the same. Immediately after dinner Shirl would hit the books. A card table in our bedroom served as her desk. A "pecking order" kept the kids' questions and problems mostly solved before they reached her. Many times I would wake up at 2 or 3 a.m. and find her nose in the books. She claimed that those hours were free of distraction and very profitable for study. I hated to see her work so hard, but it did keep her too busy to worry a lot about me.

Visits to Dr. McGehee's office became routine. Each time, a lab technician jabbed my finger with a needle, then put several drops of blood onto slides and into little vials for lab tests. I wanted to know exactly where I stood, and Dr. McGehee always told me what the white blood cell counts were. On each visit they edged upward. The 27,000 I started with gave way to 40,000 and then 50,000. I wondered how high it would go before I would have to start chemotherapy. Dr. McGehee would also measure the size of my "lumps" and finish by feeling the extent of my spleen. Somehow or other the spleen is a barometer in the blood system. Dr. McGehee was always cheerful and humorous. He did a lot for my morale.

By now the initial shock was over and I had adjusted to the idea that I was going to croak; in fact, I could even joke about it. Still, I told no one at Sperry Univac about my problem. There was no need to, as I was functioning normally.

In July, 1968, another organizational change occurred in the development ranks. Dr. Herzfeld chose to organize by function rather than location. The development activities at both the Philadelphia and St. Paul locations were placed under one director, Glen Turner, and I was put in charge of research and advanced development work. The change was agreeable for me. I had deep interest in research. After twenty-two years of fighting fires, I was ready to look into the origin of the fires.

A startling event occurred early in 1969. A letter posted by IBM arrived, telling me that I was to be presented with the W. Wallace McDowell Award at the Spring Joint Computer Conference in May. The letter caught me completely off guard. I had no idea of the significance of the award. Les Spandorfer filled me in on the details. The IEEE Computer Group made the award annually to an individual whose professional work had been outstanding in the field. The McDowell Award, a certificate and a check for $500, was established by a grant from the IBM Corporation in honor of its retired vice president. I was flabbergasted and overwhelmed at the great honor. But I wondered why me? I knew that these things did not occur miraculously, but required an effort on the part of some dedicated people in preparing the nomination. I don't know who the people were, but I can guess at a few. Thank you, from the bottom of my heart. I suspect that my good wife may have "leaked" my condition to a few intimate friends who started the ball rolling.

May arrived soon enough. Naturally I wanted to bring Shirley and my sister Fran along with me to Boston for the greatest honor of my life. Charlie Linder, an old friend and IEEE official, presented the award, which read:

> For his insight and leadership in solving primary problems of early computers and his continuing contributions that have paved the way for tomorrow's computing systems.

Charlie then gave me $500 of Mr. Watson's hard-earned money and I had no remorse in accepting it. Many friends from the past rushed up to congratulate me after the ceremony. Sid Fernback and Jim Norton had come all the way from California. Chuan Chu and many others offered words of congratulation. It took a week for me to descend from cloud nine, and I confess it was a good feeling to be recognized by my peers.

Hardly had I recovered from the McDowell Award when a letter arrived from the IEEE advising me that I was being elected a Fellow as of January 1, 1970. This was beyond my wildest dreams. The ceremony took place at an IEEE section dinner meeting in February, 1970. Dr. Granger, IEEE president, presented me with the certificate, and the citation read:

For pioneering in the development of digital computers and digital input and output devices.

These honors came along at the right pyschological time. I needed the boost in my morale to overcome the depressing thoughts of the previous two years.

Shirley was coming down the home stretch of her two year programming course, and was scheduled to graduate with honors in June, 1970. She hadn't had a break the whole time, and needed one. Our good friends, Estelle and Irv Brager, who had long wanted to visit Israel asked us to join them over the Christmas and New Year's holidays. I had never thought seriously of travelling in Israel but, something in the depths of my background was calling. The visit proved to be tremendously inspiring. The spirit and vigor of the young country stood out against the background of antiquities.

The Wailing Wall in old Jerusalem is considered one of the holiest shrines in Israel. Large groups of people were there praying, the men and women separated according to Orthodox tradition. One of the religious men at the wall informed me that if I would write a wish on a slip of paper, and then fold it and put it into a crack between the huge stones, my wish would be granted. I wrote my wish, but had a terrible time finding a crack that wasn't already occupied with someone else's wish. Even Shirley doesn't know what I wrote on the slip, but here I am today, seven years later.

I am not a religious man, but I do believe in God. My God, however, is in the form of nature rather than a being. I believe that health, life, death and most of the other things that happen to us are determined by nature. I have always tried to lead a moral life, something my parents instilled in me. Treating my fellow man fairly and dealing with him honestly has always been part of my creed. It hasn't always worked in my favor, but at any rate, I have never felt the need for religious atonement or penitence.

Pres Eckert once figured that the average life span of an organization in a dynamic industry was just a little over two and a quarter years. We were approaching that after our last restructuring. In April, 1970, a sweeping reorganization occurred. Don Neddenriep, the young engineer who worked for me on the LARC computer program, became vice president of the Data Processing Division. I was appointed Director of Technical Operations, a staff engineering function, reporting to him. Don was a very competent and ambitious young man who had risen rapidly through the ranks. He had planned his career carefully to achieve the vice presidency, including going back to school for a year to get a master's degree in business administration. At first I sensed that Don did not trust me, probably because he thought I might have resented his appointment. This was not true and in subsequent years we developed a deep respect for each other.

My assignments ranged from assessment of a new technology to accountability for the standards activities. I felt personally responsible for seeing that Sperry Univac utilized new technologies. One of these, coming on strong, was higher complexity, semiconductor, integrated circuits, especially memory. The semiconductor companies had discovered that many transistors could be placed on a chip of silicon rather than just one transistor. Furthermore, the transistors could be interconnected to form circuits such as flip-flops, similar to the basic memory element of ENIAC. The term "integrated circuit" was applied to these silicon components. The level of complexity had risen to 256 memory bits on a chip and the semiconductor vendors were known to be working on schemes for quadrupling that amount. I campaigned to drop our plated-wire memory and switch to semiconductors. Certain managers were fighting my arguments tooth and nail, reasoning we had too big an investment in plated-wire to change, but I was able to persuade the memory group in St. Paul to make the change to semiconductor memory.

Later, I instigated several studies on the advisability of having an internal semiconductor design and wafer processing capability. The studies showed that the only way we would be able to get the highly complex, customized logic circuits (LSI) for our high performance computer systems would be to design and build them ourselves. The quantities required were too small to attract the commercial vendors. Management agreed to authorize the construction of an LSI semiconductor prototype facility.

After two years of visiting Dr. McGehee, my white cell count had climbed close to the 100,000 mark. The lymph nodes in my neck had grown to large swollen areas, and I was becoming worried that people would notice the disfiguration. At this point Dr. McGehee started me on Chlorambucil, a big dose at first to bring down the white cell count. Fortunately, the medication did not generate any adverse side effects. Within several months my WBC was down to 40,000. Dr. McGehee responded by cutting down my medication to a maintenance level. My "lumps" were down to almost normal size. I was clearly doing well under Dr. McGehee's care and except for getting tired much more easily, I felt good. However, there was always the spectre of the Chlorambucil losing its effectiveness.

June 1, 1971, was a landmark day for the computer industry. Hearings on the case of Honeywell, Inc. vs. Sperry Rand Corporation commenced in the U.S. District Court of Minnesota. Honeywell charged Sperry Rand with violations of the Sherman Antitrust Act for maintenance and enforcement of an allegedly fraudulently procured and invalid patent. Sperry Rand charged infringement by Honeywell of the ENIAC patent.

The action was the culmination of events that started many years earlier. The ENIAC patent application was filed on June 16, 1947, less than one year after the ENIAC computer was officially turned over to Army Ordnance. Granting of the patent was delayed because of numerous time-consuming claims of patent interference. Consequently, the ENIAC patent (3,120,606) was not issued until February 4, 1964. It was a gigantic document containing 91 sheets of drawings, 232 columns of text, and 148 claims devoted to the fundamental principles of digital computation. The patent was obviously valuable property, and Sperry Rand had sought to capitalize on its value by asking Honeywell, Inc. to take a license under the ENIAC patent. The far-reaching implication of the patent led Honeywell to challenge its validity and enforceability; thus, the court action.

The trial ended on March 13, 1972, after 135 days with 77 witnesses presenting testimony. The judge's decision was a blockbuster. The ENIAC patent was declared invalid. Two major reasons cited were that ENIAC was put to public use prior to June 26, 1946, and even more devastating, that the invention of ENIAC was derived from the work of Dr. John V. Atanasoff.

As to the first assertion, the judge's finding of facts indicated that the ENIAC computer was used to solve an H-bomb problem, which put the machine to public use more than a year before the application filing date. It was used on an H-bomb problem, but this did not constitute public use, in my opinion.

The computer was close to completion by November, 1945, but not complete. At that time scientists at the Los Alamos Laboratory were advised by a consultant that the ENIAC computer could be used for large-scale numerical calculations to verify the feasibility of their then current H-bomb philosophy. There was urgency at that time, because the H-bomb project was being suspended, and it was necessary that the information be preserved. Therefore, it was agreed between the University of Pennsylvania and the Los Alamos people that the Los Alamos numerical calculations could be undertaken as the first shakedown test of the ENIAC computer. After an inspection of the ENIAC computer, the Los Alamos scientists recognized that ENIAC was incapable of solving their problem (principally because of its lack of memory capacity). Nevertheless, they wanted to use this tool, because they recognized its future potential. They drastically reduced the problem into a series of simpler calculations. It was their belief that the solution to the simpler calculations, when viewed in total, would indicate a trend as to the correctness or incorrectness of the H-bomb philosophy.

On December 10, 1945, the calculations were commenced. Interspersed among the actual calculation steps were calculations to which answers were known, so that the proper operation of ENIAC could be checked. Interestingly enough, the series of calculations, when viewed in total, indicated that the then current H-bomb philosophy was correct. But in 1952, when the H-bomb program was reinstituted, it was shown that the 1945-46 philosophy was *in*correct. It should also be noted that the log book showed repeated failures for the ENIAC test period and the need for corrections to the hardware. Despite the foregoing evidence of an obvious test program, the Court found that running the calculation and obtaining a supposedly correct answer amounted to public use of the ENIAC. On other prototype computer systems that I have tested, it has been necessary to run many problems over many months before inherent design errors are detected and corrected. Only after repeated shakedown runs and subsequent corrections can a computer device be considered complete. The fact that one test problem may run satisfactorily provides no guarantee that the next problem will do so. While I am not skilled in the law, I am at a loss to understand how the running of the highly classified Los Alamos test problem placed the operation in public domain.

The court further found that a demonstration given to the press in February, 1946, also served as a statutory bar. Again I cannot understand how permitting people to look at black panels and blinking lights with no disclosure of the inner workings of a machine (the ENIAC) can disclose any patentable material to the public.

The second assertion, that the invention of ENIAC was based on Atanasoff's earlier work, was even more shocking, and did a great injustice to the two outstanding inventors. The Court's conclusion was based on a visit which Dr. Mauchly made in 1941 to see Dr. Atanasoff's work at Iowa State College. Atanasoff and a graduate student, Clifford E. Berry, were working on a computational device for the solution of simultaneous linear equations. It was a rudimentary device which was worked on from 1938 to 1942, but was never completed, nor put to use. The memory hardware was crudely constructed of capacitors mounted on a rotating drum that had to be charged via a contact mechanism. Other aspects of the proposed machine indicated that it was too premature for the state of the electronic technology to support it. Curiously enough, Atanasoff's reports state that he was never able to get a flip-flop circuit to work correctly. At best, Atanasoff's device was a dead-end step in the field of computation. I cannot comprehend how this 300-tube, experimental, special purpose machine, which had no input means and no output means, which used no flip-flop circuits, which could not multiply nor divide, which was never intended to be programmable, and which, had it ever been completed, would have accomplished only one step at a time before requiring the reentry of the information (thereby, by definition, not automatic) could be held as the prototype for all of the concepts which were actually encompassed in the ENIAC.

To invalidate the ENIAC patent based on Atanasoff's work indicates a lack of understanding of how scientific accomplishments occur. Most inventions are evolutionary and have been preceded by other efforts in similar or related fields. A good example of this is the invention of the light bulb. Thomas A. Edison is universally thought of as the inventor, yet in 1820, fifty-nine years before Edison's historic demonstration, a man by the name of De LaRue first thought of the concept. In 1838, Professor Jobard built a carbon filament lamp. Groves followed in 1840 by lighting an auditorium. Frederich DeMoleyns was issued a patent that same year for an electric lamp. Starr had another carbon filament lamp in 1845. Farmer, in this country, lit up his house with a platinum wire bulb in 1859. There were many others who were also engaged in the development of the electric light bulb. The early attempts were not completely successful, the filaments burning out or the glass blackening in a short period of time. A better vacuum had to be created, and this wasn't possible until 1865 when the vacuum pump was invented by Sprengle. Powering the lamp from batteries was also not practical; the generator had to be invented. A better circuit arrangement also had to be devised so that if one bulb burned out the others could continue to function. But Edison is credited as the inventor, because he put the whole system together, not just the bulb, and therefore made it a commercial practicality. This is exactly what Eckert and Mauchly did with the electronic digital computer.

Dr. McGehee announced in 1973 that he was closing his office to return to teaching. I felt I was losing a dear friend, and so did a hundred other people who turned out at the Cricket Club to bid him farewell. Dr. McGehee referred me to Dr. McCracken, who followed the same course of treatment for the following two years.

My amateur radio activities had been on the decline, as had the sunspot cycle. There were few foreign countries remaining that I had not contacted. I had reached a plateau of 325 countries in the early 1970's. Unless there were some wars started to create new countries, or some secessions, I was out of fresh excitement.

Then a new form of amateur radio activity came to my attention: the use of repeaters, frequency modulation (FM) and the 146 MHz amateur band. At 146 MHz, line-of-sight transmission prevails. Therefore, the higher the receiving and transmitting antennas, the greater the distance that can be covered. A repeater consists of a receiving and transmitting setup located at the highest possible point, a tall building, tower, or mountain. The sensitive receiver picks up the weak signal from a low power mobile station, and retransmits it at a high power level. Thus mobile stations operating at a 1- to 10-watt level are made to sound like 400-watt stations. A good repeater can provide reliable communications for thirty to fifty miles. FM has the advantages of noise immunity, high quality audio and, if there are several stations on the same channel, it selects the stronger one, completely overriding all others. A CB'er would be very envious of this mode of communication.

I purchased several former police and taxicab radios that had been converted to the amateur band and installed them in our car. My base station was an old Bendix radio that had seen better

This haywired 146 MHz radio was salvaged from a railway car and is now operational in my basement. It serves as a base station and was used for communications via the amateur radio satellite OSCAR.

days in a railroad car. It was so old and decrepit, I sequestered it in the basement, and remotely controlled it from a neat little box over the kitchen sink. The old Bendix, a vacuum tube unit, consumed too much power to run continuously, thus thwarting my objective of calling home at any time from the car. I solved my problem by salvaging a transistorized receiver which listened twenty four hours a day on my favorite repeater channel and yet consumed no more than one-tenth of a watt of power. The two mobile units were outfitted with touchtone pads similar to those used in telephones, except mine were set to different audio tone frequencies. At home base, tone decoders were set to recognize the special tones and sound an alarm. The system worked fine! At the Philadelphia airport after returning from a business trip, I could enter my car on the parking lot, push button four on the touchtone pad, and have the alarm sound at my home in Fort Washington, more than thirty miles away. Within seconds Shirley would flip on the base station and I could talk to her all the way home. The FM quality was so good it sounded as though she were sitting in the seat next to me. Another amazing fact about

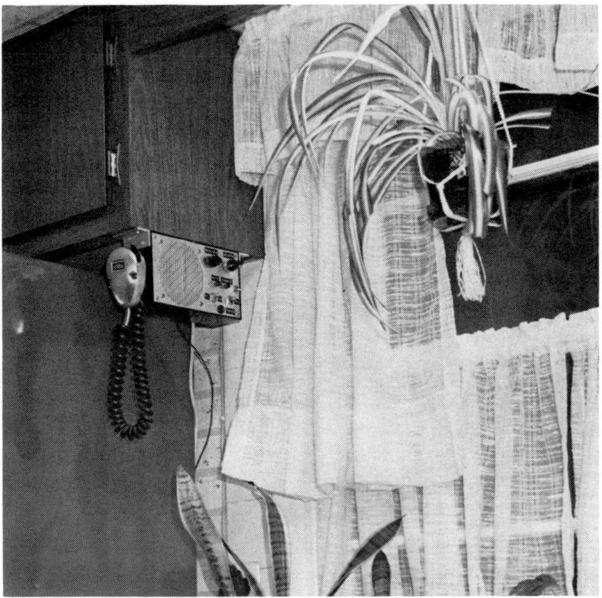

Base station in the basement is operated via this remote control box mounted over the kitchen sink. An alarm tells Shirley that I want to talk to her.

the FM repeater system is that the signal sounded exactly the same at the airport and along the route home as it did on my front driveway.

The week before Father's Day in June, 1975, was a happy one for me. My family gave me a 2-watt handy-talkie (HT) that could operate through the repeater system. The little hand-held radio proved to be a great joy. I now slip it into my briefcase for all of my business trips, and right from my hotel room, I can make many new friends on the airwaves.

One of the great thrills I received from the little HT occurred on Independence Day, 1976. A group of amateurs arranged for a spectacular event. The repeater in Philadelphia was linked via communication lines with the repeater in Boston, which was in turn linked to the repeater in Honolulu. I had an inkling that something was going to happen, so when I sat down at the dinner table that evening, I had my HT on, listening to events unfold. Somewhere between the soup and the mashed potatoes, I had a chance to hold the HT up to my lips, press the button, and within seconds was talking to Don, KH6ABF, who was in his car driving around Kahului, Hawaii. Here I was sitting at the dinner table talking to a fellow in Hawaii, with no wires attached. Will wonders never cease?

I had a chance to try out satellite communications a few years later. When Sperry Univac announced plans to set up experi-

The author at the controls of his amateur radio station W3HT.

mental satellite ground stations to transmit information between Philadelphia and St. Paul, I was motivated to do it first. An amateur radio satellite, called OSCAR 7, has been orbiting the earth for the last few years. The first equatorial crossing of each day is listed in amateur radio journals. On the weekend of my experiment, I calculated each of the one hour and fifty-five minute crossings so that I could tell when it was in range. My old Bendix base station was quickly modified to the uplink frequency of 145.925 MHz, and a telegraph key was inserted into the screen circuit of the final amplifier tubes. On the first pass after I awoke on Sunday morning, the satellite was over the Atlantic Ocean, and I was pleasantly surprised to hear dozens of European stations. I gingerly plunked the key down and listened on the downlink frequency of 29.475 MHz for my own signal, but it wasn't there.

On the next try, the satellite passed directly over Philadelphia, and this time I detected my own faint signal. The setup was working, but not well enough. The best improvement I could think of was to try my beam antenna. So, on the following satellite pass over the Midwest, I aimed my beam antenna in the northwest direction and pressed the key down again. This time the returns were considerably stronger. To prove the signal was mine, I signed my call letters several times. As soon as the key was released, I was astonished to hear KØRZ in Boulder, Colorado,

The other side of my "shack" is occupied by this personal computer system. Would you believe it is more powerful than the UNIVAC I central processor?

Boulder, Colorado 80307

KØRZ

OSCAR 7, MODE A, ORBIT 13354

Station	Date	Time	RST	Freq.	Mode
W3HT	OCT 16, 1977	1555 GMT	559	145/29	2xCW

Xmtr.	Rcvr.	Ant.	Pse QSL Tnx
FT221R	FT301	11 El/2, 3 El/10	[illegible]

P. O. Box 3214 **73, William McCaa, Jr.**

Verification card received from a contact with an amateur radio station in Boulder, Colorado via the amateur radio communications satellite OSCAR.

calling me. We established contact, my first via this amazing new means of communications, a forerunner of things to come.

Back around 1966, I could have traded my call letters W3HTF for a shorter two-letter suffix version. Old timers who obtained their licenses in the 1920's had such distinctive and coveted call letters. To those who had an extra class license and twenty-five years of service, the Federal Communications Commission granted the privilege of a two-letter suffix, but with no choice as to letters. I chose not to exercise this option. It would have been equivalent to changing my name. Recently the FCC relaxed the regulation and permitted a choice of call letters. This time I exercised the option and dropped the "F." Thus my call letters became W3HT and I became a new old timer.

On the Wednesday before Fathers Day, 1975, I developed a feeling of light-headedness. As the week wore on, the symptoms changed to a weak and dizzy feeling. I wasn't too disturbed, and assumed the distress would disappear. In fact, I had to be in good shape for the Open House for the beautiful new marketing building which had just been added to the sprawling Sperry Univac complex. My assignment was to act as the official greeter for a couple of hours. Somehow I mustered the strength to play my role, but when I got home I was exhausted. I hardly had enough strength to reach the bed. Shirley was alarmed, and on

Sunday morning, when I felt no better, she called Dr. McCracken.

As luck would have it, Dr. McCracken was just about to leave for Europe. He recommended that she take me to the Chestnut Hill Hospital for an immediate blood test. The hospital verified that something was wrong; my hemoglobin count was down to seven from a normal count of twelve to fourteen. Dr. McCracken advised Shirley, "He has to be admitted to a hospital immediately and placed under a hemotologist's care." He contacted a group of hemotology experts at the Bryn Mawr Hospital immediately and made arrangements for my admittance. Shirley could just barely drag me to the car for the long trip.

So it was that I came under the care of Dr. James Bond and his associates. After extensive blood tests the next morning, Dr. Bond explained that I had severe hemolytic anemia, a condition brought on by antibodies that had built up in my blood stream over the years. They were acting to kill the hemoglobin. He added that I would receive drugs (Cytoxan and Prednisone) to suppress the antibodies. The next few days were terrible. Getting out of the bed in the morning to shave was nearly impossible. I could hardly stand in front of the mirror and what I saw was someone with a greenish white face looking at me. For the rest of the day, all I could do was lie on the bed. My hemoglobin count continued to drop. It was now less than six. My son Art, on vacation at the sea shore, was called home. For the rest of the week, my hemoglobin count hovered in the five to six range, and I was too weak to move from the bed. I had always thought it was your muscles that gave you strength. Now I had conclusive proof it is the red blood cells.

Shirley brought in my handy-talkie at the beginning of the second week, hoping it would cheer me up. Unfortunately the nickel cadmium battery I ordered for it was several weeks away from delivery, so I asked Shirl to buy eight flashlight batteries and bring them in along with my soldering iron, solder, and some wire. I intended to wire together a temporary 12-volt supply. However Dr. Bond had decided that it was time to give me a blood transfusion. The soldering iron had just barely warmed up when in walked the nurse with the transfusion equipment and the plastic bag of blood. After being hooked up to the dripping blood supply, I resumed my soldering operation. The nurses at first were quite concerned that the mess of wiring and transfusion tubes would get hopelessly entangled or that my hot soldering iron would strike the plastic tubing and melt it. But I knew what I was doing. The temporary power supply worked, and so did the transfusion, for a while.

The new blood was literally a shot in the arm. I felt much better after the two-pint transfusion. Unfortunately, the effect did not last longer than two days before the antibodies killed the new supply and I was back in the same pallid state.

The HT provided me with some diversion from my bed. I was able to talk to my amateur radio friends as they threaded their way through traffic in the morning and pulled up to their parking places in the Sperry Univac parking lot. Soon, many people whom I had never known were calling in on the channel to find out how I was doing. One fellow, who never had a license, but listened, dropped by to see me one day. He had to walk a mile to get the bus that would take him to the hospital. The only obstacle I encountered was the silencing imposed by a nurse who kept thrusting a thermometer into my mouth. The radio communications certainly helped me through a difficult period.

The second week passed, and there was no improvement in my condition. So far the drugs had been ineffective. Dr. Bond and his associates couldn't understand why the chemicals were not working. I think my case posed a challenge to the medical profession. Not only were the old cells still being killed by the antibodies, but my blood factory wasn't generating any new ones either. Each time my hemoglobin sank to new low levels, Dr. Bond ordered a blood transfusion.

The third and fourth weeks passed, and I was in the depths of despair. The chances of ever leaving the hospital looked remote. I made all kinds of promises to myself, if I should survive, like taking my wife out to a dozen dinners and enjoying life to its fullest. Now I claim the promises were made during a period of temporary insanity.

My ever faithful wife made the long drive to be at my bedside every day. Get well cards were coming in daily from hundreds of friends. Shirley acted as a courier, bringing in my office mail each day, and returning the previous day's for file or action. I had little strength or enthusiasm for tackling the work, but it had to be done. It took me four times longer than usual to compose a memo or think of a responsive action. The going was slow, but it kept my sluggish mind occupied.

The fifth and sixth weeks passed in similar fashion except for a touch of pneumonia which was subdued with the aid of antibiotics. There was a glimmer of hope though, as I began generating new cells. The drugs were finally starting to show signs of working, just in time too, for Dr. Bond was about to remove my spleen.

At the beginning of the seventh week the doctor had me up and moving around, but not very much; my right foot had fallen fast asleep from six weeks of being in bed. Shirley took me out for walks in the hallway and on the roof terrace several times a day, with my right foot dragging behind me. Dr. Bond began to speak about going home for recuperation. I received one final transfusion, bringing the total to twelve pints, and a hemoglobin count of eight; now the count was holding. Then finally, after seven weeks in the hospital, I was on my way home. The ride was exhilarating. I felt like an immigrant in wonderland as we drove through the beautiful, lush countryside. I was glad to be alive.

I developed the deepest respect for Dr. Bond and his team. Later he told me he had been initially trained as a geo-physicist and worked as a computer programmer in doing exploration for a large oil company. Any medical doctor with that scientific background had to be good!

Within a few weeks I was back to work, my hemoglobin count returned to normal. The Cytoxan I take each day keeps it that way. As far as my friends and coworkers were concerned, it was just an attack of anemia.

In September, 1977, I celebrated thirty years of continuous service with Sperry Univac, making me the second longest tenured employee of the Eckert-Mauchly Division aside from Eckert and Mauchly themselves. Bob Roeder, who started as the machine shop foreman, preceded me by two months. There was a time when I could walk through the building and greet everyone by his first name. Today, as I walk through the building, people undoutedly wonder who I am.

In 1976, I received an additional honor, one from my own company—the Sperry Univac Presidential Excellence Award. I have had more than my share of honors in this field, more than most men receive in a life time. And for this I am most grateful. My goal in life has been achieved.

One might think that after thirty-five years of innovation, the rate of progress in the computer field would be slowing down. The fact is, technological changes are accelerating at a spiraling rate. Initially, when hardware was very expensive, as many functions as possible were relegated to software. The breakthroughs in semiconductors, from which the memories and logic circuits are made, have been nothing short of astounding. Never, in our wildest dreams in 1943, could we have envisioned a decade counter on a chassis three feet long being replaced in 1970 by an integrated circuit one-tenth of an inch square.

The revolution in the semiconductor field started when integrated circuits (ICs) first appeared in commercial computers in the mid-1960's, replacing discrete component circuits. At first, three to ten logic circuits were contained in an IC. This was called

I didn't mind receiving the Sperry Univac Presidential Excellence Award from my own company. Mr. G.G. Probst, president of the division at the time, is presenting the award.

small scale integration. Toward the end of the decade, the complexity had grown by leaps and bounds to ten to one hundred logic circuits in an IC, signalling the medium scale integration level. In the early 1970's, a large scale integration event occurred which startled the world. A whole microprocessor was placed on a silicon chip! Of course, the memory function also benefited directly from the higher complexity. Memory IC's, containing 1,000 bits a few years ago, rapidly progressed to 4,000 bits and are now at the 64,000-bit level. This progress is expected to continue.

Hardware costs have been reduced significantly and now the trend is toward implementing many of the software functions in hardware. Great strides are being made in utilizing this bonanza in low cost hardware. Error detection and correction are being built in, so that if the computer "hiccups" or falters in any way, it will not be obvious to the user. Today there are already circuits that prompt the computer, should it forget a bit in memory.

Low cost communication lines have caused a revolution in the use of terminals remote from the computer. Nearly every conceivable application has its own dedicated terminal. Everyone has seen a reservation unit, bank teller's set, or an automated cash register. At first the terminals were "dumb," doing only what they were told to do by the computer or operator. Today, many terminals are smarter because a self-contained microprocessor makes decisions for them. This trend is leading to a whole new concept of distributive processing, that is, doing as much of the processing as possible at the local site and communicating the important data to a centralized file. The advent of satellite communications opens up vast new possibilities for the transmission of information between sites. The day of computers speaking to each other in complex networks is here.

These swirling changes in technology have caused subtle social problems. Especially noticeable is the technical obsolescence of the engineer in the computer field. Within ten years after college graduation, his tools and knowledge are outmoded, and a new graduate is economically more valuable. Few other professions have this pitfall. Certainly professionals in the fields of business, law, journalism, and art do not, and those in medicine and dentistry do only to a small degree. What took me a decade to learn through a long hard apprenticeship is now being taught in one or two terms of a college course. What was formerly an art is now a science. The universities are cranking out an ample supply of Ph.D.'s in computer science. Those choosing the computer development profession had better be dedicated enough to spend hours each week in extracurricular activities that will permit them to keep up with the rapidly advancing knowledge.

The microprocessor development will cause a revolution in the industry. We are just starting to see the first wave now, with microprocessors being incorporated into radar ovens, appliances of all types, measuring instruments, automobiles, control devices, intelligent games, and other applications too numerous to mention. Within a few years the vast majority of our populace will be computer operators whether they realize it or not. The world of robots will be opened up to us with microprocessors forming the brains. Significant among the applications is the formation of a whole new hobby, home computers. Hundreds of thousands of people are already into it, but it is just scratching the surface.

I expect my own microcomputer system to be functional shortly. One of the first applications I have planned is to interface it with my amateur radio station, programming it to convert incoming Morse code to English, and display the words on the television screen. Thus, I will have traversed the path from "dits to bits," completing the cycle I started forty-five years ago.

Thus, the story of my life so far. How much longer I have to live is a moot question; only nature has the answer. But when I do leave this world, I will do so knowing that I have made a positive contribution to mankind. In looking back at the past thirty-five years, I have a deep sense of satisfaction. I consider myself lucky to have been present, at the right place and time to help in launching the computer industry. There are far brighter and more capable people than I, but the random number generator of fate did not pick them for this mission. Any degree of success which I have achieved I owe directly to Drs. J. Presper Eckert, John W. Mauchly, and J. Grist Brainerd for giving me the opportunity to work on the ENIAC computer project in the first place.

The work during the pioneer days was as challenging as anyone could have wished. It was all-consuming. Those of us in it could think of nothing but solving the complex problems, without regard to time or paycheck. What was accomplished with a handful of people then cannot be duplicated today with large staffs. The atmosphere and environment are a thing of the past. The computer industry has become big business, among the largest in the United States, and with it have come some inefficiencies. Computer developments today require the coordination of masses of people engaged in systems, circuit, logic, and software design along with representation from manufacturing, marketing, and customer engineering. Computer development has become very specialized, with personnel required in each area of expertise. Gone are the days when one man had his hands in many phases of development. Ah, nostaligia...

0111 0011

Editor's Note

Herman Lukoff passed away September 24, 1979.

Appendix

Disclosure of Magnetic Calculating Machine

A simplified method of constructing a numerical calculating machine is proposed in which some of the mechanical features of an ordinary mechanical calculating machine are retained and combined with certain electronic and magnetic devices to produce a speedier, simpler machine as well as providing additional features of utility, ruggedness and ease of repair.

A continuously rotating shaft called the time shaft, driven by an electric motor, has at least some of each of the following discs or drums mounted on it:

a) Discs or drums which have at least their outer edge made of a magnetic alloy capable of being magnetized and demagnetized repeatedly and at high speed. Suitable coils and other apparatus are provided to convert electrical pulses or other wave shapes into spatially distributed magnetized sectors on the periphery of these discs, the position and/or phase of these magnetized sectors providing a method of storing, in some usable code, those characters or digits which must be used later or indicated. It should be noted that the direction of magnetization of the sectors is unimportant and may be in any direction relative to the motion or a combination of directions, this being a well known technique. This is analogous to the use of a magnetic tape to record sound except that here linearity is of little importance.

b) Discs or drums having edges or surfaces engraved in such a way as to cause voltage to be induced in a coil arranged near the disc. In any case either the disc or pole piece of the coil should be a magnet. This disc would generate such pulses or other electric signals as were required to time, control and initiate the operations required in the calculations. This is similar to the tone generating mechanism used in some electric organs and offers a more permanent way of storing the basic signals required than would be afforded by the alloy discs referred to above.

c) Discs or drums carrying characters, usually the digits 0 to 9, which can be illuminated by a light modulating device, say a neon gas discharge lamp, and so arranged that at any desired phase of the rotating shaft, corresponding to the positions of the characters, they can be flashed thus making one of the characters on the disc visible. This stroboscope principal is to be used as the high speed indication device in this calculator.

Addition, subtraction, multiplication and division would be carried out by processes of successive addition, such as is well known in mechanical calculation machines. The alloy discs or an auxillary alloy tape could be used to store function data such as a sine table. A multiplication table might be included in this manner to appreciable speed up the process of multiplication by the method of accumulation of partial products used in mechanical calculators.

The original data or numbers might be put into the machine by means of the usual keyboards, tapes or cards. These same types of tapes or cards could be used to record the calculated results.

In the above operations some means must be provided to switch the various signals from one circuit to another. This can be done rapidly by using electronic tubes as switches. A great economy in the numbers of these switching tubes can be effected by putting all the digits of a particular number on the same disc and taking them off serially through the same switching tube. This is to be contrasted to taking the n digits of a number off through n pick-up coils and through n switching tubes. It has the advantage of reducing the number of tubes required but slows down the operation and may require the mechanical shaft system to be extended so that the alloy discs rotate slower and in synchronism with the indicator discs to allow any of the numbers on the discs to be indicated concurrently or serially. In addition to the above switching operations electronic tubes will be used to count and/or discriminate the pulses used in the system to allow composition of pulse groups from two or more sources and their deposition into other channels. Clearly the power circuits for such a system may be electronic tubes, selenium oxide rectifiers or similar devices.

The use of the binary number system is favored by such an apparatus since the switching circuits are no more complicated and the required pulse groups for representing the number are simpler. The counter circuit is also simpler and more reliable. Either discs of the etched or alloy type may be used to remember combinations required in the conversion from the decimal to the binary system and the reverse if such a system is used.

If multiple shaft systems are used a great increase in the available facilities and for allowing automatic programming of the facilities and processes involved may be made, since longer time scales are provided. This greatly extends the usefulness and attractiveness of such a machine. This programming may be of the temporary type set up on alloy discs or of the permanent type on etched discs.

The principal virtues of such a machine are largely due to the alloy discs which allow numbers to be stored indefinitely and to be put on and taken off by a conveniently controlled electric circuit, and that none of the mechanical parts have to accelerate or decelerate during the operation of the machine. The advantages of the electric control are not only that it allows rapid operation but that the design is simplified and capable of more readily being extended and interconnected to other apparatus.

Several economies of operation result. It should be cheaper to build, because the precision of the electric parts is much smaller than the equivalent mechanical parts. Maintenance should be reduced because of the reliability and long life of the electric parts, the residual mechanical parts having only very simple bearing surfaces capable of giving long life. The coil structure used to magnetize the alloy discs may be separate from those used to reproduce and demagnetize them, although in the interest of simplicity it should be possible to produce all these operations with the same coil assembly. An economy over card and tape machines may be effected since no materials are normally used up in the operation of the machine, only electric power is consumed.

J. Presper Eckert, Jr.

Copied on February 1, 1945
from three typewritten sheets
dated January 29, 1944

Bibliography

"Electronic Computing Circuits of the Eniac," A. W. Burks, *Proceedings of the IRE,* Vol. 35, No. 8, Aug. 1974.

"Mercury Delay Line Memory," I. L. Auerbach, J. P. Eckert, R. F. Shaw & C. B. Sheppard, *Proceedings of the IRE,* Vol. 37, No. 8, Aug. 1949, pp. 855-861.

"The Univac System," J. P. Eckert, J. R. Weiner, H. F. Welsh & H. F. Mitchell, Joint AIEE-IRE Computer Conf., *Proceedings,* Dec. 10-12, 1951 pp. 6-16.

"Performance of the Census Univac System," J. L. McPherson, S. N. Alexander, Joint AIEE-IRE Computer Conf., *Proceedings,* Dec. 10-12, 1951, pp. 16-22.

"Office Robots," *Fortune,* Jan. 1952, pp. 82-87.

"The BINAC," A. A. Auerbach, J. P. Eckert, R. F. Shaw & L. D. Wilson, *Proceedings of the IRE,* Vol. 40, No. 1, Jan. 1952.

"The Univac Input Output System," H. F. Welsh, H. Lukoff, et al., Joint AIEE-IRE-ACM Computer Conf., New York, N.Y. *Proceedings,* Dec. 1952, pp. 2-19.

"The Election and Univac," Charles Collingwood, Third Annual Computer Applications Symposium, *Proceedings,* Oct. 9-10, 1956.

"Model Making Problems in Election Forecasting," Max A. Woodbury, Third Annual Computer Applications Symposium, *Proceedings,* Oct. 9-10, 1956.

"Youth Masters the Big Brains," T. B. Morgan, *Look,* Nov. 26, 1957, pp. 105-109.

"Design of the UNIVAC-LARC System: I," J. P. Eckert, J. C. Chu, A.B. Tonik & W. F. Schmitt, Eastern Joint Computer Conf., *Proceedings,* 1959, pp. 59-65.

"Design of the UNIVAC-LARC System: II," H. Lukoff, L. M. Spandorfer & F. F. Lee, Eastern Joint Computer Conf., *Proceedings,* 1959, pp. 59-65.

"Sperry Rand: Still Merging," *Fortune,* March 1960.

"Sperry Rand: Clearing Skies?" *Forbes,* April 1, 1964

"*Electronic Digital Systems*, R. K. Richards, John Wiley & Sons, Inc., 1966.

"Were Early Giant Computers a Success?" H. Lukoff, *Datamation*, April 1969, pp. 77-82.

"Univac Comes in From the Cold," *Business Week,* Nov. 22, 1969, pp. 160-163.

"*The Computer from Pascal to von Neumann,* Herman H. Goldstine, Princeton University Press, 1972.

"Fading Species," *Datamation,* Nov. 1, 1970, pp. 41-43.

"Opinion of the District Court of Minnesota," 180 *USPQ,* pp. 673-773.

"*The Origins of Digital Computers,* Brian Randell, Springer-Verlag, 1973.

Glossary

A and B registers

Arithmetic (A) registers act as a fast intermediate storage for data used or produced by the arithmetic unit.

Index (B) registers contain values that are added to or subtracted from the operand address to select a new address prior to or during the execution of an instruction.

access time

The time interval between the request for stored data and the delivery of that data.

accumulator

A register in which the result of an arithmetic or logic operation is formed.

address

A label name or number identifying a location where information is stored in a memory.

alphanumeric

A character set that contains letters, digits, and usually other characters such as punctuation marks. Also called alphameric.

arithmetic unit

That portion of the computing system that contains the circuits that perform arithmetic operations.

binary

Two state, as in a binary circuit or binary code. The states are usually denoted by a 1 and a 0.

binary-coded decimal notation

A quantity having any value up to ten represented by four binary bits.

biquinary coded decimal

A grouping of four bits to denote one of ten values. The three least significant bits can have one of five values; the most significant bit can have one of two values.

bit
Abbreviation for a binary digit—0 or 1, the smallest unit of information.

breadboard
Circuits spread out, usually on a flat board, for maximum accessibility during the checkout period.

bus
A common signal or power line which may connect various parts of the system.

byte
A grouping of eight bits to denote one character.

cathode follower
A type of vacuum tube circuit having a current gain but no voltage gain. Useful for driving low impedance transmission lines.

cleargate
A lengthy signal used to clear or reset logic circuits.

clock
A high speed signal that synchronizes operations in the arithmetic unit, memory, and other units.

compiler
A computer program that translates a higher level language program into machine code that can be executed by the computer.

computing unit (CU)
Also called central processing unit (CPU). That portion of a total system devoted to arithmetic computation. Circuits that control the interpretation and execution of instructions.

control unit
The portion of the computer system that generates the synchronizing signals to control the arithmetic unit, memory, or I/O.

crystal oscillator
A circuit using a quartz crystal to generate accurately timed repetitive signals.

cycling unit
A basic unit used in computing systems that generates fundamental timing signals of a repetitive nature. The signals aid in synchronizing the various parts of the system.

debouncing
An electrical contact, instead of producing a single electrical "make" or "break," actually bounces and produces many makes

and breaks scattered over a very short period of time (microseconds to milliseconds). Debouncing is a circuit technique for producing only one single make or break with each operation of the switch contacts.

decade counter

Electronic circuits capable of being stepped through ten stable states upon applying appropriate signal inputs.

decimal

A number system using the base ten.

decimal adder

A combination of logic circuits that arithmetically add two decimal or coded decimal numbers.

decoder/encoder

A device for converting from one form of coded information to another. Decoding converts from a complex code to a simpler one. Encoding does the reverse.

delay line

Electrical circuit usually made of inductances and capacitances that produces a propagation delay.

design verification routine (DVR)

A test program devised to test every aspect of the system and validate its design. Used to disclose logic errors.

digital

Pertaining to discrete values (usually 2) as contrasted to analogue, which is continuous and may assume any value.

diode (germanium, silicon)

A two-terminal semiconductor device that allows current to flow in one direction. Physically made of germanium or silicon. Used in logic gates and as power rectifiers.

direct coupled

A circuit design that responds to direct current signals, that is, signals that maintain their state for an indefinite period.

drive

The output capabilities of an amplifier or logic circuit. A logic circuit is said to have eight drives when it can provide input to eight identical circuits. (Same as fan out)

drum file

A large diameter drum having its surface coated with magnetic material. It is capable of storing millions of bits in tracks around the drum. Its access time is relatively slow, 30,000 to 50,000 times slower than main storage, but the cost per bit is also much less.

duty cycle
Percentage of the time period that the signal is active.

dynamic testing
Testing of components, subassemblies, or systems under rapidly varying conditions, as opposed to static testing which tests at an unchanging value.

electrostatic memory
A memory system that stores bits as electrostatic charges on the face of a cathode ray tube.

encrypted
Information that is encoded with a key so that it is no longer recognizable, and written in secret code or cipher.

executive routine
Programs resident in memory that handle most of the bookkeeping, scheduling, and control functions.

fan out
The number of logic gates that can be driven by the output of one gate. (Same as drive)

flip-flop
A logic element which may be set or reset into either one or the other of its two stable states.

floating point representation
Numbers having the decimal point placed anywhere within the number and usually used with a power of ten exponent.

function table
ENIAC terminology for manually set up, stored constants representing the values of a mathematical function. Equivalent to an alterable read-only memory.

Also used in BINAC and UNIVAC computer terminology to refer to the diode matrices that encoded machine code instructions set up in a register or to control signals that operated the appropriate logic gates. It was the hardware equivalent of microprogram control.

gate, logic gate
Fundamental elements used in combination to perform computer logic operations. Fundamental types are AND, OR, NAND and NOR.

grasshopper fuse
A type of fuse, which when blown, exhibits a raised arm. An alarm contact is also provided.

ground strap, ground plane
Means of simulating an infinite conductor of theoretically zero resistance at earth potential.

higher level language

A language for writing computer programs that is more natural and easier to use than the machine language. Examples are FORTRAN, COBOL, and BASIC.

IC

An integrated circuit (IC) using semiconductor technology to place and interconnect transistors, diodes, resistors, and capacitors into operational circuits on one silicon chip one-tenth to two-tenths of an inch on a side.

indexing memory address

A means of modifying the memory address without changing the instruction. Accomplished by adding the contents of an index register to the address.

input/output (I/O)

Refers to peripheral devices which interface with the system to convey information into and out of the computer.

input/output processor (IOP)

A separate computer optimized for handling input/output functions. Acts to relieve the CU of these chores.

instruction

Information fed to the control unit of a computer to direct its sequence of operations.

instruction code

A predefined operation that is executed in a computer and is described in machine language.

instruction overlap

The initiation of the next instruction prior to the completion of the current one.

internal register (high speed register)

Fast registers provided to facilitate arithmetic and control operations.

KHz, MHz

Abbreviation for kilohertz and megahertz, equal to 1,000 and 1,000,000 cycles per second, respectively.

levels of logic

The number of logic gates between retiming points.

logic

Fundamental elements interconnected into arrays that accomplish the arithmetic and control functions in a computer.

magnetic amplifier

A device using the saturation properties of a magnetic material to act as an amplifier.

mainframe
A term applied generally to larger cabinets of the system including the central processor, memory, and I/O processor.

memory
A means for storing the bits constituting the data and instructions.

mercury memory
Storage of acoustic pulses as bits in a mercury delay line.

multiplexing
A means of sending many different signals through one channel.

nanosecond
One billionth of a second (10^{-9} seconds)

neon bulb
A small bulb filled with neon gas that glows with an orange color when an appropriate voltage is applied. Used to indicate the 1 or 0 state of a vacuum tube circuit.

noise, ringing
Extraneous signals that interfere with normal circuit operation.

nondestructive readout (NDRO) memory
A type of memory that can be read without destroying the contents. Ferrite core memories, for example, are destructive and therefore require another cycle for restoring the read data.

non-return-to-zero (NRZ)
A method of encoding information that results in the signal remaining active when all 1's are present. More information may be conveyed in the same time period than the conventional return to zero system.

oscilloscope
An instrument utilizing a cathode ray tube that can display the amplitude of a signal as a function of time. Thus electrical signals can be seen on the television-like display.

parity bit
An extra bit appended to the bits that form a character to make the total number of bits odd. Used to detect the dropping or picking up of a bit.

plated-wire memory
A series of small diameter wires plated with a very thin continuous film of magnetic material. A grid of wires overlaying the plated wires creates magnetic fields which magnetize the plated areas in the clockwise or counterclockwise direction corresponding to the storage of 1 or a 0.

potentiometer
A three-terminal variable resistor with an adjustable center connection.

power supply
Device for converting from commercial power to power suitable for operating logic and memory circuits, and peripheral devices.

propagation time
The time that it takes for a signal to pass from the input to the output of a logic circuit.

pulse
A digital signal that is active for a short period and then returns to the quiet state.

pulse former
A circuit that reshapes and resynchronizes logic signals.

program control
Under control of the executing program rather than the operator.

real time
Instantaneous response to a current event, for example, live television.

saturated
No further output from the device is attainable even though the input continues to increase.

semiconductor
Transistors and integrated circuits fabricated from silicon or germanium.

serial operation
Flow of information through a computer using only one channel. Results are developed serially—one after the other—rather than simultaneously as in parallel operation.

set/reset
Control signals used to trigger a logic circuit into its active or inactive state.

strip transmission line
A means for transmitting high frequency signals. Consists of two flat conducting strips separated by an insulator. Can provide lower impedances than the coaxial transmission line.

supervisory control panel
A panel containing operating and diagnostic switches and indicators. Used by the operator to control the system and by the serviceman for maintenance purposes.

synchronization
A means for forcing two or more circuits to operate in step with each other.

taper pin
A small (⅝"L × ⅛"D) cone-shaped piece of rolled metal crimped on the end of wire. Makes electrical connection with a female counterpart when inserted under a controlled pressure.

test vehicle
An abbreviated sample of the final product used to test the validity of the design.

word
A multiple number of bytes, often four, but can be more.

X-Y drivers, X-Y memory selection
X and Y refer to the dimensions of a memory array; X is one dimension, Y the other.

Drivers provide high currents for the X and Y lines during a read or write operation. The coincidence of current in the X and Y lines selects the specific memory location.

0111 0011
The binary coded decimal equivalent of "73," the traditional signoff used by amateur radio operators to say "best regards."